100 GREAT GARDEN PLANTS

100 GREAT GARDEN PLANTS

William H. Frederick, Jr.

Timber Press
Portland, Oregon

Copyright © 1975 by William H. Frederick, Jr.

Published by arrangement with Alfred A. Knopf, Inc.

Library of Congress Cataloging in Publication Data
Frederick, William Heisler, (date)
100 great garden plants.

Bibliography: p.   Includes index.
1. Ornamental trees. 2. Ornamental shrubs.
3. Ground cover plants. I. Title.
SB435.F86   1975   635.9′32   74–21280
ISBN 0-88192-027-4

Printed in Hong Kong by Colorcraft Ltd.

Timber Press, 1986
9999 S.W. Wilshire
Portland, Oregon 97225

This book is affectionately dedicated to my wife,

Nancy Greenewalt Frederick,

and my children,

Richard Holland Frederick,

Peter Crawford Frederick,

Margaretta Semiramis Frederick,

Rebecca Greenewalt Frederick.

CONTENTS

III. Shrubs 83

ACKNOWLEDGMENTS

Writing this book has been a delightful moment in my life. The gardening experiences recounted here have called to mind many beautiful memories of the good gardeners I have been fortunate enough to know. It is with the warmest affection that I acknowledge the debt I owe to those who encouraged my love of plants and gardens and passed the torch of knowledge on to me. From my Grandfather Frederick I absorbed a husbandman's attitude toward all that grows. My first experience with the passion to plant and with that magic moment of ordering the spring seeds was witnessed and encouraged shamelessly by my grandmother. My own mother made me face design decisions squarely at an early age, while my father taught me both patience and standards of excellence. Laura Woodward, an aunt, taught by example. I have yet to see finer cowslips than hers grown anywhere in Delaware.

My friendship with Semiramis Marr Paulson in my early teens was probably one of the most fortunate happenings in my life. Some fifty-five years my senior, she began gardening at the age of sixty on a few stony acres at Charlestown, Maryland. She grew trees and shrubs from all over the world, and gardened as though she were going to live forever. At sixty-five, she planted three-foot white pines along either side of a walk because she had always wanted a path where she could "walk on pine needles." She did just that for a number of years before she died. Her special love was Narcissus; until her death, in her late eighties, she continued to grow new hybrids from seed—a project needing three years to produce blooms. She was extremely well-read and corresponded with horticulturists here and abroad. It was from her I first heard of Liberty Hyde Bailey, Ernest H. Wilson, George Slate, and Guy Wilson.

My luck continued when I found that Swarthmore, the college of my choice, was the home of the Arthur Hoyt Scott Horticultural Foundation. I found myself not only in the midst of one of the best collections of woody and herbaceous ornamental plants in the United States, but also in close contact with John Wister, the Director, Harry

Wood, Superintendent of Buildings and Grounds, and Gertrude Smith (now Wister), special editorial assistant. Good fortune was indeed with me. Any kid with a passion to learn about plants could not have landed in the midst of a more knowledgeable and generous trio. John Wister's encyclopedic knowledge of plants, and love for them, taught me that choices are hard to make: nearly every ornamental plant has a valid use under some conditions. Harry Wood, trained early in the English school of gardening, made me fully aware of the very highest standards of horticultural excellence. Gertrude Smith was the very best sort of teacher. Every question received a thoughtful answer, opening the door to a hundred new questions.

As a landscape nurseryman, I was extremely fortunate in having William Earl Hamilton as my first superintendent. With wide experience in growing ornamentals, landscape planting, and large tree moving, he would never let me be satisfied with any job that could not be classified as excellent. During this period I met Jacques LeGendre, one of the finest plantsmen this country has ever known. Annually he and John Gruellemanns, founder of Wayside Gardens, would search European nurseries, botanic gardens, and private gardens for little-known or forgotten treasure with which to tease the palate of the American gardening public. His standards were tough; only those plants which were the best came back to be propagated at his Gulf Stream Nursery, and subsequently marketed by Wayside.

During this same period two landscape architects whose work I had been admiring at a distance became first-hand acquaintances and inspiring friends. Both have set landscape-design standards to which our culture will aspire for many years. One of these men, Thomas Church, originated designs for American gardens that have brought landscape architecture in this country out of the copycat period left from the 1920's and made gardens an important functional part of our lives. The other, the Brazilian Roberto Burle Marx, both an artist and a plant lover, has applied all of the best aspects of a rich international cultural heritage in developing abundantly rich garden designs. I am deeply humble in my appreciation for the teaching and guidance of all of these friends, each of whom seemed to arrive in my life at just the right moment.

The writing of this book would not have occurred had it not been for Jerome Eaton, formerly director of Old Westbury Gardens and himself a noted horticultural author. The idea for the book was Jerry's and it was through his persuasion that it began. He has been a very patient friend and a wise counselor throughout. The quality of this book would have been considerably poorer had it not been for Dr. George H. M. Lawrence. George read the first draft of the manuscript as the result of my plea for assistance on the origins and histories of various plants. What came back was thorough scholarly notes and a host of delightful anecdotes too fascinating to be omitted. In this respect much of the book is really his.

In addition, many other people have cheerfully assisted me in this task. Special thanks go to Dr. Russell Seibert, Mr. Everitt Miller, Dr. Donald G. Huttleston, and Mrs. Enola Jane N. Teeter at Longwood Gardens; to Dr. Richard A. Howard and Mr. Robert S. Hebb at the Arnold Arboretum; to Dr. John L. Creech and Dr. Gene Eisenbeiss at the U.S. National Arboretum; to Dr. David Bates at the Liberty Hyde Bailey Hortorium; and to Miss D. M. Staples at the Royal Horticultural Society's Garden at Wisley. Grateful acknowledgment is also made to the following nurserymen: Bert Flemer (F & F Nurseries), J. Herbert Alexander (Dahliatown Nurseries), Richard A. Simon (Bluemount Nurseries), William Flemer, III (Princeton Nurseries), J. Peter Vermeulen (John Vermeulen & Son, Inc.), and E. Sam Hemming (Eastern Shore Nurseries). Three secretaries have helped to make order out of my chaotic penmanship: I am most appreciative of the fine jobs done by Mrs. A. W. Fretz, Mrs. Henry J. Winkler, and Mrs. David Goehringer.

William H. Frederick, Jr.
Ashland Hollow
June, 1975

INTRODUCTION TO THE SECOND PRINTING

The reprinting of *100 Great Garden Plants* ten years after original publication has brought to light two sets of important facts of which all readers should be aware. The first has to do with minimum winter temperatures in the area where I live (near Wilmington, Delaware) and may well be true of the area in which you are gardening.

The average minimum temperature in the 10 year period prior to original publication of this book was 4.9°F. In the 10 year period since then the average minimum temperature has been -6.88°F and what is more important the last 4 years have had lows as follows:

      1982 -10°F
      1983 - 7°F
      1984 -14°F
      1985 -14°F

This means that *the climate has changed* and the *plant hardiness zone map* on page xxii *is no longer reliable for determining what hardiness zone you live in.* In my case I no longer live in Zone 7 (minimum temperature 0°-7°F). More accurately I now live in Zone 5 (minimum temperature -20° to -10°F). I urge you, therefore, before using this book, to get minimum temperature figures from your local U. S. Government Weather Bureau for at least the last five years. From this you can determine in what hardiness zone you now live. (See temperature ranges and zone designations in the lower right hand corner of page xxii.) With this in hand you will be able to determine which of the 100 plants should be hardy in your garden as the hardiness zones given for each plant are, to the best of my knowledge, accurate.

Contrary to my statement in the Introduction I have had to eliminate the following plants (included in the 100) from the palette I use in this area:

      Magnolia grandiflora
      Diospyros kaki
      Ilex aquifolium 'Ciliata Major'
      Berberis wisleyensis (formerly inaccurately listed as *Berberis*
          triacanthophora)

>*Elaeagnus pungens* 'Fruitlandi'
>*Ilex cornuta*
>*Stranvaesia davidiana* 'Undulata'
>*Genista sylvestris* 'Lydia'
>*Hedera helix* 'Conglomerata Erecta'

In addition, although I still use the following here they are used with qualifications:

>*Abelia* x *grandiflora* is treated as a cutback shrub and is a perfectly satisfactory plant used in this way.
>*Arundo donax, Chimonanthus praecox, Mahonia bealei, Hedera helix* 'Baltica', and *Phyllostachys aureosulcata* have suffered winter injury more than once. I therefore use them in very protected areas only.

This does not mean that I am no longer as enthusiastic as ever about these plants. It means only that the northern limit of their use must be geographically south of here.

Changes like this are all part of the challenge and excitement of gardening. In my own case the loss of the above plant friends has led me to know, admire, and use some other plants which are hardy to at least -14°F.

The greatest loss has, of course, been with broadleaf evergreens. In the LARGE TREE category I have come to rely on the handsome *Cedrus libani* var. *stenocoma,* hardy at the Arnold Arboretum in Boston, instead of *Magnolia grandiflora.* In the SMALL TREE category, *Ilex aquipernyi* 'San Jose' makes an outstanding substitute for *Ilex aquifolium* 'Ciliata Major'. The new *Ilex* x *meservei* cultivars 'Blue Maid' and 'Blue Stallion' with their glossy dark green leaves came on the market just in time to take the place in the SHRUB category of *Berberis wisleyensis* (formerly inaccurately listed as *Berberis triacanthophora*), *Elaeagnus pungens* 'Fruitlandi', and *Ilex cornuta.*

Likewise, the relatively new *Stranvaesia davidiana* 'Watnong Procumbent' seems to be hardy to -14°F thus providing a delightful substitute for *Stranvaesia davidiana* 'Undulata'.

The increased availability and fall and spring flowering characteristics of *Prunus subhirtella* 'Autumnalis' have been a great plus, making up for the loss of *Diospyros kaki* (SMALL TREE category). *Callicarpa dichotoma* (purple berries in the fall), *Euonymous alata* (red fall foliage and corky winter bark), and *Prunus* x *cistena* (wine colored foliage all season) also provide first rate SHRUB substitutes for the broadleaf evergreen shrubs mentioned above.

A number of new ground covers (predominantly herbaceous) have come to have positions of importance as GROUND COVERS in my work, making up for the loss of *Genista sylvestris* 'Lydia' and *Hedera helix* 'Conglomerata Erecta'. One of the best of these is a hardy geranium, tough in nature, sporting attractive pink flowers in late May, and fragrant foliage (Retsina wine) which is winter persistent and presents attractive red, orange and green coloration to individual leaves. This is *Geranium macrorrhizum* from southern Europe.

Thus it can be seen that the palette has not decreased in number. It has simply changed, a tribute to the vast cornucopia of good garden plants available to us.

The second important fact is that three of the plants included in the 100 have become subject to disease problems since the original writing.

Ilex pedunculosa was probably sited poorly in my ignorance of its native habitat which turns out to be moist woodlands in northern Japan. When grown here in full sun on dry slopes it is invariably a failure due to attacks of the bacterial blight, *Corneybacterium ilicis*. When it is sited properly this is not a problem.

Both *Sciadopitys verticillata* and *Calocedrus decurrens* have been subject to canker attacks for the first time. The cause of those on the Umbrella Pine has been identified as *Diploidia* and a regular spray program has this under control. The cause of the cankers on *Calocedrus* has not been identified. A spray program has been started but there are no conclusive results at this writing. In both instances the trees were not experiencing any stress due to siting and the problem has only occurred in the last four years. Therefore, pathologists tend to blame the incidence of trouble on some change in general environmental conditions such as the lower winter temperatures or an increase in air pollution. There is nothing definitive on this as yet. I would not hesitate to recommend continued use of *Ilex pedunculosa* and *Sciadopitys verticillata* as long as the caveats indicated are heeded. I am sure that there are many places where *Calocedrus* will continue to grow healthily and a few more years of experience may well indicate a control for the problem I am experiencing.

Aside from correction of minor errors in the original text and attempting to make the text current taxonomically I feel comfortable leaving the message as it was originally. The section of the Introduction called *How to Use This Book* has been revised to reflect the climatic change and update recommendations on finding sources. A few more books have been added to the Bibliographies in an attempt to assist the reader who wishes additional information.

I am grateful to Richard Abel for his encouragement in his project.

William H. Frederick, Jr.
Ashland Hollow
26 January 1986

INTRODUCTION

A gardener, by my definition, is anyone whose curiosity has been piqued by even a single living plant and who feels even the slightest urge to experience the joy of placing a few plants together in the earth to achieve an effect.

This is a book for gardeners by a gardener, an attempt to share both a knowledge of plants and of design experience. It is not an encyclopedia and not a textbook. It is meant to be a visit with you in my own garden, where the greatest of gardening joys is trading plants and discussing failures and successes in achieving landscape effects. This book's observations and recommendations are based entirely on first-hand experience. For this reason, any recommendation it contains has the advantage of being tested and practical— but also, I must warn you, the disadvantage of not covering every possible alternative for *your* garden.

Further, this book is an attempt to combat the schizoid tendency in American garden thinking, whereby trained horticulturists care nothing about landscape design and professional landscape architects know nothing about plants. All too frequently, the horticulturist thinks carefully about selecting the right plant for the right spot from a cultural viewpoint and rates highest that garden which has the most varieties of plants—*horticultural zoo though it may be!* For his part, the landscape architect does a fine job of designing gardens that function well for the persons living in them; he designs spaces with good proportions and beautiful forms and shapes; he effectively balances shrub massings to specimen accents. Yet with a few exceptions the landscape architect knows little and cares less about what varieties of plants he uses. Because of lack of discipline and control, the living picture painted by the horticulturist is as unsatisfying as a gourmand meal. And at the same time the landscape architect's picture is bland and without savor because he has missed the opportunity for full enrichment, failing to make use of all the excitement and stimulation available from our contemporary ornamental plant world. *Both* approaches are essential, the warp and woof of a fine garden.

Good private gardens are more important today than ever before. We suffer anxieties from a world largely out of our control, a world overpopulated and daily becoming less beautiful due to various forms of pollution, a world where the possibility of nuclear self-destruction seems ever greater, and where there seems to be less and less communication between people. Because of rampant standardization, our personal physical world is equally out of control. Mass production and mass merchandising techniques seriously limit our choices of consumer products, whether they be a washing machine, a TV set, clothes, a new car, or even a house. Opportunities for expressing our own originality (let alone our own personality) are seriously reduced. The private residential garden can be the one big exception to this rule. The space around our house is ours to do with as we wish. We can make choices and commitments and tailor this personal environment to satisfy our own needs, functional, intellectual, and aesthetic. Here is a part of our lives we can indeed control.

Gardening can be a civilized person's most rewarding and exciting activity. As fast as our curiosity is satisfied by acquaintance with one plant, we discover five more we would like to know. We have no sooner applied our scientific background and exercised our ingenuity in solving one cultural problem than we see a hint of an even better answer and have a new temptation to explore. While we are relishing with great satisfaction our own creation of a well-balanced landscape picture, a stimulating color combination, or a dramatic textural effect, almost immediately new possibilities creep into the mind and we're off again on a new project. A single lifetime seems too short for the richness of this experience. It is never ending, always expanding.

As, in this book, we visit my garden together, I suggest we discuss individual plants as we come upon them, *always considering how they relate to a total picture.* Generally speaking, any pleasing effect that you enjoy in any garden is the result of thoughtful consideration by the gardener involved. This consideration process is called planning or designing. And whether you are modifying a small part of your own existing garden or just beginning with a new home, the same planning or designing begins with an understanding of the practical uses you may wish to make of the area involved.

Such use may include a driveway and possible parking area for extra cars. A landscape designer often has the opportunity to provide a transitional area between car and house which can serve as a kind of "air lock" between the pressures of the outside world and the warmth and security of the home. It can likewise serve to reduce at an agreeable pace the physical scale of our daily environment from office or supermarket to the size of our own living room.

We may wish to create a picture to be viewed from one or more windows of the house, or to extend the size of one or more rooms by creating outdoor living areas. We may wish to provide space for active recreation such as badminton, croquet, tennis, or swimming. Another possibility is to set aside space for some intensive form of hobby gardening—vegetables, roses, or an herbaceous border. Or we may wish to provide a sort of retreat: a place to which we can walk and be secluded from the house. Not all of these functional uses will be desirable on any one property, but some of them will. Of course, there may be other, more specialized requirements too: I have professionally encountered requests for a breeding pool for fish, a place for a collection of contemporary sculpture, a place for an aviary. In any event, it is with these practical and personal functions that we must start planning, for if our garden is not able to satisfy such needs it will be unsuccessful.

Next, we must look carefully at the site. Does it have any particularly unique existing features? Is there a very fine old tree, grove of trees, rock or rock outcropping? Is there a particularly desirable view? It would be a great loss of opportunity if such assets were ignored, for not many are lucky enough to have them. Likewise, we must consider *ourselves*—is there some present or past interest of our own that should be expressed? A willow tree or apple tree you held in affection or esteemed as a child could now be a key feature in a new garden. Perhaps you have been intrigued by the history of a certain species of tree such as *Franklinia alatamaha* or *Metasequoia glyptostroboides.* Around a grove of these a garden could grow. Or, if disciplining plants satisfies an inner yearning, how about lovingly developing a handsome topiary as your personal garden feature? To feature natural assets and personal yearnings thoughtfully gives a garden strength of character and can make the difference between one which is mediocre and one which is rich and satisfying.

All of these considerations have to do with creating the bones of a garden. Just as in contemporary art, the forms of our gardens may be rectilinear or curvilinear; and, careful thought must be given to the three-dimensional proportions of spaces and the transition from one space to another. There are many good books on the subject of pure garden design; they are most rewarding to read.*

*See Bibliography, "Books About Garden Design," page 205.

The following two planning guidelines are extremely helpful to remember:

1. *It's the space left over that counts.* Suppose you are dealing with the squarish piece of real estate bounded by the back of your house and the rear and side boundary lines of your property. And suppose you plan to use this space as an outdoor living area with a certain amount of grass for lawn games, surrounded by plantings both to lend privacy and to provide changing interest during various seasons of the year, as seen from the house. The total area is now in lawn. On first impulse, it would seem that your attention should be primarily given to selecting plants that you like and arranging attractive combinations of them around the periphery of the area. Although this is important, the end result will not necessarily be successful unless you decide ahead of time what shape the lawn area should be. If you will study various gardens that you admire, you will discover that grass or other ground cover not only ties all the other elements in the picture together; more important, the strength or weakness of the picture—the impact or lack of impact of the garden area—depends on whether this "space" has a clearly thought-out definition and is attractive in its form and proportions. Hence the dictum that "it's the space left over that counts."

2. *Always work to a "center of interest" in any garden area.* We've all read books that we dubbed failures because there were too many themes or plots without one that was dominant, or too many characters given equal importance. In the same sense, presumably we've all seen plantings involving one each of a number of varieties of plants and realized that this was an unsatisfying picture. Any area within your garden can suffer from this fault. When featuring a particular tree, you must arrange the plantings and structures to show off this tree, and emphasize its dominant positioning and its color and textural relationship with other plants in the garden. As soon as you try to feature other single trees in the same area, you will have dissipated the effect. I have worked with clients possessed of three garden ornaments from "Grandmother's garden" which they wanted to feature in the same area, and I had to explain that it was better to put two in storage and give one a chance to assume full sway in pulling the picture together. Of course, this is not to say that the center of interest cannot be more than one object, for a clump of three trees of one kind or even a small grove can occasionally be a very special feature. Likewise, several pieces of sculpture, if they appear successfully as a group, could come off very well. The important challenge is *to create a point of emphasis*—so that

regardless of where you look in the garden, the eye is subtly led back to that point.

In this book we will *start* with individual plants—a hundred of them to be precise. But in addition to discussing their cultural and historical personalities we will also spend considerable time on ways in which you might group them with other plants in your garden. Plant grouping becomes a matter of "orchestration" or "choreography" involving both the size and shape relationships of plants now and ten or twenty years from now, the textural quality of these plants, and the effect of such changing seasonal characteristics as flower color, summer foliage color, fall foliage color, fruit characteristics, and bark characteristics.

In choosing shapes and textures, it is generally true that while like shapes and like textures create a feeling of quiet and harmony, if carried to an extreme the result is boredom. Contrasting shapes and textures provide interest and richness, but when carried to an extreme create chaos. Obviously, these opposing forces must mesh in a harmonious balance all aimed at continually returning the eye to a dominant center of interest.

Because it is *possible* to have something of interest going on in the garden at every season of the year, it is easy to get carried away. The larger, older gardens in this country and abroad seldom made this mistake. The garden would be composed of a number of small gardens, each featuring a combination of special beauty or interest at one or at the most two times of the year. Assuming that you have a sufficiently computer-like mind to plan out a blooming-fruiting-foliage sequence that provides changing interest all year, the question remains whether this is really desirable in our present-day smaller gardens. For some who thrive on horticultural stimulation it may be appropriate. I suspect that for the majority of us the fun of looking forward to one or two really fine displays a year with sensory resting periods in between is a richer experience. This assumes, of course, that the garden is of sufficiently good design that the eye is satisfied by its two-dimensional and three-dimensional form, and by the arrangement of shades of green and textures of green during the off season.

This book contains one hundred plants. My object has been to select only my own favorites, plants that I have grown rewardingly myself and which I can recommend. I feel strongly that too many gardening books fail to discriminate, to take a stand and speak with enthusiasm about that which is truly excellent. I hope that this will be a helpful approach in our present horticultural world, when any one of us may be overwhelmed with the choice of more than 7,000 kinds of ornamental plants from all over the globe.

I have selected one hundred plants that are especially useful, as well as particularly beautiful and exciting, and have attempted to state clearly their virtues and their faults. They come from thirty-six botanical families. Twenty-seven are native American plants. The balance have been introduced to this country from all over the world, starting in the days of the early settlers. The story of plant exploration and introduction is an exciting one; the bibliography section beginning on page 205 contains a selection of books on the subject. Of the seventy-three alien plants, thirty-six are from China, Japan, and Korea, three from Siberia and Asia Minor, and eleven from the European continent. The remaining twenty-three are clones of species from these areas, hybrids between species from these areas, or clones of these hybrids.

In thinking of attractive combinations in which these one hundred plants can be used, many others are mentioned. I hope this will challenge every reader to search for further information and more catalogs, to use his imagination, to think more deeply about his garden design, to plant more thoughtful combinations and groupings. I hope, in short, that he will become a true gardener, and join the ranks of those enjoying one of the richest experiences life can offer.

How to Use This Book

To assist you in locating plants of a particular height, the plants in this book have been grouped by size into four categories: large trees, small trees, shrubs, and ground covers.

In the case of each plant, average measurements are given in the form of *effective landscape height* and *effective landscape spread*. (Note that these are not necessarily the greatest dimensions to which the plant has been known to grow under the most ideal conditions. Rather, they are the effective heights at which the plant matures under average garden conditions.) Under these average conditions, trees may take ten to twenty years to mature, while shrubs may take five years and ground covers as few as two. These time relationships emphasize the fact that new plantings must give priority to those plants maturing at the larger sizes. When the plant's residence is likely to be permanent, spacing should be calculated on the basis of mature dimensions. When residence is intended to be shorter, spacing may need to be closer in order to provide the "finished" look sooner. The tendency among many gardeners is to space plants more closely than will be advisable when they mature. This practice is not undesirable so long as the gardener is willing to weed out and even redesign as crowding occurs.

Plants in each of the four categories are further designated as those which are valued chiefly for their *structural qualities* in creating landscape pictures and those which are valued for adding some particularly significant *seasonal interest.* It is very important to think about plant choices in terms of these two categories and to make certain that a garden has good "bones," or structure, before considering the enrichment of the scene with those plants providing seasonal interest.

In developing a home landscape plan based on the uses made of various parts of the yard, I have emphasized the need for defining these spaces as eye-pleasing shapes. Once these shapes have been determined, the next step is to develop a planting which will define the open space. It is not enough that plants be selected which give attractive blossoms in the spring or pretty berries in the fall. If the garden is going to have strength of character at all times of the year we must start our planting design with a core of plants with *structural qualities.* If the plot is large, for instance, we might want to select three large evergreen trees (such as Nordmann's Fir) and five deciduous trees with a strong branching structure (such as Washington Hawthorn) for the "bones" of our grouping. In a smaller garden, we might use three small trees of good form (such as Redleaf Plum) and six highly structured shrubs (such as Warminster Broom). In each case these plants would be selected and placed on our plan before we really began fleshing out the picture with plants of predominantly seasonal interest. If a garden, landscape scene, or plant grouping has good structure it will be successful all year. If it doesn't, no amount of color or texture can make the picture totally satisfying.

Not all of the 100 plants will be hardy everywhere, or easy for every reader to grow. All of them thrived in the area where my own garden is located; namely, latitude 39°, 45' north, and longitude 75°, 40' west – approximately 30 miles southwest of Philadelphia in 1975. The terrain is rolling piedmont 350-400 ft. above sea level. The average annual rainfall is 40 in. The soil is predominantly acid.

At that time we fell in what is known as Hardiness Zone 7, described as having an average annual minimum temperature 0° to

10°F. The climate has now at least temporarily changed with temperatures below -10°F in three of the last four years, putting us in Hardiness Zone 5. (See Introduction to the 2nd Printing.)

The zone numbers listed with each plant and the related temperature ranges found in the lower right hand corner of page XXII will be helpful in deciding how hardy a plant will be in your area. First, however, it is important to check the minimum winter temperatures of the last 4-5 years with your local U. S. Weather Bureau as the geographical bands shown on the Plant Hardiness Zone Map can no longer be totally relied on due to the climatic shift. (These zones and the plants growing in them were determined by a committee of the American Horticultural Society on the basis of average minimum winter temperatures and contributed to the publication of the Plant Hardiness Zone Map by the United States Department of Agriculture in 1960. The zone hardiness ratings assigned to the plants are still perfectly valid even though the map is less useful than it was.)

Plant hardiness is, of course, a very complicated subject and, in addition to temperature, depends also on the type of soil, moisture conditions, and wind protection in each individual garden. Since these other factors are both variable and to a degree controllable, the minimum winter temperatures do end up being the most critical factor. To this extent the zones are helpful as a guideline.

Of the 100 plants covered in this book, seven are hardy as far north as Zone 2, six in Zones 3-4, thirty-five in Zone 5, thirty-five in Zone 6, and seventeen in Zone 7.

For several plants the currently acceptable Latin name is followed by a second Latin name in parentheses, which is commonly used and known but now outdated under botanical rules. Botanical name changes are notoriously poorly publicized among horticulturists, and outdated names continue to be used in trade and amateur circles for many years after a change (for example, very few horticulturists have ever heard of *Calocedrus,* the currently acceptable name for *Libocedrus*).

Not all the plants discussed are necessarily readily available commercially. The nature of mass production horticulture in this country is such that the very best are not always grown. This is partly due to a lack of demand from our amateur gardening public; there is reason to hope that the situation will improve as our demands become more vocal.

Finding sources for some of the less common varieties can involve the gardener in a challenging treasure hunt. Your local garden center or landscape contractor may sometimes be helpful in locating hard-to-find varieties. These sources should know that in almost every part of the United States there are trade organizations which periodically publish more or less complete lists of material available in wholesale nurseries. These lists, although not usually including really rare plants, give a much greater number of varieties than any one retail outlet can regularly stock. (An outstanding example of such a trade organization is Landscape Materials Information Service, Inc., which publishes such lists twice a year to member firms from Maine to Maryland and west to Wisconsin.) The success of this approach depends on a particular firm in your area being a member of such an organization and being willing to accommodate you with a special order.

The Brooklyn Botanic Garden, as part of their *Plants and Gardens Handbook* series, has published *Nursery Source Manuals* in 1969, 1977, and 1982. These listings are very well done and extremely helpful while the information is current (for perhaps a year or two after publication). It would be a great boost to American gardening if such manuals could appear annually.

The reader service editors of such national gardening magazines as *Horticulture, Flower and Garden*, and *American Horticulturist* can be very helpful in suggesting sources, as can the garden information centers found at flower shows and associated with horticultural societies and public gardens in larger cities. Members of horticultural societies frequently have the privilege of advertising their needs in the society's publication.

In rare instances, a plant discussed in this book may not, at the moment you are looking, be available from *any* commercial source. This means that you must find where such a plant is growing *and* learn to start the plant yourself from seed, cuttings, or grafts. Local arboreta and botanical gardens frequently can be helpful in supplying propagation material or, if they don't have the desired plant, helping you find an institution where the plant is grown. Seeds of rare plants are made available to members on an annual basis by several horticultural societies (i.e., Royal Horticultural Society and American Horticultural Society) and some plant societies (i.e., The American Rock Garden Society). Information on how to propagate plants is usually available from horticultural societies, local arboreta and botanic gardens, or your local county agent's office.

In any case, the search can be intriguing and the result much more satisfying than settling for readily available plants which are mediocre or second best.

SEE INTRODUCTION TO THE SECOND PRINTING.

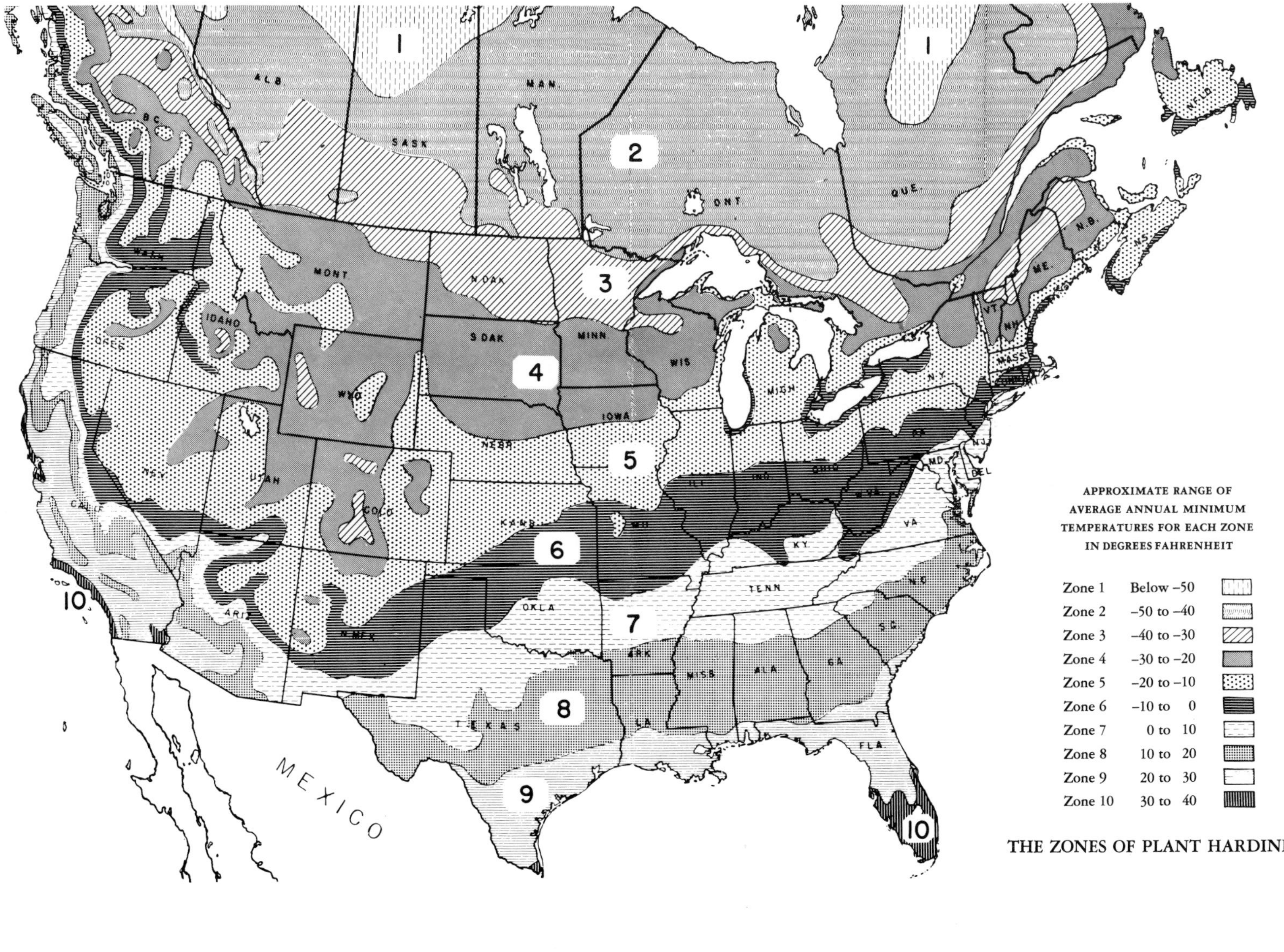

1
2
3
4
5
6
7
8
9
10
ALB.
B.C.
SASK.
MAN.
ONT.
QUE.
N.B.
N.S.
NFLD.
WASH.
ORE.
CALIF.
NEV.
IDAHO
MONT.
WYO.
UTAH
ARIZ.
COLO.
N.MEX.
N.DAK.
S.DAK.
NEBR.
KANS.
OKLA.
TEXAS
MINN.
IOWA
MO.
ARK.
LA.
WIS.
ILL.
MICH.
IND.
OHIO
KY.
TENN.
MISS.
ALA.
GA.
FLA.
S.C.
N.C.
VA.
W.VA.
PA.
N.Y.
MD.
DEL.
N.J.
VT.
N.H.
ME.
MASS.
MEXICO
APPROXIMATE RANGE OF
AVERAGE ANNUAL MINIMUM
TEMPERATURES FOR EACH ZONE
IN DEGREES FAHRENHEIT
Zone 1 Below −50
Zone 2 −50 to −40
Zone 3 −40 to −30
Zone 4 −30 to −20
Zone 5 −20 to −10
Zone 6 −10 to 0
Zone 7 0 to 10
Zone 8 10 to 20
Zone 9 20 to 30
Zone 10 30 to 40

THE ZONES OF PLANT HARDINESS

100 GREAT GARDEN PLANTS

I
LARGE TREES

Trees are not automatically thought of as plants, but to any landscape planner trees are of prime importance. Large trees, because they tend to grow more slowly and occupy a greater portion of space during most of their lives, deserve our first consideration in this book. The seventeen examples discussed here include both evergreen and deciduous species, and all will reach an effective landscape height of 25 feet or more. One or two may grow to 100 feet or more under ideal conditions, but most mature in the 40-to-60-foot area. They may be further distinguished, in terms of landscape use, by predominantly structural qualities and by their function in providing the garden with interest at various seasons. The ten trees included mainly for their structural qualities range from *Fagus sylvatica* 'Laciniata' (common name, Cutleaf European Beech) with its strong horizontal lines to the dense nondirectional background foliage of the *Magnolia grandiflora*. Those primarily of seasonal interest include blossoming trees, species remarkable for their bark in winter, and one noted for the splendor of its autumn leaves.

1

STRUCTURAL INTEREST

Evergreen
Effective landscape height: 50-60 feet
Effective landscape spread: 25 feet
Zones 5-6
Pinaceae (Pine Family)
Native range: Caucasus and Asia Minor

Abies nordmanniana
Nordmann's Fir

Nordmann's Fir is the epitome of what everyone thinks of as the perfect "Christmas tree." In form it is a very regular, pointed cone and is clothed with lustrous dark green needles. W. J. Bean (1970) refers to it as "one of the handsomest, and in most places, best . . . growing of the firs." The branching is very symmetrical; the branches mildly ascendant. The needles are fat and glossy, dark green above, silvery green below. These are ranked horizontally on either side of the twig and angle toward the twig tip. Twig bark is tan; trunk bark is bronzy-gray with horizontal markings. The effect from a distance is of rich, gray-green branch tips with dark green shadows within, a truly inspiring sight.

In scale, Nordmann's Fir is a large plant and would not remain an appropriate size for a small garden very long. When space is no problem, I like it best when three or more plants can be grown in association, well spaced apart, creating a grove-like feeling. I can think of nothing finer than associating Nordmann's Fir with Serbian Spruce *(Picea omorika)* in a grove. The Serbian Spruce is gray-green and has an open conical habit with gracefully arching branches, making a fine contrast with the stiffness of the fir. I would use approximately one-third Serbian Spruce, two-thirds Nordmann's Fir, allowing the lighter colored, more delicately formed Serbian Spruce to act as highlighting for the mix. This arrangement could well stand on its own; if seasonal interest is desired, a large massing of the Doublefile Viburnum *(Viburnum plicatum forma tomentosum)* could be included. The highly light-reflective white, flat-topped blossom clusters of this plant would add a rich glow to the grove in late May.

A similar relationship might be developed when highlighting a grove of Nordmann's Fir with several of the yellow-green *Pinus griffithii* 'Zebrina.' The underplanting in this case might have a winter interest emphasis using large masses of the golden variegated evergreen Elaeagnus, *Elaeagnus pungens* 'Maculata,' and occasional plants of the red-twigged Japanese Maple, *Acer palmatum* 'Senkaki.'

In a slightly smaller-scale situation three Nordmann's Firs might serve as background for a single Bigleaf Magnolia *(Magnolia macrophylla)* and a grouping of five or six White-flowered Dogwood. *Magnolia macrophylla* has enormous, bold, light green leaves, and in summer these and the tree's 12-inch white flowers would be considerably dramatized by the background of dark needles. The leaf buds of the Magnolia are just at the uncurling stage when the Dogwood blossoms peak. At this stage the fuzzy, silver-gray-green of the Magnolia leaves makes a marvelous highlight for the entire scene. The dogwoods would of course provide colored foliage and red fruit in the fall. In winter their dense horizontal branching contrasts happily with the open, ascendant habit of the larger Magnolia tree.

Abies nordmanniana was named for Alex von Nordmann, a Finnish botanist and professor of zoology, who discovered the tree in the mountains of Crimea in 1837. It was distributed in Britain a few years later by Charles L. Lawson of Edinburgh and was growing in Monza near Milan, Italy, as early as 1845. There are a number of fine old plants growing in the vicinity of Easton, Maryland. Since many of our finest firs and spruces do not do well where summers are hot, this is another big plus for *Abies nordmanniana.* A nurseryman named Hemming, who was with Easton's old Canterbury Nurseries in the 1920's, noted several handsome

Abies nordmanniana

specimens of this plant doing well in the area. His son tells us that there were "three fine specimens at 'Fairview' and another old one at Wye Mills, near the Wye Oak. This one used to stand above the surrounding trees as you drove down the old Centerville Road." The father was responsible for growing and popularizing *Abies nordmanniana* in the Easton area—an excellent example of the importance of careful observation of local performance of alien plant materials.

2

Betula nigra
River Birch, Red Birch

SEASONAL INTEREST

Deciduous
Effective landscape height: 50 feet
Effective landscape spread: 50 feet
Zone 5
Corylaceae (Hazelnut Family)
Native range: United States—Massachusetts and Minnesota to Florida

It is a mystery to me how this outstanding American plant can be so little known and used in this country. There is no finer plant for winter effect—not even the white Paperbark Birch of New England. Sometimes single-stemmed, sometimes multiple-stemmed, the trunks are always very straight and closely angled to the vertical. From a distance, their color is off-white with shadings of the softest, most incredibly beautiful warm pink. The trunks are seen through a veil of horizontal to ascendant branches, cherry-brown in color, and terminating in the finest, most delicate twigs. Moving closer, the viewer is entranced by the subtle color and textured detail of the bark. Some trunks are smoother, and exfoliate in larger patches than do others; some are rougher, and the bark comes off in smaller wrinkles and crinkles resembling ancient paper that has become wet and then dried. Where the off-white bark has peeled, the new underbark is a beautiful peach color; the back of the curling old bark, on the other hand, is deeper, in pink to bronze shades. This baroque mixture is punctuated by triangles of black, where side branches meet the trunks. The leaves are roughly diamond-shaped, a bright, cheerful green in spring and a good yellow in fall. The form is narrow and vertical when young, becoming round-topped with age and broadly so in dry locations.

There is no finer native scene than River Birch, Winterberry *(Ilex verticillata)*, the green twigs of Greenbriar *(Smilax rotundifolia)*, and the tawny tan of Poverty Grass *(Aristida dichotoma)*; no gardener with a yen for the naturalistic could be criticized for trying to imitate it. A more sophisticated use of the plant could well be with broadleaf evergreens of winter interest, such as the red-berried *Aucuba japonica* 'Longifolia' featured among the strap-shaped leaves of Lilyturf (*Liriope muscari* 'Big Blue'), and backed by Canadian Hemlock *(Tsuga canadensis)*. On the other hand, a strictly deciduous combination with interlocking groves of *Betula nigra* and Paperbark Maple *(Acer griseum)* under-planted with Baltic Ivy (*Hedera helix* 'Baltica') would make a most satisfying scene for the long winter months. The similar barks and contrasting tree forms would be an entrancing subtlety.

River Birch is commonly native in lowlands and along stream banks of eastern North America, where the soil is moist, even covered with water during several weeks of the year. The tree is very adaptable, however, and I have seen it doing perfectly well on higher sites several miles from water. Charles Sprague Sargent, long-time director of the Arnold Arboretum near Boston, pointed out an interesting adaptation River Birch makes with its environment in that the seeds ripen when water is at its lowest level, in the early summer and fall, and soon germinate in the moist, rich soil. Thus the young plants have gained a foothold by the time the waters return.

This plant is but one example of how we have foolishly neglected our natives when selecting plants for gardens. With White-flowered Dogwood and American Holly as notable exceptions, American gardeners have yet to open their eyes to such fine natives as American Beech *(Fagus grandifolia)*,

Betula nigra

American Plane Tree *(Platanus occidentalis)*, Virginia Juniper *(Juniperus virginiana)*, Staghorn Sumac *(Rhus typhina)*, Sassafras *(Sassafras albidum)*, Sour Gum *(Nyssa sylvatica)*, Joe Pye Weed *(Eupatorium purpureum)*, Iron Weed *(Vernonia novaboracensis)*, Butterfly Weed *(Asclepias tuberosa)*, Virginia Bluebells *(Mertensia virginica)*, and Bluets *(Houstonia caerulea)*, to mention just a few.

River Birch has been enthusiastically cultivated in Europe since its introduction there in 1736. There are records of both Peter Collinson and Phillip Miller, prominent British gardeners of the day, writing to John Custis at Williamsburg for seeds of the plant in the 1740's.

3

STRUCTURAL INTEREST

Evergreen
Effective landscape height: 50-70 feet
Effective landscape spread: 9 feet
Zone 6
Cuppressaceae (Cypress Family)
Native range: United States—Oregon and northern California

Calocedrus decurrens (*Libocedrus decurrens*)

Incense-cedar, California White-cedar

This native American conifer is uniquely beautiful both in form and color. The narrow fastigiate habit is notably dramatic. Because the top is not usually sharply pointed, however, and the manner in which the foliage is carried gives somewhat lumpy lines to the tree, there is a soft and aged quality about the form which is utterly charming. The color of the aromatic foliage is a bright green that persists all winter, unlike another familiar plant of the same form, Pyramidal Arborvitae (*Thuja occidentalis* 'Pyramidalis'). If you have ever seen *Calocedrus* growing in an arboretum closely associated with other needle evergreens, you will know that the quality of the bright green foliage, even when seen with its many relatives, is truly distinctive. Upon close examination, you will note that unlike most other conifers the needly branches are held in a near vertical fashion (always twisted slightly), thus allowing sunlight to get to both sides of the needles and causing them to be uniformly green on both surfaces. The trunk or trunks are generally much thicker at the base in proportion to the height of the tree than are those of other conifers. The bark is composed of long, narrow scales which periodically slough off revealing an attractive cinnamon-colored underskin. The same quality carries through to the smaller stems and twigs where there is a more curly exfoliation.

Whether used as a single phallic specimen or grouped as a shivery grove, *Calocedrus* really carries the show and other associated plant material becomes secondary. In a grove, I find the urge for little more than a ground cover of grass or interlocking patches of Variegated Liriope (*Liriope muscari* 'Variegata') and one of the evergreen Ivies—preferably, if your climate is mild enough, the bigleaf *Hedera canariensis.* Singly, the tall narrow spike is shown off most effectively by contrasting it with both tall rounded forms such as Yulan Magnolia *(Magnolia denudata)* and Star Magnolia *(M. stellata)* and distinctly horizontal forms such as Corkbark Euonymous *(Euonymous alatus)*, Washington Hawthorn *(Crataegus phaenopyrum)*, Yellow-flowered Dogwood *(Cornus officinalis)*, and Doublefile Viburnum *(Viburnum plicatum forma tomentosum).*

Because of the rapidly increasing caliper of the trunk, large specimens must carry exceptionally large balls of earth to be moved successfully. This becomes an expensive operation and makes it desirable to start your planting with smaller sizes. The root system is fleshy and therefore can suffer damage if moving is done during freezing weather. The plant is not terribly demanding but will really thrive in moist, deep loam. There are no serious foliage pests. The tendency of the tree to throw multiple stems can be a disadvantage in snowy areas. I have seen a handsome allée turned into an eyesore by a heavy, wet snow that broke out whole trunks leaving adjacent stems naked and ugly. For this reason either

Calocedrus decurrens

single-stem plants should be selected or the gardener should commit himself in advance to keeping multiple stems cabled together.

Incense-cedar is to be found from Oregon to Baja California and Nevada. It was discovered in 1846 by the American explorer John Charles Fremont and introduced to the European gardening public by the Scottish explorer John Jeffery (a member of the Oregon Association of Edinburgh) in 1853. The wood has been used for pencils, cedar chests, and cigar boxes. The native form of the tree is not always as fastigiate as is that of plants traditionally grown in gardens.

4

Cladrastis lutea
American Yellow-wood

SEASONAL INTEREST

Deciduous
Effective landscape height: 50 feet
Effective landscape spread: 50 feet
Zones 3-4
Leguminosae (Pea Family)
Native range: United States—North Carolina to Tennessee

Yellow-wood has a quality of elegance about it that is characteristic of no other shade tree. The branches rise from a proportionally stout trunk in an ascendant manner, to form a beautiful dome-shaped top. The handsome form is accentuated by the marvelously smooth, silvery-gray bark on older branches and trunks. This contrasts well with the black-brown of the newer growth shoots. The compound foliage is a handsome dark yellow-green; each leaf is composed of five to seven broadly oval, pointed leaflets, with the larger ones at the outer extremity, somewhat like those of hickories. The 12-inch pendulous clusters of white, fragrant flowers superficially resemble black locust or wisteria, and add a very decorative quality to the early June picture. The fall coloration is a handsome orange to yellow.

Cladrastis's umbrella-like quality provides the perfect canopy for shading a terrace or a spot of lawn. The roots are deep enough so that grass and other plants grow well in its shade, though it is certainly handsome enough to be featured as a free-standing specimen. On the other hand, its form also makes it desirable when framing a doorway or other feature in conjunction with other plantings. I like to use a combination of evergreen material with it, such as Dwarf Japanese Yew (*Taxus cuspidata* 'Nana'), Leucothoë *(Leucothoë fontanesiana)*, and *Pachysandra terminalis*, in order to dramatize the beautiful gray trunk.

If the gardener persists in the removal of side branches for a few years, the tree can be encouraged to take a more upright vase shape, closely resembling a small American Elm. Pruning when necessary should be done in early summer, for spring pruning causes the tree to bleed profusely. *Cladrastis* is easily transplanted; average garden soil will do. It may not bloom consistently every year, sometimes putting on a performance only every third year.

The wood itself is yellow, hence the name. The French botanist Francois Michaux is responsible for introducing the tree to gardeners in western Europe about 1808, and it has been grown there with enthusiasm since then. It received the Award of Merit from Britain's Royal Horticultural Society in 1924.

Cladrastis lutea

5

Fagus sylvatica 'Laciniata'
Cutleaf European Beech

Not exactly the ideal tree for the small place, or for the person seeking immediate effect, this garden aristocrat is of such outstanding merit that it should be given first consideration when these factors do not apply. In form this Beech is densely pyramidal, but the generally horizontal branches are sufficiently irregular in length and direction that the Beech's

STRUCTURAL INTEREST

Deciduous
Effective landscape height: 60 feet
Effective landscape spread: 65 feet
Zone 5
Fagaceae (Beech Family)
Native range: central and southern Europe

Fagus sylvatica 'Laciniata'

form, rather than being crisp, is wispy. This characteristic is enhanced by the close spacing and narrow diameter of the twigs, and the fineness of the leaves. The olive-green leaves are alternate, narrowly pointed, and deeply cut. The summer effect is charming in somewhat the same way as a kid with slightly mussed-up hair. As with most European Beeches, the young foliage in the spring is an absolute joy of soft gray-green. The fall foliage is a rich bronze, while the winter character is one of sturdy gray strength.

It is, of course, handsome as a freestanding specimen on a big expanse of lawn. Because of its denseness, it is a good plant for screening—even lending itself, in small-scale situations, to being used in hedge form. If you're lucky enough to have a bottom-land garden, place the Beech with some big boulders and with the contrasting forms and textures of *Magnolia grandiflora* or *Magnolia macrophylla* (similar form—broadleaf texture), Yellowgroove Bamboo, *Phyllostachys aureosulcata* (similar foliage—vertical form), the dinner-plate-size leaves of the Japanese ground cover, *Petasites japonica* (different form and different texture), and an accent of the pendulous leaved grass, *Erianthus ravennae*. This will certainly provide a textural treat.

It is curious that our American Beech *(Fagus grandifolia)* has shown no tendency to leaf variation at all while the European Beech has varied tremendously. The Cutleaf Beech was introduced into the United States in colonial times.

In England this plant received an Award of Garden Merit from the Royal Horticultural Society in 1969.

6

Fagus sylvatica 'Pendula'

Weeping European Beech

Weeping Beech is an extremely strong design statement in any landscape setting in which it occurs. This is both because of its distinctly pendulous nature and because of an air of venerableness that it evokes. The latter quality is especially noticeable in winter when it is leafless and the gray, gnarly, iron-like quality of the trunk and branches is clearly visible. The smooth bark contributes a muscle-like quality to the whole form. The picture sustains interest as the changing quality of light produces a variety of fascinating shadow patterns. This structure is concealed in summer by a dome of typical Beech leaves, although the pendulous nature of the plant is still apparent.

Fagus sylvatica 'Pendula' is a slow-growing, long-lived tree. As such, it is an appropriate plant for use in institutional (campus, park, or club) settings, where it can remain undisturbed for more than one generation. Because it is attractive at any age, however, there is no reason why any contemporary home owner, even when space is limited, should not consider enjoying its beauties for at least a portion of its life span. Such an attitude might make the Beech expendable after a certain number of years. I find this a perfectly acceptable viewpoint on the basis that *any* plant not at the moment appropriate for its location is a weed and may properly be treated as such. So much for the urge to enrich our contemporary lives!

One major drawback of any Beech is the surface rooting characteristic. This makes it extremely difficult, if not impossible, to establish permanent lawn or other plantings beneath their limbs. How-

STRUCTURAL INTEREST

Deciduous
Effective landscape height: 50 feet
Effective landscape spread: 65 feet
Zone 5
Fagaceae (Beech Family)
Native range: central and southern Europe

ever, since this area is generally hidden by the pendulous branches, it is not a major drawback.

Aesthetically, of course, Weeping Beech must be classified as a "character" tree. As such, an association with other plants with irregular lines only dissipates its effect, whereas associating it with strong architectural forms emphasizes its great beauty. Such forms may be truly architectural. Or they may be other plants used in architectural ways, or plants that are in themselves architectural.

In the early period of large estate development in this country, in the style known as English landscape school, *Fagus sylvatica*, in all its forms, played a large role. Today, *Fagus sylvatica* 'Pendula' is often used as a specimen plant with the very strong, clean rectilinear forms of contemporary architecture. Often the only other associated materials will be a rock, some pebbles, and a large patch of ground cover. This stark simplicity is refreshing, provides the perfect foil for the Beech, and conversely the Beech provides a marvelous softening quality to the architecture. The same net result occurs where a specimen Weeping Beech is used in the foreground of a view backed by a crisply trimmed hedge. Such a situation might exist where a Hemlock hedge *(Tsuga canadensis)* provides background for an exuberant planting of deciduous Azaleas or Tree Peonies. The Beech in the foreground, by virtue of its branching structure, would lead the eye down to the horticultural display. The hedge would provide a strong horizontal line which would, by contrast, emphasize the irregular character of the Beech.

A less formal variation on this theme would be to use the Beech in a similar manner in the foreground, with a planting of studied, occult balance behind. The Beech, in this case, would be to left of the center of the view. Directly behind it would be a long, dense, mounded sweep of hybrid Rhododendron terminating on the right in a grouping of three very neatly pyramidal conifers such as Nordmann's Fir *(Abies nordmanniana)*. The Rhododendrons in this case individually have softer curves to their form than with the Hemlock hedge above, but a strong horizontal line is created by the long sweep of their use, and strong angular lines are produced by the dense conifers.

Another version would be simply to plant an informal grouping (of a single variety) of small trees or shrubs (behind the Beech), selecting a variety which has a very distinct horizontal habit. Such plants as Sargent's Crab Apple *(Malus sargentii)*, Winged Euonymous *(Euonymous alatus)*, or Pfitzer Juniper (*Juniperus chinensis* 'Pfitzeriana') might be used.

It is interesting that European Beech *(Fagus sylvatica)* has been so variable. W. J. Bean in *Trees and Shrubs Hardy in the British Isles* (Vol. 2, 1973) lists 23 clones. American Beech, on the other hand, doesn't seem to mutate at all. There appear to be significant shades of difference among individual plants called *Fagus sylvatica* 'Pendula' even. Two of the oldest Weeping Beeches in the United States are thought to be different enough to be of distinctly separate origin. One is the famous Flushing Weeping Beech, planted in 1847 by Samuel Parsons, a Flushing nurseryman who brought it back from Europe that year in a pot. The other is a superb specimen growing near West Chester, Pennsylvania, which is believed to have been planted about the same time. It is 65 feet in spread, 50 feet in height and there are two distinct rings of outrigger trees—the result of pendulous branches rooting. The West Chester tree is not so tall as the Flushing tree (as of 1968) but is broader and has more ascendant terminal branchlets. One of the most curious forms of European Beech is *Fagus sylvatica* 'Tortuosa,' which has been found over the years in Denmark, Germany, and two locations in France. According to J. R. P. van Hoey Smith, all of these locations are in a straight line across the face of Europe, and he speculates that this mutation may have occurred because of the influence of an ancient radioactive meteor.

Fagus sylvatica 'Pendula'

7

Gymnocladus dioica
Kentucky Coffee-Tree

SEASONAL INTEREST

Deciduous
Effective landscape height: 100 feet
Effective landscape spread: 65 feet
Zone 5
Leguminosae (Pea Family)
Native range: United States—New York to Nebraska and Tennessee

Kentucky Coffee-Tree's value as a landscape plant lies both in its rugged winter silhouette and its dramatic summer foliage. The rather vertical round-topped form is structured by a few heavy branches with twigs terminating in fat, blunt tips. In matured plants the topmost branches have the somewhat serpentine character of old native Persimmon trees, all the more dramatic because of their wide spacing. Many of the lower branches descend downward in a somewhat pendulous manner. There is a handsome, vertical, scale-like pattern to the bark on the trunk. This progressively becomes more curling as the eye moves out the branches. This exfoliating quality is very teasing to the viewer on a winter day—and downright spectacular when decorated with snow!

The foliage, which is tremendous in proportions, is pink when unfolding, an attractive blue-green during the summer, and yellow in the autumn. The leaves are singly and doubly compound, up to 26 inches or more in length. A typical leaf has nine lateral rachides, each with eleven leaflets. The leaf-stalk is reddish. A curious effect is produced in the fall by the leaflets falling and leaving the naked common stalk on the branch for some time. The white flowers are not particularly conspicuous, with female flowers on trees separate from those that bear the smaller male flowers. Large bean-like fruits 6–10 inches long are in attractive scale with the foliage during the summer and an extremely decorative part of the winter silhouette of the female tree. Residents of Kentucky and Tennessee in early days roasted and ground these seeds to make a coffee-like beverage—hence, the common name Kentucky Coffee-Tree.

At any time of year this open, sturdy plant radiates "health and vigor." It is very undemanding, thriving in average garden soil and—like all members of the pea family—manufacturing its own nitrogen. It is not a good shade tree because of the open habit, because the leaves come late and drop early, and because it is very slow-growing. However, in situations where space is not at a premium and time is not of the essence, this rugged American beauty has much to offer.

8

Koelreuteria paniculata

Goldenrain-Tree, Varnish-Tree

This medium-sized tree is an excellent example of one that is valuable both as a shade and flowering tree. Handsome, dark green foliage clothes the irregular branching, round-topped structure. The large (6–18-inch-long) compound leaves are composed of small (1–4-inch) leaflets with an interestingly toothed edge. There are usually seven pairs of leaves plus a tip leaflet to each leaf. The leaves are thick on the tree and the shade is most satisfactory. The blossom spikes in late June project 12–18 inches beyond the foliage, are a very cheerful yellow, and consist of quantities of small flowers arranged with the delicacy of jewels in a tiara. Both the color and texture contrast handsomely with the foliage and relieve any concern we may have about going without flowers once "spring is past!" The blossoms are followed in July and August by clusters of light green, lantern-like seed pods, which are extremely ornamental. In spring the new growth is an attractive reddish-orange color, making an intriguing sight against the tan-colored twig and branch growth. The foliage turns yellow in the fall.

SEASONAL INTEREST

Deciduous
Effective landscape height: 30 feet
Effective landscape spread: 40 feet
Zone 6
Sapindaceae (Soapberry Family)
Native range: China, Korea, and Japan

Koelreuteria paniculata

Goldenrain-Tree makes a fine statement alone, and provides excellent shade for any kind of an outdoor living area. There are many choices for blooming companions where it is used primarily for its blossom effect. Under its boughs the handsome blue Hydrangea (*Hydrangea macrophylla* varieties) and spiky, white-blossomed Black Snakeroot *(Cimicifuga racemosa)* may be planted in drifts and surrounded with a ground-cover planting of chartreusey Variegated Liriope (*Liriope muscari* 'Variegata'). This makes a very cool and cheerful combination. A "hotter" but even more colorful scheme would combine the white-flowered Oakleaf Hydrangea *(Hydrangea quercifolia)* with large drifts of the soft yellow Day-lily, *Hemerocallis* x 'Hyperion,' and the rusty-orange Butterfly Weed *(Asclepias tuberosa)*. Another alternative where space is not limited: a single Goldenrain-Tree could be featured against a mass planting of the fine, gray-foliaged Willow, *Salix elaeagnos*, backed by a clump of four or five Redleaf Plums *(Prunus cerasifera* 'Thundercloud'). The finer, contrasting foliage shapes of the willow and plum would emphasize the dramatic textures of the leaves and flowers on the *Koelreuteria*. Also the contrasting gray and wine foliage masses would anchor the bouquet-like *Koelreuteria*, with its striking, bright yellow, conical flowers.

Koelreuteria dislikes winter planting and cold, wet soil. I recommend spring planting and a sunny site that is well drained. Good loamy soil is ideal although it adapts readily to light, sandy, and gravelly soils. For some reason its bark is attractive to sap suckers whose attentions if allowed to continue for several years can kill the tree. Goldenrain-Tree is very easily raised from seed, making an excellent project for children.

According to John Wister (1947), the French Jesuit d'Incarville discovered *Koelreuteria* and sent it to Paris in 1750. It was in commerce in the United States in 1790 and listed at that time by the Prince Nursery on Long Island. In England, *Koelreuteria paniculata* received an Award of Merit from the Royal Horticultural Society in 1932.

9

Magnolia heptapeta
(M. denudata, M. conspicua)
Yulan Magnolia

SEASONAL INTEREST

Deciduous
Effective landscape height: 40 feet
Effective landscape spread: 30 feet
Zone 6
Magnoliaceae (Magnolia Family)
Native range: central China

Yulan Magnolia carries itself with a noble bearing at all times of the year and puts on a breathtaking display of waxy white flowers early every spring. This tree is slow-growing and has the reliable, sturdy look typical of plants with this characteristic. The pyramidal form is structured by a dense branching habit; the older branches and trunks have a smooth, tannish-gray bark. The flower buds, enclosed in large scales and covered with gray fuzz, are conspicuous all winter, adding a touch to its winter habit which signifies health, robustness, and a real promise of spring. The pure white flowers are born in profusion in April. They carry 3-inch petals which are extremely light-reflective. At first upright (forming handsome cups), they later spread out in a most voluptuous manner. Foliage follows the flowers and gives a heavy cover to the crown. The leaves are oval (3–6 inches long and 2–3½ inches wide) and are a clean, medium green all summer. The fruit is spindle-shaped and about 5 inches long.

Yulan Magnolia is truly one of the aristocrats of the landscape, and would be a prime candidate for the garden which could have only one tree. Because, whether single- or multistemmed, it can be "limbed up"—have its lower limbs removed without spoiling its beauty—it can double as both a shade and flowering tree. Its good winter habit makes it a desirable feature near a window of the house. Because of the excellence and earliness of the blossom effect, a flowering scheme can be built around it which sets the standard for the entire season.

One possible combination might feature *Magnolia heptapeta* as a single specimen against three or

four plants of its blooming companion, the Yellow-flowered Dogwood *(Cornus officinalis)*. The Dog-woods would remain lower in height, the mass as well as the individual branching habit emphasizing the horizontal, contrasting with, and thereby emphasizing, the taller, more vertical quality of the Magnolia. The foreground might well be planted with a potpourri of blues, such as the creeping *Phlox stolonifera* 'Blue Ridge,' early blue Grape-hyacinths *(Muscari armeniacum)*, and the large blue-flowered Periwinkle (*Vinca minor* 'Bowles'). The quality of delicacy in the fine yellow flowers of the Dogwoods and the foreground flowers would seem by contrast to show off the heavier, sculptural charm of the white Magnolia cups.

Another combination might use Yulan Magnolia and its blooming mate, the white-flowered Manchu Cherry *(Prunus tomentosa)*, as a background planting to feature the yellow-flowered Winterhazel, *Corylopsis glabrescens*. I would aim for one mature Magnolia in the far back, faced with four or five Cherries; three Winterhazels could then be closely clustered off-center in the foreground. The vertical stems of the Winterhazel would make a happy contrast with the horizontal habit of the Cherries; the pendulous sharp yellow blossoms of the Winterhazel would have a happy background in the less relaxed white mix of Magnolia and Cherry blossoms. This scene could be further enhanced by a great foreground carpet of white-flowered bulbs such as the white *Chionodoxa* and white Grape-hyacinths (*Muscari* sp.) and this might be spiced with a clump of the beautiful, white trumpet Narcissus, *Narcissus* x 'Beersheba.' The result would be a rich spring symphony of whites and yellows, as contrasted with the previous alternative involving whites, yellows, and blues.

A cold February and March suit this plant best, as such weather holds the buds back until there is less chance of the plant flowering early and the blossoms being destroyed by a late frost. This is, of course, one of the gambles involved in planning early spring blooming combinations. The reward is so great in the case of *Magnolia heptapeta,* however, that it's well worth the risk.

Yulan Magnolia had been cultivated in China for at least 1,300 years before its introduction to England in 1780 under the sponsorship of Sir Joseph Banks. It was commonly planted near temples and in the Imperial Gardens. Unfortunately, it was neglected for a number of years in England, where it was long thought to be half-hardy and treated as a conservatory plant (until 1826 or later). It reached the United States in the 1820's, soon after its acceptance in England as an outdoor plant, and enjoyed considerable popularity here for a number of years. This was unjustifiably eclipsed by later introductions such as the pink Saucer Magnolia *(Magnolia soulangeana)*, of which it is one parent, and related hybrids. Its slow rise to eminence in England was probably due to the relatively greater interest in *Magnolia grandiflora,* the evergreen member of the family, introduced from the United States between 1724 and 1738. Yulan Magnolia now occupies a position of high respect in England, having received an Award of Garden Merit from the Royal Horticultural Society in 1936 and its First Class Certificate in 1968. It is to be hoped American gardeners will awaken to its charms and make wider use of it in the future.

10

Magnolia grandiflora
Southern Magnolia, Evergreen
Magnolia, Bull-bay

William Flemer III has called *Magnolia grandiflora* "one of the world's choicest flowering trees." I feel that this praise is entirely justified because it comes very close to meeting the request for an ideal plant I heard made by an inexperienced gardener shopping

STRUCTURAL INTEREST

Evergreen
Effective landscape height: 40 feet
Effective landscape spread: 25 feet
Zone 7
Magnoliaceae (Magnolia Family)
Native range: United States — North Carolina to Florida, and west to Texas

in a garden center. "The plant," she explained, "must grow fast, not get too big, have big shiny green leaves all year, and large fragrant red flowers continuously for several months." *Magnolia grandiflora* does grow fast and doesn't get terribly large in the mid-Atlantic states. It has really handsome, thick, oval, dark green leaves, 5–8 inches long, and so glossy as to look as though they had just been polished. The blossoms are not red (contrary to the specification of the above-mentioned woman) but a spectacular creamy white, 8–12 inches across (usually composed of six very waxy petals), and sport a cluster of attractive yellow anthers in the center. The blossoms appear fairly continuously during late June, July, and August and are richly fragrant. The fruit matures in late summer through early fall, and consists of cucumber-like pods with a tan velvet coat. These split open at maturity revealing shiny, red-coated seeds of considerable beauty.

The overall character of the tree is dense and pyramidal, giving it a distinctly architectural quality. As such, it is a great asset in the winter landscape. Except for the possibility of contrasting it with a group of bright, yellow-green needly evergreens such as *Juniperus chinensis* 'Armstrong' it needs the company of few, if any, other evergreens to enhance its winter effect. I find great magic in a winter scene featuring *Magnolia grandiflora* with plants of good bark and twig color such as River Birch *(Betula nigra)*, Yellowgroove Bamboo *(Phyllostachys aureosulcata)* and *Kerria japonica* (both with green stems), and Redtwig Dogwood *(Cornus sericea)* or the Japanese Redtwig Maple, *Acer palmatum* 'Senkaki.'

If it is being used in a large-scale situation, deciduous trees of contrasting form and foliage are this Magnolia's best companions. These might include Willow Oak *(Quercus phellos)*, Goldentwig Weeping Willow (*Salix alba* var. 'tristis'), Japanese Pagoda-Tree (*Sophora japonica* 'Regent'), Golden-larch *(Pseudolarix amabilis)*, and Cutleaf Beech (*Fagus sylvatica* 'Laciniata').

Where less space is available, the emphasis could well be placed on featuring the Magnolia in a potpourri of summer bloomers, selecting from any of the following which are hardy in your area: Mimosa (*Albizia julibrissin* 'Rosea'), with its pink powder-puff blossoms, *Vitex agnus-castus* 'Latifolia' (blue-purple spikes), blue and pink Althaea (*Hibiscus syriacus* 'Blue Bird' or *H. syriacus* 'Woodbridge'), pink Crape-myrtle *(Lagerstroemia indica)*, light yellow Day-lilies (*Hemerocallis* x 'Hyperion'), or *Tamarix* 'Pink Cascade.'

Magnolia grandiflora has been called "the glory of Southern gardens and the envy of Northern gardeners" because it was believed for years that it would not grow north of its natural range, North Carolina. With the increasing demand for broadleaf evergreens in the 1940's and 1950's, many traditionally "Southern" plants were tried farther north. The plants of *Magnolia grandiflora* that were sent North from Southern nurseries had been grown from seed; as with any seedling population, there was a great variation in the Magnolia's tolerance of severe winter conditions. Some plants survived happily on Long Island and in northern New Jersey. Selections from seedling populations have consciously been made for qualities other than hardiness, and some sixty to seventy varieties have been named. However, compared with the amount of breeding effort put forth on roses for instance, relatively little breeding has been done with evergreen magnolias. The chief exceptions are the work of J. C. McDaniel at the University of Illinois and of the plant breeders at the U.S. National Arboretum. From the latter source has come *Magnolia* x 'Freeman' which will withstand the cold winters of Urbana, Illinois. Of the *Magnolia grandiflora* seedling selections, *M. grandiflora* 'Empire State' was selected by H. Harold Hume as the best tree on Long Island. My own favorite is *M. grandiflora* 'Edith Bogue,' a selection that has proven reliably hardy in Montclair, New Jersey.

In its native range it is a lowland tree with a marked preference for moist, rich soil. It is therefore surprising to learn that it seems to grow well under a variety of conditions including those of the inner city. The heavy waxy coating on the leaves probably

Magnolia grandiflora

accounts for this tree's extra resistance to air pollutants. In the North *Magnolia grandiflora* is, of course, subject to mechanical injury from snow damage. This is not too serious a problem, however, as the tree responds quickly with lush new growth from any damaged area. Plants of *Magnolia grandiflora grown from seed* are often quite old (twenty years or older) before having their first blossom. You will often hear the claim made that one variety or another will produce flowers when quite small. This is really because it was produced as a *cutting, layer, or graft* (as would be the case with any horticultural variety). The home gardener is generally better off selecting a named variety which has qualities (particularly hardiness) suited to his requirements and which has been propagated asexually, thus ensuring blossoms at an early age.

Magnolia grandiflora has been well appreciated in Europe since its early introduction there in 1734. A fine old specimen at Malmaison was a great favorite of the Empress Josephine.

Aborigines generally have taken more interest in and shown more concern about fragrance than gardeners today. Alice Coats (1965) tells us that the Indians would not sleep under a *Magnolia grandiflora* because of the overpowering scent of its flowers—"one of which if kept in a bedroom, could cause death in a single night." However unbelievable that claim may be, such a concern is laughable in my own area where the plant is relatively rare and the scent on a summer evening the greatest treat imaginable!

11

Nyssa sylvatica
Sour Gum, Black Gum,
Tupelo, Pepperidge

SEASONAL INTEREST

Deciduous
Effective landscape height: 90 feet
Effective landscape spread: 50 feet
Zone 5
Nyssaceae (Tupelo Family)
Native range: United States—Maine to Texas and west

This large, lush-foliaged, native American tree provides us with absolutely spectacular red coloration in early fall. It has a straight trunk, quite orderly horizontal branches to the ground, and a regular pyramidal form when young. This is in contrast to its mature shape, when most of the lower branches disappear (except for occasional "feathers"), and a smaller rather horizontal crown with some branches pendulous, most irregular, is retained high up on the trunk. The twigs are lush and stubby. The leaves are about 6 inches long, generally oval and pointed at both ends, thick, and extremely lustrous. The fruit is a dark blue berry appearing in midsummer. The overall effect of these trees when young is that of good health and great vigor; older trees have the aura of venerable giants.

Nyssa is a handsome addition to any garden. A needly background of gracefully branched Canadian Hemlock *(Tsuga canadensis)* emphasizes all its fine qualities. This might be contrasted with a broadleaf foreground planting of Adam's Needle *(Yucca smalliana)* in large-scale situations, or Lilyturf *(Liriope muscari* 'Big Blue') where smaller scale is more appropriate. Although *Nyssa* does equally well whether planted on hillside or in hollow, it is natively found most often in bottomland or actually adjacent to water in some form. It is a natural, therefore, as a key feature in a pond planting and combines well with those other early fall performers: Asiatic Sweetleaf *(Symplocos paniculata)*, with its shiny blue berries, and Franklin Tree *(Franklinia alatamaha)*, with its yellow-centered, white, camellia-like flowers. These would all, in turn, be enhanced by that great textural combination: Japanese Butterbur *(Pestasites japonica)*, known for its enormous round leaves, and Maiden Grass (*Miscanthus sinensis* 'Gracillimus'), with its neat vertical grass foliage.

Sour Gum has been very little used in American landscaping because it has a notoriously sensitive root system, and transplants very poorly when normal nursery techniques are used. More recently, it has proven to be an excellent subject for container growing, and is now readily available in and easily transplanted from five-gallon cans. Since larger sizes of the plant do present a moving problem, gardeners must be content to plant a small tree and wait. Because the reward is so great, I have no hesitation in recommending this course of action.

The British have grown it enthusiastically since its introduction into their country from Virginia wetlands in the early 1700's. Peter Collinson, writing to John Bartram in the later decades of the century, repeatedly requested seeds of the Tupelo.

The Royal Horticultural Society has recognized the merits of this tree on three occasions: it received the Award of Merit in 1951, a First Class Certificate in 1968, and the Award of Garden Merit in 1969.

12

STRUCTURAL INTEREST

Evergreen
Effective landscape height: 60 feet
Effective landscape spread: 50 feet
Zone 5
Pinaceae (Pine Family)
Native range: northwest China

Pinus bungeana
Lacebark Pine

Lacebark Pine combines the charming characteristics of a good short-needled pine, a Birch clump, and a Sycamore. The needles, carried in bundles of three, are an attractive yellow-green, rather evenly spaced over the crown. The tree is often multistemmed, and the branches are ascendant. It is usually round-topped, not sharply pyramidal. Its most outstanding feature is its multicolored bark. Basically brownish-gray, the bark exfoliates in irregular peels, revealing dark apple-green and lighter yellow-green patches. Sunlight filtering through the needles makes changing shadow patterns of great magic on the variegated bark. There is apparently considerable genetic variation in this bark characteristic, for some trees become mottled at earlier ages than others and some are more strongly exfoliated than others. In fact, some very old trees in China are reported to have trunks which have turned completely white.

Because it is very hardy and of interest all year, Lacebark Pine must surely be classified as one of the aristocrats of the garden. It makes a fine specimen plant. In fact, it is used most effectively this way in a formal garden at the U. S. National Arboretum in Washington, D.C. A fine tree form, multistemmed specimen is centered in and shades a brick landing in the steps leading to the arboretum's Azalea garden. Adjacent plantings feature such broadleaf evergreens as Dwarf Chinese Holly (*Ilex cornuta* 'Rotunda') and Evergreen Magnolia *(Magnolia grandiflora).*

Pinus bungeana

Lacebark Pine is a wonderful plant in a winter setting both because of its interesting bark and because its small-scale, light green needles are an excellent contrast for broadleaf evergreens. I have always found *Camellia* gardens somewhat dull from the point of view of landscape interest. Solid plantings of their heavy foliage are not a particularly inspiring sight even when relieved by the trunks of handsome old hardwoods. This can be remedied by the addition of an occasional Lacebark Pine, which both lightens the whole effect and provides, by virtue of its trunks, an occasional focal point. The addition to such a scene of drifts of evergreen ground covers such as a small-leaf ivy like *Hedera helix* 'Shamrock' and the chartreusey Golden Variegated Liriope (*Liriope muscari* 'Variegata') would add the superlative touch of color and textural interest.

To feature a specimen *Pinus bungeana* in a sunny situation, one might well develop adjacent evergreen plantings emphasizing various shades of green. I think particularly of the shiny dark green Japanese

Holly, *Ilex crenata* 'Compacta,' the yellow-green Juniper, *Juniperus chinensis* 'Armstrong,' bronze-foliaged Leucothoë *(Leucothoë fontanesiana)*, and the dark green, shrub-like Ivy, *Hedera helix* 'Conglomerata Erecta.'

Pinus bungeana is slow-growing and undemanding in its requirements. It was named after a botanist from St. Petersburg, Alexander von Bunge (1803–1890), who explored many areas of northeastern Asia, and wrote extensively of his findings. For many years he was professor of botany at the University of Dorpat. He first saw the plant in 1831 in the environs of Peking, where it had been planted for its remarkable white trunks. It was first introduced to the Western world by Robert Fortune in 1846 and was first named in honor of von Bunge in 1897. Subsequently it was seen in great quantity as a forest tree by Ernest H. Wilson during his plant explorations in western China.

13

STRUCTURAL INTEREST

Evergreen
Effective landscape height: 45 feet
Effective landscape spread: 40 feet
Zone 2
Pinaceae (Pine Family)
Native range: western United States and Canada to Texas and Baja California in Mexico

Pinus flexilis
Limber Pine

This somewhat variable American native is both tough and attractive. It is a hardy Rocky Mountain plant, tolerant of both low temperatures and drought. In addition, the branches are so flexible that it sheds snow loads very effectively. In fact, some plants have branches so pliable that they can be tied in knots! The needles are short (2¼ inches), rather blue-green, and are thickly congested on the branches. Individual needles have a slight curl as hairs in a well-used paint brush. The tree itself (at least in our Eastern climate) is rather squat and round-topped and very thickly branched. This dense mound-like quality might be unattractive if it were

not for the charming, irregular, wispy quality of
the branch tips. These always have an attractive
twist to them and are generally ascendant. The bark
is a medium gray with horizontal markings, and the
new buds highlight the foliage with their light tan
coloration. Some variants have bluer foliage, longer
needles, and a more open pendulous habit. I find
them all extremely attractive.

Because of its dense slow-growing quality, *Pinus
flexilis* is valuable for use on small properties. It
has some of the admirable characteristics of White
Pine *(Pinus strobus)* but is much less overwhelming.

Limber Pine, because of its blue-green coloration,
makes an interesting winter companion for bronzy
foliages and other plants having a blue-gray tint. For
instance, a single *Pinus flexilis* might be featured
against the bronzy, willow-like foliage of five red-
fruited *Cotoneaster salicifolia* 'Flocossa,' these in
turn backed by three or four twiggy, gray-barked
Star Magnolia *(Magnolia stellata)*. Or, a single gray-
green barked Korean Dogwood *(Cornus kousa)*
might be featured in a sea of bronze, pendant Leucothoë *(Leucothoë fontanesiana)*, using three Limber
Pines as the background. Limber Pine could also be
an excellent background for featuring three plants
of the dramatic broad-leaved Leatherleaf Mahonia
(Mahonia bealei) in a mass planting of Redtwig Dogwood *(Cornus sericea)*.

Anyone who enjoys conifers as a group could make
an extremely pleasant planting using interlocking
groves of *Pinus flexilis, Pinus cembra* (Swiss Stone
Pine), *Pinus parviflora* (Japanese White Pine), and
Pinus aristata (Bristle-cone Pine). All are gray to
blue-green in color. All are short needled and slow-
growing. The interest in this case arises from the
intriguing variation in size and form. The Swiss
Stone Pine is very narrow and columnar, while the
Japanese White Pine is very open and irregular. The
Bristle-cone Pine is so slow-growing that it might
just as well be treated as a true dwarf and used as a
small "feature grove" midst all the rest.

First known in 1823, as a result of the Long ex-
pedition to the Rocky Mountains, it did not become

Pinus flexilis

a garden subject until 1861, although it was known to some European botanists as early as 1847. It was named a new species by Edwin P. James (1797–1861), physician-botanist in the Long party, who worked later at the Smithsonian.

14

Quercus phellos
Willow Oak, Peach Oak, Water Oak, Swamp Oak

STRUCTURAL INTEREST

Deciduous
Effective landscape height: 50 feet
Effective landscape spread: 30 feet
Zone 6
Fagaceae (Beech Family)
Native range: United States—New York, south along Eastern seaboard to Gulf States

Willow Oak comes close to being the perfect shade tree. As a very small plant it develops a strong central leader, with horizontal to ascendant branches. This habit quickly matures into a rigid frame with a round-topped, pyramidal shape. At maturity the ascendant branches often predominate, giving the tree a vase shape. At any rate, the branches never have that depressing, crowding, downward thrust so typical of Pin Oak. The twigs are abundant and very fine, having a softening effect on the tree's basically sturdy form. The root system is deep and compact making it easy to transplant and enabling the owner to grow a good crop of grass beneath its boughs. The leaves, as the name implies, are very linear, like willow leaves, seldom more than ½ inch wide but running up to 5 inches long. These are a medium yellow-green, densely clothing the crown and providing excellent shade. The foliage turns a good yellow in the fall and because of the small size of the leaves is easily managed from a leaf raker's viewpoint.

Aesthetically, Willow Oak has a tough, reliable-looking frame but, because of the fine foliage, none of the coarse and overwhelming aspects of other oak, maple, and linden varieties. As such it is ideal where a generous-sized shade tree is needed on a small property.

The foliage has a cool-looking quality which is very refreshing on a hot summer day. This can be emphasized by planting broader-leaf plant materials with it. In the small garden, this might be a Rhododendron and Leucothoë grouping below its branches. In more spacious surroundings adjacent trees might include such broadleaf beauties as Empress-Tree *(Paulownia tomentosa)*, Bigleaf Magnolia *(Magnolia macrophylla)*, or Common Catalpa *(Catalpa bignonioides.)*

In my area, which approaches the northern part of the Willow Oak's range, spring or late winter planting is recommended over fall planting. Plants set out in the fall often winterkill, whereas those planted early in the year do not. One can speculate that this is because the tree is slower than other species of oak to go into a state of dormancy in the fall.

Its timber is valued for pilings, general construction, boat building, and other uses where bending qualities are important. Although it is commercially mature at seventy years or less, trees of one hundred fifty years of age are common.

In its natural lowland habitat it often grows up to 100 feet with a trunk diameter of 4 feet. It is as fast-growing as any other really good shade tree and takes on a shade-providing form very quickly, maturing under *average* garden conditions at around 50 feet.

Quercus phellos is a good example of another American native which is an excellent garden subject. It was early cultivated in this country, introduced into Europe by 1723, and had become a regular export item from William Prince's nursery at Flushing, Long Island, by 1800.

Quercus phellos

15

STRUCTURAL INTEREST

Deciduous
Effective landscape height: 75 feet
Effective landscape spread: 65 feet
Zone 2
Salicaceae (Willow Family)
Native range: Europe and North Africa to central Asia

Salix alba var. *tristis*

Goldentwig Weeping Willow

This large tree is of outstanding value in the garden all year because of its pendulous habit, and is of very special interest in the wintertime because of the yellow color of its twigs. *Salix alba* var. *tristis* is a fast grower, often putting on four feet of growth in a single year. This quality contributes to the general impression of lushness so characteristic of this tree. The twigs are very fine, and the streamers long. The round-topped form has the feeling of a good head of thick, long hair, neatly combed. The yellow color of the twigs becomes brighter as spring approaches. The buds visibly fatten earlier than most trees, and the small leaves are one of the earliest and most convincing evidences that spring may really be coming at last. Alice Coats (1965) states that "the Willow seems to have been considered the emblem of spring long before it was adopted as the 'Palm' used in processions on Palm Sunday in some of the colder parts of Northern Europe, where the early Christian people were unable to find the true palm leaf." When full blown, the leaves are yellow-green above, white below. As breezes wave the weeping branches, the overall effect is gray-green.

Weeping Willow is practically a storybook tree because of its traditional association with water. And, indeed, there is no finer association than a single freestanding Willow on green lawn at a pond's edge. The pendulous habit leads the eye downward to whatever activity or reflections may occur at the water's surface.

The pendulous form is useful in many garden settings simply to keep the eye within the garden rather than allowing it to fly skyward. It is best associated with rounded or horizontal forms. Vertical forms only contradict its downward motion and set up an unpleasant tension. As a specimen lawn plant in a relatively small-scale situation, Goldentwig Weeping Willow would be appropriately backed by a combination of rounded, dark, broadleaf evergreens such as Roundleaf Osmanthus *(Osmanthus rotundifolius)* or Roundleaf Japanese Holly *(Ilex crenata* 'Compacta') and the horizontal branching Paperbark Maple *(Acer griseum)*. The broad, dark green texture would emphasize the fine texture and yellow color of the Willow by contrast. The bronze, horizontal character of the Maple would provide a rich background.

Alternatively, in a larger-scale area the nearer background plants might be 'Nellie R. Stevens' Holly *(Ilex* x 'Nellie R. Stevens') or Chinese Holly *(Ilex cornuta)*. The silhouette plants in the far background could be either Coffee-Tree *(Gymnocladus dioica)* or Mossycup Oak *(Quercus macrocarpa)*. Again, the Hollies possess broad-textured evergreen foliage, and the form and textural strength of the silhouettes of these background trees contrast with the silhouette of the Willow.

Salix alba var. *tristis*, of course, makes a good *background* plant for a multitude of garden situations. Suppose, for instance, that your objective was to feature a plant or a sculpture that was of strong horizontal design by planting a background strong in winter interest. In fact, suppose the plant to be featured was a Tanyosho Pine (*Pinus densiflora* 'Umbraculifera'). This plant is characterized by ascendant, irregular orange-brown trunks topped with a very flat, yellow-green crown. Immediately around the Pine might be a ground-cover planting of bronze-foliaged Leucothoë *(Leucothoë fontanesiana)*, behind this an extensive planting of *Kerria japonica* (with its vertical, bright green stems—which in mass would read as a strong horizontal), behind this several plants of the red-berried, bronze-foliaged Willowleaf Cotoneaster (*Cotoneaster salicifolia* 'Flocossa'), and behind this one or more Goldentwig Weeping Willows. The broad bronze foliage of the Cotoneaster and Leucothoë would provide stimulating contrast for the yellow-green of the Pine,

Salix alba var. *tristis*

while the fine yellow and green characteristics of the Willow and *Kerria* would relate to these same elements in the Pine. The Willow, the Cotoneaster, and the Leucothoë are all pendulous in nature, providing contrasting form for the horizontality of the Pine and associated *Kerria* planting. This is a rich grouping to which the Willow makes a major contribution.

Salix alba var. *tristis* is well worth searching out in preference to the Babylon Weeping Willow *(Salix babylonica)*, both because of its yellow twigs and because it is considerably hardier (Zone 2 versus Zone 6). Because of an unfortunate confusion of nomenclature in the nursery trade, this Willow is sometimes offered under the names *Salix vitellina* 'Pendula' and *Salix niobe*. There also seem to be some forms in the trade with longer, more pendulous branches than others. Certainly these plants should be sought out when making a purchase.

Weeping Willows are weak wooded, dropping a shower of twigs in every wind storm and occasionally being major victims of heavy ice storms. For this reason they should not be used where neat maintenance is a high priority. Because Willows are most effective when lush, they are best used where their high moisture requirements are naturally satisfied.

Salix alba var. *tristis* has been in this country since colonial times. In Great Britain it received the Award of Garden Merit in 1931.

16

Sciadopitys verticillata
Umbrella-pine

STRUCTURAL INTEREST

Evergreen
Effective landscape height: 30-40 feet
Effective landscape spread: 12-18 feet
Zone 6
Taxodiaceae (Taxodium Family)
Native range: central China

Without a doubt, Umbrella-pine is the most visually stimulating texture plant we can grow in the mid-Atlantic region. The needles are a bright, fleshy green (not the least bit wiry, as in the needles of true pines), 3½ inches long. They are arranged in whorls, twenty to thirty in a group, like the ribs of an umbrella, with bud clusters in the center of each whorl. There are often long stem sections (up to 4 inches) between whorls, thus dramatizing all the more successfully the intriguing arrangement of lush needles. The stems are rusty tan with newer growth a lighter green. The plant is usually quite dense and is a narrow vertical, starting out pyramidal and eventually taking on more of a cigar form. Unlike many conifers, Umbrella-pine naturally retains its lower limbs.

In a landscape, Umbrella-pine is valuable for its texture, for its vertical form, and for the *bright* green quality of its winter foliage. In a planting of broadleaf evergreens such as *Rhododendron* x 'Boule de Neige,' Drooping Leucothoë *(Leucothoë fontanesiana)*, and Baltic Ivy (*Hedera helix* 'Baltica') or Leatherleaf Mahonia *(Mahonia bealei)*, Round-leaf Osmanthus *(Osmanthus rotundifolius)*, and Variegated Liriope (*Liriope muscari* 'Variegata'), Umbrella-pine adds great magic with its contrasting fleshy needles, and provides very positive structure with its sentinel form.

In my own garden, a low mound around a secluded pool is planted with a grove of Umbrella-pines. The ground is covered with *Sedum kamtschaticum,* whose broad light green foliage further enhances the solo performance of the *Sciadopitys.* This grove-type use of tall, narrow evergreens is well worth considering for its dramatic impact. It is an informal way of creating a space within your garden. It has none of the gloom of a "roofed-over" area. The height of the trees relative to the visitor brings forth some of the feeling of awe experienced midst the pillars of a cathedral or in a Sequoia forest.

Umbrella-pines are very, very slow-growing when young. A three-year-old plant may only be 3–4 inches tall. Once they reach 18 inches, however, they move faster, and established plants will often put on 8–10 inches per year. Nurserymen must charge a high price for these gems because of the unusually long

Sciadopitys verticillata

time they take to reach marketable size. *Sciadopitys* do best in rich bottomland soil. They must, however, be provided with very good drainage; standing water is fatal. They are happily not susceptible to any fatal diseases. The foliage may bronze in the wintertime if they are in a windy spot. Winter foliage color is at its very best when other evergreens shield them from early morning sun.

Sciadopitys verticillata was introduced into this country from Japan by George R. Hall, M.D., about 1861. Interestingly enough, it was he who also introduced one of our most persistent pest plants, Honeysuckle (*Lonicera japonica* 'Halliana'). My own feeling is that he can be forgiven the latter deed on the basis that the Umbrella-pine is one of the very finest "aristocrats of the garden."

17

Sophora japonica 'Regent'
'Regent' Pagoda-Tree
Regent Scholar-Tree

SEASONAL INTEREST

Deciduous
Effective landscape height: 30-40 feet
Effective landscape spread: 50 feet
Zone 5
Leguminosae (Pea Family)
Commercial origin

Of top quality as a medium-sized shade tree, Pagoda-Tree also presents us with handsome flowers during the summer. The branch structure is ascendant and the crown is round-topped. With minor training, it is vase shaped enough to make a really fine street tree. The bark on older tree trunks is dark greenish-brown and handsomely fissured; the new twigs are a quite bright green. The open, compound foliage (6–10 inches long) is composed of tiny oval leaflets (nine to fifteen of them, 1–2½ inches long). They are a polished blue-green, and very resistant to insect damage. The total effect on a hot day is one of great coolness. From the richly clothed crown the pyramidal clusters of creamy white, pea-like flowers blossom forth during July and August. The leaves retain their rich green quality until destroyed by frost in the fall.

Sophora, an easy tree to grow, comes highly recommended even for city conditions (a handsome parking lot at the Bethlehem Steel Company in Bethlehem, Pennsylvania, is delightfully shaded by Pagoda-Trees).

Because the youngest trees seem to be subject to winterkill for two or three years until the root system is well established, I definitely prefer spring planting and a well-drained site.

Because of the refinement of its foliage and its generally neat habit and appearance, *Sophora* features well as a specimen in a nicely manicured, crisply defined lawn plot of a contemporary garden. Ornamental grasses in variety, such as Giant Eulalia (*Miscanthus sinensis* 'Giganteus'), the medium-sized, chartreuse-foliaged Zebra Grass (*Miscanthus sinensis* 'Zebrinus'), and the lower-growing Fountain Grass *(Pennisetum alopecuroides)*, and a low, compact, broad-leaved ground covering of Pachysandra *(Pachysandra terminalis)* or Baltic Ivy (*Hedera helix* 'Baltica') make a happy combination with *Sophora*. The contrasting textures and shades of green provide a cooling subtlety, while the grasses produce blossom interest throughout the latter part of the summer.

Sophora japonica is a native of China, where it was often planted around Buddhist temples. It has been widely planted in Japan for many years. The French missionary Pierre d'Incarville sent seeds of this plant and Tree of Heaven *(Ailanthus altissima)* to the Jardin des Plantes in Paris sometime after 1740. Pagoda-Tree reached the United States by 1747 and was grown in the Elgin Botanic Garden in New York City by Dr. David Hosack in 1811.

When grown from seed, the variation among progeny is tremendous. In the same batch, I have had fast-growing giants and plants so slow and dwarf that they would make charming bonsais. Recognizing this quality of variation, William Flemer III of Princeton Nurseries embarked on a program of planting seeds from the best upright forms and re-

Sophora japonica 'Regent'

peatedly selecting the progeny. This in turn gave rise to the widely acclaimed 'Regent' clone. In addition to having an ascendant form, excellent foliage, and especially large flowers, it grows extremely fast. Regent's history is a very happy example of the important but independent parts played by the plant collector, the botanic garden, and the plant breeder successively in providing us with good garden plants.

II
SMALL TREES

Small trees, like large trees, are useful both to give form to a garden and to provide points of seasonal interest. The twenty discussed here have an effective landscape height of 25 feet or less. Many are typical single-stem trees, but some verge on shrubbiness, with multiple stems and grove-like habits of growth. Also included—even though it is technically a form of grass—is a tall bamboo, because both in general appearance and design function it resembles a small tree. As in other sections, each entry is labeled to indicate whether its primary use is structural or for seasonal display.

18

Acer griseum
Paperbark Maple

SEASONAL INTEREST

Deciduous
Effective landscape height: 25 feet
Effective landscape spread: 15 feet
Zone 6
Aceraceae (Maple Family)
Native range: central and western China

Paperbark Maple certainly gets my highest vote for being a small-scale, "all-season" patio tree. The form is an upright oval. Cleanly rounded, the crown is thickly clothed with compound leaves, each composed of three leaflets. The foliage is a good medium green in summer and turns wonderful shades of red and orange in the fall. The real clincher comes when the foliage drops, revealing more completely *Acer griseum*'s fascinatingly beautiful skin. The trunk, the predominantly ascendant branches, and even the smaller twigs are covered with intriguing curls of bark. These are most dramatic on the trunk and main branches, where the paper-thin flakes are all rolled on a vertical axis. Older bark is a rich, shiny, purpley-brown, while the newly revealed layer is a striking orangey-cinnamon.

When you stop to think that for six months out of every year, those of us in the northern half of the United States look at leafless trees, the importance of good-looking bark is very apparent. Winter light playing on the branches of Paperbark Maple is a cheerful and stimulating sight. For that reason I would place the tree where it can be seen clearly from one of the most frequently used rooms of the house. By planting companion plants such as Red-stem Dogwood *(Cornus sericea)*, Drooping Leucothoë *(Leucothoë fontanesiana)*, and *Bergenia cordifolia*, which reaffirm the plum colors of the older bark, you will make the orangey underbark sing out in contrast. On the other hand, a very subtle planting using the gray, broadleaf, Fragrant Elaeagnus *(Elaeagnus pungens* 'Fruitlandii'), the blue-gray, horizontally branching *Juniperus chinensis* 'Pfitzeriana Glauca,' the striking, deciduous, arching, Whitestem Raspberry *(Rubus cockburnianus)*, and the blue-needled ground cover, *Juniperus horizon-talis* 'Wiltonii,' plays up the whole drama of rich contrasting shades of brown in *Acer griseum* itself. A touch of early spring joy could be added in the first combination with a mass planting of Winter Aconite *(Eranthis hyemalis)*. In the second, *Crocus fleischeri* would be a charming subtlety, with its narrow white petals and red and yellow flower parts.

Fortunately, Paperbark Maple is hardy quite far north in the United States, is not particular as to soil or location, and is easy to grow. Unfortunately, it has been scarce in the trade, and expensive when available. There is an explanation for this in that it has proved very difficult to propagate in quantity because the embryos in the seeds fail to develop and the germination rate is rarely more than 5 percent. Fortunately, techniques have now been developed for growing this plant from cuttings, by applying heavy doses of indolebutyric acid to the cutting wood. Special care, however, is required in bringing these through the first winter after rooting. Therefore, Paperbark Maple, although more readily available, is still expensive to produce.

Acer griseum has been known to the Western world since it was first collected by Adrian Franchet of France in 1894. It was introduced to gardens by Ernest H. Wilson, when working for the British nursery firm Messrs. Veitch, to whom he sent the seed from the Hupeh and Szechwan provinces of China in 1901. Paperbark Maple provides yet another example of the great enrichment that hardy exotic plants have brought to American gardens.

In England this plant received the Royal Horticultural Society's Award of Merit in 1922 and Award of Garden Merit in 1936.

Acer griseum

19

Amelanchier canadensis
Shadblow, Serviceberry

SEASONAL INTEREST

Deciduous
Effective landscape height: 25 feet
Effective landscape spread: 15 feet
Zone 5
Rosaceae (Rose Family)
Native range: United States—Maine to Georgia and Iowa

The fragile, fleeting beauty of this American native is an irreplaceable part of the richness of an American spring. In late April the fat buds finally unfurl, producing first the grayish young foliage and soon after the upright racemes of delicate white flowers. The odor of the flowers is somewhat unpleasant at close range, and the petals fall after only three days if the weather is warm. The leaves are oval, pointed, and woolly white on both surfaces when young. The latter quality produces a silvery effect, along with the blossoms, that is very charming in its light-reflective quality. Maroon-purple berries succeed the blossoms in early summer, only to be devoured greedily by the birds. The fall foliage is yellow to red. Shadblow sometimes grows as a single-stem tree; more often it is found as a large multistemmed shrub. The bark is a purple-brown. The twigs are very fine and rather a silvery gray. The buds are handsome all winter, thick, fat, and catkin-like on the fine twigs, and purplish with gray pubescent markings.

Shadblow is a rich but subtle delight, and its use should be carefully planned so that more spectacular beauties do not overwhelm it. In this respect it is ideal for small gardens and is a charmer with diminutive spring bulbs such as Grape-hyacinths *(Muscari armeniacum)*, Guinea-hen-flowers *(Fritillaria meleagris)*, and early species Tulips. If used in sufficient quantity, it would, in a larger garden, be handsome featured with its blooming mate the Royal Azalea *(Rhododendron schlippenbachii)*.

Amelanchier is subject to all the ills of members of the rose family—lacewing fly, red spider, various scales, and fire blight—in areas where any of these may be a problem. It is easy to transplant.

The name "Shadblow" memorializes the fact that it blooms when the shad ran in the unpolluted rivers of New England, where it was a much-admired shrub at an early date.

Amelanchier canadensis received an Award of Merit from the Royal Horticultural Society in 1938.

20

Aralia spinosa
Hercules Club,
Devil's Walking Stick

STRUCTURAL INTEREST

Deciduous
Effective landscape height: 12-15 feet
Effective landscape spread: indefinite
Zones 3-4
Araliaceae (Aralia or Ginseng Family)
Native range: United States—southern Pennsylvania to Texas

"Dramatic" and "exotic" are the adjectives which describe the finer qualities of this native, and refer primarily to the leaves and flowers rather than its winter character. Whether grown as a single-stem "tree" or allowed to follow its natural bent and develop into a shrubby clump or dense grove, the appearance is gaunt in the winter. The light tan vertical trunks branch little, carry no twigs, are well covered with spines, and terminate abruptly. The real fun starts in the spring when the foliage, with its bronzy hue, first unfolds. Individual leaves eventually reach 3 to 4 feet in length, and are very broad, taking on a blue-green cast. Each leaf is composed of seventy-two or more leaflets, 3–4 inches long and arranged in six to eight pairs on each of seven to nine secondary stems. The leaves are carried in a very horizontal fashion at the top of the trunks and give a generally flat-topped appearance to the plant. From this "platform" in summer arise vertical plumes of creamy white flowers up to 3 feet in height. These are followed in late August by black berries which are made more showy by the bright pink stems on

Aralia spinosa, close-up of trunk and leaf blade

which they are carried. The foliage itself often turns a good scarlet in October.

Aralia spinosa is an exciting and dramatic plant, and definitely not your cup of tea if you prefer to deal in subtleties. It also has certain practical drawbacks. It is thorny; not the perfect tree if there are small children in the family. It will seed itself about the garden, and will also spread by suckering from its wide-ranging roots. The wood is soft and pithy and therefore it is not long-lived.

There are many instances, however, where *Aralia* is extremely useful. Because the leaf shapes of our native hardwood trees are so similar, a view into a woodland often needs one spot of dramatic foliage to add charm and character to the scene. This is best achieved by clearing away enough of the larger native trees to open up a "light" hole in the tree canopy where the *Aralia* can be planted. It will "reach" for the light and at the same time be "spotlighted." The effect is especially good when viewed from a higher elevation. I recall one woods-enclosed pond garden on Long Island where the "touch" of one *Aralia* clump at the water's edge pulled the whole picture into a satisfying focus. The very capable landscape designer Al Vicks has used this trick for years in his highly stimulating "wild gardens" at the Philadelphia Flower Show.

Devil's Walking Stick frequently comes into its own where a single dramatic plant is needed for a bold statement with a piece of contemporary architecture.

For the person who has the urge for a real departure in an exotic, erotic, almost jungle-like direction, Devil's Walking Stick is certainly a key plant. In a large-scale situation, it could be contrasted with the broad foliage of such trees as *Magnolia grandiflora, Magnolia macrophylla, Paulownia tomentosa,* or *Catalpa bignonioides;* or, in a smaller-scale situation, it could be featured as the dominant plant, and underplanted with such big broadleaf companions as *Clerodendrum trichotomum* (heart shape), *Petasites japonica* (platter-like), and *Bergenia cordifolia* (cabbage-like). The grass-like foliages of Giant Reed *(Arundo donax)*, which reaches 15 feet in height, *Miscanthus sinensis* 'Giganteus,' 12 feet; *Miscanthus sinensis* 'Gracillimus,' 6 feet; Yellow Day-lily (*Hemerocallis* x 'Hyperion'), 2 feet; and blue-flowered Lilyturf (*Liriope muscari* 'Big Blue'), 12 inches, planted with these would provide an appropriately rich setting for the stimulating *Aralia spinosa.*

Although Devil's Walking Stick favors a rich, heavy soil, poorer soil is to be preferred if healthy long-lived plants are the object. In rich soil the wood, always soft and very pithy, becomes especially so, making it more subject to freezing, rotting when wounded, and a generally shorter life expectancy.

There are very similar *Aralias* from Manchuria, Korea, Japan *(A. elata)* and China *(A. chinensis)*, but our native Devil's Walking Stick, *A. spinosa*, seems to be the most satisfactory performer in the mid-Atlantic region.

21

Chionanthus virginicus
Fringe-Tree

Since John Bartram (through Peter Collinson) introduced it to England in 1736, European gardeners have considered this American native to be one of our most beautiful and striking plants. Yet it is as yet only rarely used in this country—a great shame, I feel! The tree, a relative of Forsythia, is small and often multistemmed, with an attractive rounded habit. The leaves are a clear, slightly glossy, dark green, narrowly oval in shape and 6–8 inches long; they turn a good yellow in the fall. White blossoms appear in late May and are unusual in form and unbelievably attractive. As the name implies, they hang like fringe from the twigs, in racemes as much

SEASONAL INTEREST

Deciduous
Effective landscape height: 15 feet
Effective landscape spread: 15 feet
Zone 5
Oleaceae (Olive Family)
Native range: United States—New Jersey and Pennsylvania to Florida and Texas

as 8 inches in length. It is as though a suspended white thread had branched in the manner of a deer antler, first to one side and then to another. The blossoms are followed by hanging clusters of blue berries on the female plants. An unjustified reputation for being difficult to transplant may have contributed to its lack of acceptance in the United States. However, its unpopularity is more likely due to the natural perversity of gardeners who, from time immemorial, have clamored for the exotic and ignored treasures at home.

Fringe-Tree prefers moist but well-drained soil. It reportedly is subject to the same scale that attacks the lilac, its close relative, but I have never observed this problem in my area. It does leaf out extremely late, and I frequently have to persuade clients that it is not dead when the leaves have failed to appear with those of other trees in early May. Because the tree comes easily from seed, this is the way it is traditionally reproduced. However, both because there is considerable variation among seedlings in the size of the flowers, and because the blossoms of the male plants are larger, a large-flowered male clone should be selected and propagated by grafting or budding.

The bloom of the Fringe-Tree occurs at a time when our gardens are rich with blossoms. Hence, there are many desirable combinations in which it is useful. *Chionanthus* makes a marvelous terrace or patio tree. Featured under these conditions, the blossoms can be appreciated close up amidst herbaceous plantings, including the purples and blues of the *Iris germanica* clones, the pink *Geranium sanguineum* 'Prostratum' *(Geranium lancastriense)*, and chartreuse of *Alchemilla mollis*, all tied together with such grays as *Stachys olympica, Artemesia stelleriana, Euphorbia Myrsinites*, and *Thymus serpyllum lanuginosus*. In a larger area, clumps of *Chionanthus* could be massed against the deep pinkish-maroon of River's Purple Beech (*Fagus sylvatica* 'Riversi') or Redleaf Plum (*Prunus cerasifera* 'Thundercloud') and dressed down with the pinkish-lavender lilac *Syringa* x *henryi* 'L. H. Lutece.' It is a charming asset wherever used and highly recommended.

Chionanthus virginicus

In England, *Chionanthus virginicus* received an Award of Merit from the Royal Horticultural Society in 1931.

22

Cornus kousa
Korean Dogwood

This garden aristocrat really does do our native Dogwood at least one better! It is a wispier, more delicate small tree by virtue of its finer twigs, the longer, straighter internodes of its new growth, and the long, more narrowly pointed flower buds. The branching habit is extremely ascendant when young, more horizontal with age. There is considerable winter interest found in the bark of older branches and the trunk. This is caused by irregular exfoliation, resulting in an extremely attractive mottling of light gray, dark gray, and greenish-tan.

The flowers, unlike those of our native Dogwood, appear after the plant is clothed with its oval, narrowly pointed 4-inch leaves. The blossoms are large, with the white bracts pointed (not rounded and notched) and of a fresh, reflective white. They are at their peak a good three weeks after our native Dogwood. These inflorescences are borne on long stalks, more vertically erect than their native counterpart. Each rests on its stalk in a strictly horizontal position, and because they clothe the branches rather thickly, the total effect is one of spectacular delicacy—giving a somewhat oriental mood.

The fruit is most curious, resembling large red raspberries, and is effective in early fall. The autumn color may be anywhere from purple or brownish-purple to scarlet.

Whereas *Cornus florida*, our native, is almost as attractive to look up at as down on, *Cornus kousa*

SEASONAL INTEREST

Deciduous
Effective landscape height: 20 feet
Effective landscape spread: 15 feet
Zone 6
Cornaceae (Dogwood Family)
Native range: Japan, Korea, and central China

is definitely better when seen from above. At a distance the effect is enhanced by a black-green background material such as Canadian Hemlock *(Tsuga canadensis)*. An attractive all-seasons combination might combine Korean Dogwood, Canadian Hemlock, and Chinese Stranvaesia (*Stranvaesia davidiana* var. *undulata*). The latter evergreen shrub has clusters of white blossoms at the same time as *Cornus kousa*. These too are followed by attractive, frosty red berries, effective later in the season than those of the *Cornus*. Hence, the winter picture would contrast the needled evergreen of the Hemlock with the broadleaf, berried *Stranvaesia* and feature the mottled Dogwood bark.

Alternative June color combinations might include Korean Dogwood with the pink, jewel-like blossoms of Mountain-laurel *(Kalmia latifolia)*, the lavender cascades of Fountain Buddleia *(Buddleia alternifolia)*, and a ground cover of the herbaceous, delicate, blue-flowered *Amsonia tabernaemontana*. Or, for a different June treat the white blossoms of *Cornus kousa* might be blended with the soft gray foliage of *Elaeagnus angustifolia* as a white-gray background for such old-fashioned shrub roses as *Rosa* 'Fantan LaTour' (small, double, soft pink to white blossoms), *Rosa* 'Camaieux' (small, double, pink blossoms), and *Rosa centifolia* 'Muscosa' (the common moss rose).

For some reason *Cornus kousa* does not transplant as well in small sizes as some trees. I recommend starting with a 5–6-foot size or larger. Good, well-drained garden soil is the basic requirement. If this is supplied at the outset, fertilization is not recommended. Pruning is seldom necessary.

Cornus kousa was grown in this country by 1875. In England it has justifiably received awards from the Royal Horticultural Society: First Class Certificate in 1892, Award of Merit in 1958, and Award of Garden Merit in 1969.

23

Cotinus coggygria var. *rubrifolia*

Purpleleaf Smoke-Tree,
Purpleleaf Wig-Tree

STRUCTURAL INTEREST

Deciduous
Effective landscape height: 15 feet
Effective landscape spread: 20 feet
Zone 6
Anacardiaceae (Cashew Family)
Commercial or garden origin

Where space permits, this irregularly branched large shrub adds a note of real magic to the garden both because of its colored foliage and because of its ornamental fruiting panicles. The young foliage in the spring is a marvelous purpley-wine color. As the season progresses, older leaves fade to a duller black-green, veined with lighter green. Especially in moist summers this serves as the perfect background for younger, more highly colored foliage carried on pinky-purple, yellow-flecked new stem growth. Whatever the stage of the leaf development and color, there is overall a milky-blue "bloom," which adds a very special quality. The large quantity of purplish stem parts to the 8-inch-long fruiting panicles makes a very fine-textured ornament, that contrasts handsomely with the broadleaf foliage. As this fades to a gray color later in the season, it is easy to imagine from a distance that these are puffs of smoke.

Whereas the redleaf Plum (*Prunus cerasifera* 'Thundercloud') is a very orderly and compact garden subject, *Cotinus* has the rangy, irregular quality of its Sumac relatives. New growth is multidirectional and can be quite extensive, as much as 3 to 4 feet in one season. When given lots of space and spared any stiff design constraints, it makes a lush and voluptuous garden subject from June to September.

Its coloration works equally well with orangey-tan, pink-purple, and gray-blue companions. Plume-poppy *(Macleaya cordata)* has large fig-like blue-green leaves covered with the same marvelous

Cotinus coggygria 'Foliis Purpureis'

milky "bloom" as that of *Cotinus coggygria* var. *rubrifolia*. Because of this and plume-poppy's wonderful tan inflorescences, it and Purpleleaf Smoke-Tree combined with bright orange flowers such as those on the annual *Tithonia rotundifolia* 'Torch' makes a very stimulating picture.

In June there is a very happy pink-purple combination in my own garden. The maroon-flowered Tree Peony, *Paeonia* x 'Black Pirate,' picks up some of the *Cotinus* color and grows in a sea of the cheerful purple flower spikes of *Salvia* 'East Friesland.' This is planted with a carpet of the soft pink perennial *Geranium sanguineum* 'Prostratum' *(Geranium lancastriense)* in the foreground. All of the participating flower colors pick up components of the *Cotinus* foliage color and thereby emphasize its rich and unusual qualities. An equally delightful alternative might be a bedding combination of dark lavender Heliotrope and two shades of tender Geraniums *(Pelargonium hortorum)*: 'Genie,' which is light pink, and 'Springfield Violet,' shocking purple-pink.

In the gray-blue direction I like the feathery blue-green foliage of *Tamarix* 'Pink Cascade' with *Cotinus coggygria* var. *rubrifolia*. There is an almost metallic quality about the needly *Tamarix* foliage, which becomes very lively when combined with the broad purple foliage of the Smoke-Tree. The pink blossoms of the *Tamarix*, which appear during the summer, are cheerful and feathery. Their bawdiness is just sufficiently restrained by the dulling qualities of the *Cotinus* to make a delightful subtlety. The *Tamarix* should best be seen against the Smoke-Tree. This combination might be backed by a handsome Blue Atlas Cedar (*Cedrus atlantica* 'Glauca'), and color and texture repeats made in the foreground with interlocking sweeps of 'Crimson Pygmy' Barberry *(Berberis thunbergii* 'Crimson Pygmy') and the blue-foliaged Juniper, *Juniperus horizontalis* 'Wiltonii.'

Cotinus is sometimes fussy about being transplanted. Once established, however, it thrives even in poor, stony soils. In fact, rich soils tend to encourage more growth and fewer flowers, as does a super-abundance of moisture. Although this quality of lushness is attractive, I tend to prefer leaner situations because there has been some trouble in recent years with a disease called verticillium wilt *(Verticillium albo-atrum)*, which is associated with unusual vigor or rankness. There is no control for this other than pruning out dead wood below the point of infection and burning it.

The green-leaf form of Smoke-Tree is native over a wide area from southern Europe to central China. It has been important as a dye plant, the twigs yielding a yellow color known as "young fustic." It was growing in English gardens by 1656 and was listed in nursery catalogs in this country by 1790. Because individual plants generally carry flowers of only one sex, it is important to select only plants that are characteristically heavy with female blossoms in order to assure a good supply of "smoke." This problem is pretty well solved for us in the case of the red-foliaged forms. These are asexually propagated from plants which have been selected for varying degrees of purple and red in the foliage and for their good flowering qualities. In addition to var. *rubrifolia*, other red-foliaged cultivars are, 'Velvet Cloak,' which was introduced by Coles Nursery in Ohio, 'Nottcutts Variety,' introduced by Nottcutt Nurseries in England, 'Royal Purple,' introduced by the Messrs. Kromhout of Boskoop, Holland, and 'Rubrifolius.' Because the color qualities may be affected by soil and climate conditions, it is impossible to say which of these is the very best without growing them all together under the same conditions. To my knowledge, this has never been done.

Cotinus coggygria var. *rubrifolia* is highly regarded in England, where it received an Award of Merit (1921) and an Award of Garden Merit (1930) from the Royal Horticultural Society.

24

STRUCTURAL INTEREST

Deciduous
Effective landscape height: 25 feet
Effective landscape spread: 25 feet
Zone 5
Rosaceae (Rose Family)
Native range: southeastern United States

Crataegus phaenopyrum
Washington Hawthorn

For gardeners concerned about winter interest in the landscape, this small tree gets my strongest recommendation. Not only is its winter habit extremely attractive, but its display of red berries is spectacular. The habit is broad and upright, but the branches have a distinctly horizontal dominance. Associated with its very sturdy-looking frame is a thick coating of fine twigs, rather angular in quality and loaded with 1¼-inch-long thorns. The gray bark is smooth on young twigs and fissured and flaky on older trunks. Overall, there is the same aura of sturdy respectability one feels with American Beech or White Oak, though on a smaller scale, of course. The fruit is about the size of a pea (¼–5/16 inch), turning from orange to scarlet in color. These berries are borne in large, pendulous clusters. They become effective in October and, unlike most other fall berry-bearing plants, continue to spread their charm well into the winter. In fact, the haze of red caused by the quantity of relatively small fruits is probably at its very best when snow is on the ground.

Washington Hawthorn continues to uphold its position in the late spring, when the attractive clusters of white flowers make an excellent show. The lustrous three-to-five-lobed, maple-like leaves (up to 3¼ inches long) densely clothe the tree all summer and turn scarlet to orange in the fall.

Because of its thorns, *Crataegus phaenopyrum* makes an excellent barrier planting. Because of its denseness, it makes an excellent deciduous screen or windbreak plant. Even in the winter, the dense branching habit gives visual protection and according to scientific measurement does more to slow down and disperse high wind velocity than a dense evergreen planting.

From an aesthetic viewpoint, its highest value is for winter interest. An attractive red, bronze, purple scheme might feature four Washington Hawthorns against three of the dense, pyramidal *Ilex aquifolium* 'Ciliata Major.' If foreground planting seems desirable, this might be composed of drifts of the bronzy, broad-leaved Leucothoë *(Leucothoë fontanesiana)* and the needly, purple-foliaged Andorra Juniper (*Juniperus horizontalis* 'Plumosa'). The gray bark and twigs of the Hawthorn would be echoed in the purple Juniper and contrasted with the bronzy broadleaf qualities of the *Ilex* and *Leucothoë*. The entire scheme would be highlighted by the sparkle of the berries.

Another approach might be to go for an all gray-blue relationship. This might consist of a single Blue Atlas Cedar (*Cedrus atlantica* 'Glauca') as background with three Washington Hawthorns set in a sea of the low-growing *Juniperus sabina* 'Tamariscifolia.' An accent clump of three gray-leaved *Yucca glauca* would complete the picture. Gray bark, gray needles, and broad gray leaves would provide a subtly intriguing textural combination for the delicacy of the red berries.

A totally different tack would be to make a play on shades of green, with heavy emphasis on contrasting forms. A single red-berried Hawthorn featured against a large clump of the green-stemmed Bamboo *Phyllostachys aureosulcata* and a mass of the dark green English Weeping Yew (*Taxus baccata* 'Repandens') would provide all of the cheer associated with the red and green of "Merry Christmas." The horizontal lines of the Hawthorn would find stimulating contrast with the verticality of the Bamboo and the pendulous nature of the Yew.

Washington Hawthorn will thrive under a variety of conditions. It is especially useful because of its ability to handle sites that are windy and characterized by poor soil conditions. As with other native

Crataegus phaenopyrum

Hawthorns, there can be problems with fire blight or cedar-apple rust in areas where either of these diseases is prevalent.

The American Hawthorns have entertained botanists for a number of years because of the tendency for one geographic form to blend by slight variation into the next. Some botanists have divided the genus into more than 1,000 species! I am in complete accord with Dr. Donald Wyman (1965), who states: "If only one Hawthorn was to be selected from the many native or exotic types available in North America today, the Washington Hawthorn would be the first one to consider."

25

SEASONAL INTEREST

Deciduous
Effective landscape height: 25 feet
Effective landscape spread: 18 feet
Zone 7
Ebenaceae (Ebony Family)
Native range: China, Korea

Diospyros kaki

Oriental Persimmon, Chinese Persimmon, Kakee (Japan), Date-plum

This important Chinese fruit tree is a most handsome ornamental, and a completely sufficient reward for the effort and persistence that may be needed to obtain and establish the plant. The structure of the tree is graceful and full of character, often superficially resembling an old and undisciplined apple tree. Often characterized by lack of a central leader, it is always open within and heavily clothed with fine twigs at its outer extremities. The bark of the older wood is vertically fissured and black-gray, while the younger growth is smooth and a lighter tan. Whereas the main inner branches are ascendant, the upper branches and twigs tend to bend over to the horizontal or below, giving a round-topped effect. The 2½–3-inch or larger tomato-like fruits can change this habit to one that is positively pendulous. The leaves are oval and pointed, 4¼ inches long by 2⅝ inches wide. They are thick, dark green, and glossy, resembling healthy *Camellia* foliage in their reflective quality. Before the leaves drop in the fall, there is often a brief moment when they turn a delightful Chinese red. Then, when the leaves do fall, as dramatically as if the curtain had been pulled aside, the full impact of the bony structure hung with orange orbs makes its full impact. The fruits are smooth and glossy, a delightful light tangerine orange, and carry just a hint of white blush. This drama occurs in late October and November, at a time when most other ornamentals have passed their prime.

Oriental Persimmon is such a remarkable tree that it deserves a featured spot in any garden. The feature could be a single specimen, a grove of three or more, or a very geometrically arranged orchard. The irregularity of the leafless habit sparkling with orange fruit contrasts well with a more formal, controlled, hedge-like situation composed of evergreens such as needly Yew (*Taxus* x *media* 'Densiformis') or the small broadleaf evergreen foliage of "Old English" Boxwood (*Buxus sempervirens* 'Suffruticosa'). Such a situation might be highlighted with a ground cover of the chartreuse-foliaged Variegated Liriope (*Liriope muscari* 'Variegata') and made to sparkle with the small, yellow berries of a planting of Yellowberry Firethorn (*Pyracantha coccinea* 'Aurea'). Contrasting textures and shades of green are the key to the Oriental Persimmon's use in an informal planting. Dark green broadleafs such as *Ilex* x 'Nellie R. Stevens' and Luykens Cherry-laurel (*Prunus laurocerasus* 'Otto Luykens') and the lighter green, grassy foliage of Zebra Grass *(Miscanthus sinensis* 'Zebrinus') and the lemon-yellow Day-lily (*Hemerocallis* x 'Hyperion') serve to emphasize the highly unusual qualities of the Oriental Persimmon tree.

In addition to the ornamental qualities of the plant, the fruit at its best is very good to eat and should not be associated with the small astringent fruits of our native Persimmon. On a worldwide basis, more persimmons are grown, it is believed,

Diospyros kaki

than almost any other cultivated fruit (mangoes and bananas are notable exceptions). The Japanese alone have eight hundred varieties of persimmon. In both Japan and China there are special varieties for drying, eating out of hand, and so on. They were reported growing in the United States as early as 1828. The generally recognized date of introduction is, however, 1856, after Commodore Perry had obtained seed during his visit to Japan to promote trade relations. In 1870 the first grafted varieties were introduced from Japan by the United States Department of Agriculture. These were distributed to the Gulf States and California. Many other varieties were subsequently introduced and interest here ran quite high. Around 1900 an evaluation program was undertaken at the U.S. Plant Introduction Station at Chico, California, and new varieties were released by the station starting in 1917. By the early 1930's there were more than 2,000 acres in Oriental Persimmons in California and more than sixty named varieties and two hundred seedlings being tested at Chico. The industry unfortunately declined during the Depression, the Chico collection was boiled down to sixteen superior varieties, and recently, because of budgetary restrictions, that station was closed.

The focus in this country was obviously on developing Persimmons for warmer climates. The Chinese have for centuries grown Persimmons in much colder areas, and a very few nurserymen and amateur gardeners have pioneered this effort in the United States. An excellent discussion of the successes and failures has been prepared by Dr. Merlin M. Brubaker, a fine gardener living near Wilmington, Delaware (see "Oriental Persimmons," *Horticulture*, September, 1972, p. 40).

The varieties most successful in the mid-Atlantic area have been 'Great Wall' and 'Otome.' Culturally, there are two main problems here. In the first place, the growing season is a little short for the complete maturation of fruit. As a result, the fruit must be picked just before the temperature drops to below freezing and artificially ripened. Secondly, the plants are poor transplanters. The Chinese solved this problem by planting a seed where the plant was to grow. Once the seedling was well-established, they grafted the variety they desired onto it. Because we do not have this sort of patience, the general practice here has been to plant commercially grafted plants and hope that the root system would establish itself fast enough to support the fresh graft, something which our short growing season doesn't exactly encourage. The native Persimmon *(Diospyros virginiana)* has traditionally been used for understock in these colder areas. One pioneering nurseryman felt that grafting was more successful if kept 18 inches above soil level. Unfortunately, the grafts on his plants often died out and the understock took over. There is a theory now that *Diospyros lotus* may have a more transplantable root system and be perfectly hardy.

As a result of these problems, there are at the moment no nurserymen in the Northeastern United States offering plants of *Diospyros kaki* that are locally grown. The problem then is to get a fresh, dormant plant from a grower in a more distant—presumably milder—area to your home at a favorable planting time in the spring. No small order! The surer but slower alternative, of course, would be to follow the Chinese system.

Because the Persimmon-growing areas in China are rich in limestone, it is felt advisable to add crushed limestone to the soil in which Persimmons are planted. The leaves are tough and resist most pests. The named varieties, which are, of course, all female, set fruit freely without benefit of pollination by male trees.

The name *Diospyros* comes from *Dios* (divine) and *pyros* (wheat), for a total meaning of "celestial food"!

26

STRUCTURAL INTEREST

Evergreen
Effective landscape height: 18 feet
Effective landscape spread: 12 feet
Zone 7
Aquifoliaceae (Holly Family)
Garden origin

Ilex aquifolium 'Ciliata Major'

Bronzeleaf English Holly

This vigorous, pyramidal evergreen is the fulfillment of every gardener's fantasy of what a Holly tree should look like. The foliage, during the growing season, is a dark, glossy green, with an occasional olive tinge. The large, oval leaves have a slight wave to the margins and are regularly spined. The berries are large, fat, and dark red. In addition, the new shoots of this selection have very decorative purple bark, and the foliage itself changes to a marvelous bronze color during the fall and winter. There is no more sparkling picture than the dark red berries of this Holly seen against its bronze foliage on a sunny winter day.

English Hollies in general are more easily established and perform better in the cool, moist climate of the British Isles or the Pacific Northwest than the East coast of the United States. A few of the more than two hundred variants being grown in the United States today, however, seem especially adaptable to our Eastern conditions. *Ilex aquifolium* 'Ciliata Major' is, in my opinion, the finest. American Holly *(Ilex opaca)* varieties are, of course hardier but rank much lower in terms of landscape effectiveness.

Ilex aquifolium 'Ciliata Major' should be grown in full sun for the foliage and stem characteristics to show themselves most prominently. The location selected should be out of the strong winter wind and in a spot with good air and soil drainage. Good topsoil rich in organic matter is essential. Supplemental watering should be carefully timed to get this plant to establish quickly. As with all berry-bearing English Hollies, there must be a male

English Holly which blossoms at the same time planted nearby if a good crop of fruit is desired.

Ilex aquifolium 'Ciliata Major' is so handsome that it is a worthy addition to almost any plant combination. When featuring it, Spreading Junipers used in mass are particularly valuable for the contrast in texture. A fine color relationship with the Holly's bronze foliage might feature interlocking ground-cover plantings of *Juniperus chinensis* 'Sargentii' (gray), *Juniperus horizontalis* 'Plumosa' (purple), and *Juniperus horizontalis* 'Wiltonii' (blue). Other larger shrubs that might be added to fill out this charming winter picture would be the Yellowtwig Dogwood (*Cornus sericea* 'Flaviramea') and the yellow-berried form of the deciduous Winterberry Holly (*Ilex verticilata* 'Chrysocarpa').

Ilex aquifolium 'Ciliata Major'

The group of Hollies generally referred to as "English" includes not only blood of *Ilex aquifolium* (native to Europe, Africa, China, and the British Isles), but also *Ilex perado* (native to the Azores and Canary Islands) and *Ilex perado* var. *platyphylla* (native to the Canary Islands). As a result, among Holly authorities there is some confusion regarding botanical identity and origin. "English" Hollies have been garden favorites for many years, and the number of variations here and abroad is quite impressive. 'Ciliata Major' is currently classified by the Holly botanist Dr. Gene Eisenbeiss as a garden form of *Ilex aquifolium* and considered distinct from *Ilex* x *altaclarensis* (*Ilex aquifolium* x *I. perado*) 'Camelliafolia,' which it closely resembles in appearance. 'Ciliata Major' is distinctive, he claims, in being more regularly spined, with more distinctive wavy margins to the leaves, and characterized by a more bronzy leaf coloration during the winter. This variety has been known as a distinctive garden plant since before 1852, when it was mentioned by Dr. H. R. Goeppert, director of the Breslau Botanic Garden. Its more precise origin is unknown. Mrs. F. Leighton Meserve, the well-known Holly breeder and nurserywoman from Long Island, on the other hand, feels that 'Ciliata Major' and 'Camelliafolia' are the same plant, the former produced by cuttings taken from the apron of a mature tree, the latter from cuttings taken higher up. In a letter to me she stated, "The higher up the cuttings are made, the more entire the leaves are." She would group the varieties 'Father Charles,' 'Ciliata Major,' 'Laurafolia,' and 'Camelliafolia' all together as 'Camelliafolia.'

27

STRUCTURAL INTEREST

Evergreen
Effective landscape height: 25 feet
Effective landscape spread: 15 feet
Zone 6
Aquifoliaceae (Holly Family)
Native range: eastern United States

Ilex opaca 'Arden'
Berry-bearing American Holly

American Holly is certainly an aristocrat of the American woodlands, and a most adaptable tree for landscape purposes. Always pyramidal in habit, the plant in sunny conditions generally carries horizontal branches right to the ground, with a heavy covering of dull green leaves. Under the shade of larger trees, lower branches are generally absent, and the foliage is less dense and often has more gloss and a darker color. The variety 'Arden' has typical medium-sized leaves, slightly curved and spiny. The leaf stems are purplish; the berries, often yellow at first, later turn to bright scarlet; and the foliage takes on a bronze cast during the later part of the winter. 'Arden' has proven to be a good nursery tree because it propagates readily from cuttings, develops a central leader as a young plant, and, most important, the females set a heavy crop of fruit every year.

To be sure, no American Holly can hold a candle to a thriving specimen of English Holly such as the lush *Ilex aquifolium* 'Ciliata Major.' However, the English Hollies will only thrive under rather specialized conditions in the Eastern United States, whereas *Ilex opaca* 'Arden' will thrive under a variety of conditions—hence it has many landscape uses. If you have the time to wait or the resources to purchase a large specimen, it will of course make a handsome shade tree for the lawn or patio. There is a marvelous example of this at Longwood Gardens, in Kennett Square, Pennsylvania, where six enormous, gray-stemmed giants shade the big terrace in front of the main conservatory. American Holly is most responsive to trimming and makes an excellent hedge for windbreak or screening purposes—reaching heights of anywhere from 6 to 20 feet. At the Governor's Palace in Williamsburg, Virginia, the delightful "maze" is made of clipped hedges of American Holly. The plant is very effective as a formal trimmed espalier as well.

My own greatest enthusiasm about the plant is associated with memories of a winter pasture scene I chanced upon one time in the country west of Elkton, Maryland. Birds had seeded an abandoned, gently undulating farm field to conical American Holly, vertical Red-cedar *(Juniperus virginiana)*, horizontal White-flowered Dogwood *(Cornus florida)*, and the intricately branched Black Haw *(Viburnum prunifolium)*. Cattle had been turned to pasture here after the plants were of mature size, so that what I saw was an informal grouping of this mixture of great American natives, as it were, on flowing lawn. One could do much worse than to imitate this scene. The sparkle of red berries against broad, spiny Holly leaves is only accentuated by contrast with the black-green vertical cedars. The conical form of the Holly is dramatized against the horizontality of the Dogwood and Black Haw. And, what's more, the combination provides interest at every season of the year.

In smaller-scale situations, the same general principles can be followed. Contrast the conical form of 'Arden' Holly with a background planting of the roundish-shaped, bronzy-leaved, red-berried *Cotoneaster salicifolia* 'Flocossa,' repeating the rounded form in smaller scale in the foreground with the fine-textured Threespine Barberry *(Berberis triacanthophora)*, whose fall and winter foliage colors are apple-green and red. Give a horizontal

Ilex opaca 'Arden'

dark evergreen base to the whole picture with a mass planting of Helleri Dwarf Japanese Holly (*Ilex crenata* 'Helleri'). To this I would add just a touch of spice with a clump of six to eight *Yucca smalliana*. The sword-like leaves of this plant would provide an exciting foliage contrast all year, and its vertical 6- to 8-foot flower spikes would enliven the scene in June, at a time of year when the Holly is usually least interesting.

The quality of the foliage and berries on an American Holly is, of course, very closely related to the quality of the soil in which it is grown and the care it receives. Good, well-drained soil is recommended; annual feeding certainly helps guarantee richer foliage color. Male or pollinator forms of American Holly must be grown nearby (within, say, a quarter-mile) if *Ilex opaca* is to produce a good reliable crop of berries.

Because the plant occurs naturally over a wide range (Cape Cod to Florida, west to Missouri and Texas), because there is considerable variation in leaf shape, plant form, and berry-bearing quality, and because the plant has been desired for Christmas decorations since earliest times, many forms have been selected for garden and orchard use. The recently published *International Check List of Cultivated Ilex* (U.S. Department of Agriculture, 1973 *b*) lists more than 1,000 named cultivars. Tests are currently being conducted at the New Jersey Experiment Station at New Brunswick to evaluate many of these. The home gardener will, of course, run a much better chance of getting a good garden plant if he buys a named variety with qualities suited to his needs rather than a seedling whose mature qualities are unknown. The variety 'Arden' is the best of several garden clones which have performed well for me. It was found in a woods near Arden, Delaware, by Guy Nearing and described by him in 1922. It was introduced through Arden Nursery, Arden, Delaware, in 1926, and by Tingle Nursery, Pittsville, Maryland, in 1939.

28

Ilex pedunculosa
Long-stalk Holly

STRUCTURAL INTEREST

Evergreen
Effective landscape height: 20 feet
Effective landscape spread: 15 feet
Zone 6
Aquifoliaceae (Holly Family)
Native range: Japan and central China

This evergreen, red-berried Holly is unique because of its foliage, which resembles that of a pear tree, and the stems of its berries, which are unusually long. The foliage is a shiny dark green; the leaves are pointed ovals (1–3 inches long), which curl slightly downward lengthwise. The plant is usually shrubby, multistemmed, densely foliaged, and femininely mounded. The berries are shiny red, hanging either one or two on 1½-inch stems. They sparkle against the green foliage; because of their pendant characteristic, they are delightfully gem-like.

Long-stalk Holly is one of the hardiest of the evergreen Hollies and unfortunately one of the least well-known. This may be true because it is too often seen with rather olive-colored foliage. In some cases this is caused by a genetic variation, in others it may be due to poorly drained clay soil and too much sun. My recommendation is to see the plant before making a purchase (in order to obtain one which has good foliage quality), and to plant it on a site slightly shaded from the hottest sun and in well-drained soil rich in organic matter. It is essential to have a male (staminate) plant of *Ilex pedunculosa* nearby in order to have a berry crop.

Long-stalk Holly is valuable for the intriguing winter interest it can generate; it seems to come alive particularly when contrasted with deciduous material that is horizontal or horizontal-to-ascendant in form. It provides an excellent berry-sprinkled, broadleaf background for the spidery, light yellow blossoms of the Witch-hazel hybrid *Hamamelis mollis* 'Pallida.' An attractive bronzy touch could

be added to such a planting by covering the ground with *Cotoneaster dammerei* 'Skogholmen.'

It can be nicely featured against such horizontal branchers as Paperbark Maple *(Acer griseum)* or Corkbark Euonymous *(Euonymous alatus)*. Both have interesting bark and twig characteristics, which contrast with the dense quality of Long-stalk Holly. Associated foreground plantings could well be of materials which are characteristically light green or chartreuse. *Kerria japonica* would provide this quality with its twigs, Variegated Liriope (*Liriope muscari* 'Variegata') with its foliage.

Ilex pedunculosa was introduced to this country from Japan in 1892 by Charles S. Sargent, founder of the Arnold Arboretum, and again from different sites in the Hupeh province of China in 1901 and 1907 by Ernest H. Wilson.

29

STRUCTURAL INTEREST

Deciduous
Effective landscape height: 20 feet
Effective landscape spread: 25 feet
Zone 5
Rosaceae (Rose Family)
Garden origin

Malus × 'Red Jade'
Red Jade Crab Apple

This hybrid Crab Apple is a real charmer for its pendulous form alone. Almost everything about the branching habit is pleasantly serpentine. First the branches curve downward from the trunk, then up a bit, moving outward and gracefully downward again. The trunk has a sensuous twist in the early stages which is less dominant as the plant matures into a more regular mound, broader than it is tall. Even at this later stage, however, the serpentine characteristic of the branches persists, allowing occasional branch tips to break the lines of what might otherwise be a boringly rigid form.

In addition, it has strong seasonal interest twice during the year. In early to mid-May the branches are covered with attractive pink buds which open to white blossoms. These produce ½-inch or larger fruits, which turn cherry red in the fall. The fruit is clustered with the leaves on short spurs, from which it hangs on cherry-length stems. The picture is equally striking whether the red fruit is seen with the bright green foliage, or after leaf fall has dramatized the plant's irregularly pendulous habit.

Plants with pendulous forms are valuable assets to the designer and include such choice aristocrats as Weeping Beech (*Fagus sylvatica* 'Pendula'), Golden-twig Weeping Willow (*Salix alba* var. *tristis*), Willowleaf Cotoneaster (*Cotoneaster salicifolia* 'Flocossa') as well as Sargent's Weeping Hemlock (*Tsuga canadensis* 'Pendula'). Considerable interest is added to any garden scene by contrasting horizontal, vertical, and pendulous forms. Generally, when vertical forms (having upward motion) and pendulous forms (having downward motion) are the sole elements in a composition, a disturbing tension is produced. Pendulous and horizontal forms together make a restful composition. All three types together are satisfactory if the horizontal elements predominate with one of the other two.

For example, a pleasant, large-scale planting might feature three of the early lilac *Syringa* x 'La-Martine,' as a vertical clump accent against a background grouping of seven or eight horizontally branched dwarf Burning-Bush (*Euonymous alatus* 'Compactus'), and three large specimens of the weeper, Red Jade Crab Apple. The horizontal and pendulous forms thus are predominant. The vertical accent of this scene adds a note of excitement not massive enough to be disturbing. (This combination would incidentally provide an attractive pink-lilac color combination in May from the flowering Lilac and Crab Apple and in the fall the brilliant red foliage of the *Euonymous* with the cherry-red fruit).

With less space available, a single specimen *Malus* x 'Red Jade' might be featured against a mass planting of the rather "loose," nearly pendulous shrub *Spirea thunbergii*. While these two forms would relate to each other, a carpet of *Phlox divaricata* in the foreground providing horizontality might

Malus x 'Red Jade'

Malus x 'Red Jade'

contain an accent clumping of six *Iris pumila*—providing a tease of verticality. This grouping would provide an exciting spring show of color. The fine foliage and charming white flowers of the *Spirea* would provide a delicate background for the pink of the Crab and light blue of the Phlox. The accent of, say, five light blue *Iris pumila* 'Blue Denim' and one dark purple *Iris pumila* 'Sambo' would provide the finishing touch.

'Red Jade' is only one of the many varieties of ornamental Crab Apples, which are defined as any apple *(Malus)* with fruit 2 inches or less in diameter. There are three European species of Apple, nine from the United States, and seventeen from eastern Europe and Asia. More significantly, there are hundreds of hybrids requiring constant re-evaluation and selection. Some are alternate-year bearers as is *M.* x 'Red Jade.' Many are subject to fire blight, scale, and borers.

Malus x 'Red Jade' is certainly a uniquely fine plant. It originated at the Brooklyn Botanic Garden in 1935 and was introduced by it in 1953. Plant patent 1497 was granted for it on July 17, 1956, and assigned to the Brooklyn Institute of Arts and Sciences.

30

Phyllostachys aureosulcata
Yellowgroove Bamboo

STRUCTURAL INTEREST

Deciduous
Effective landscape height: 25 feet
Effective landscape spread: indefinite
Zone 7
Gramineae (Grass Family)
Native range: China

There is absolutely no substitute for the exotic effect of this hardy bamboo. Whether a cluster of six stems or a grove of half an acre, it provides a symphony of verticality which no native plant can offer. The color of the canes varies, but when growing happily, the majority of the larger ones are usually dark green with darker green above the nodes and a whitish blush below. The smaller stems are often yellow-green, with less of the dramatic contrast at the joints. The charming accent-like spacing of the nodes varies considerably, sometimes being as little as 4 inches and sometimes as great as 9½ inches. The branches are horizontal to ascendant and very fine in texture. The leaves are small, narrow, and sharply pointed. They have the appearance of having been sprinkled at many different angles, and provide a delightful hazy mist through which the strong design qualities of the canes are seen. The outer stems in any clump often lean out, and some branches take on a pendulous quality as the foliage becomes heavy. This gives a graceful quality to the entire clump or grove, creating an overall effect resembling a fountain. Seen from inside, each grove has an arrestingly "clean" appearance. The ground is usually covered with a coating of light tan leaves from prior years, and there is no detracting vegetation around the closely spaced stems. In winter, frost turns the leaves a tan so light as to be almost white. Old leaves hang on the twigs until spring and contrast handsomely, often in a curled state, with the green shades of the canes.

Because of Bamboo's exotic quality, I like to use it for dramatic impact. Contrasted with the largest broadleaves we have, Rhubarb *(Rheum rhaponticum)* or *Petasites japonica*, with its dinner-plate-size foliage, it makes an unforgettable impression—especially when used as a background for a pond or small lake. In a drier situation, it might create an equally striking effect with a planting of Oakleaf Hydrangea *(Hydrangea quercifolia)* and a ground cover of *Sedum acre*. The *Sedum acre*, being a very light green, would reflect light upward, bringing out the shades of green in the Bamboo. The Hydrangea would provide excellent coarse texture and a long season of interest with dramatic white flowers, chartreuse seed heads, and wine-colored fall foliage.

The chief problem with growing Bamboo is controlling its spread by underground runners. This *is* possible and is discussed under the heading *Arundinaria viridistriata* (pages 180–1). I have seen a dra-

Phyllostachys aureosulcata

matically effective use of Yellowgrove Bamboo as a screening plant in a 3-foot strip between neighboring driveways. The paving of the driveways controlled its spread, and its narrow vertical growth habit provided privacy even for second-story windows.

The culms are widely used for fishing poles, and the new young shoots are edible. There are a total of two hundred and fifty species of Bamboo, most of which are tropical. *Phyllostachys aureosulcata* is one of the two species hardy as far north as Philadelphia. It was first introduced from Tang-si, Chekiang province, China, to America in 1907 by Frank Meyer, the well-known plant explorer of the United States Department of Agriculture. It became popular in Europe soon after World War I.

31

Pinus densiflora 'Umbraculifera'
Tanyosho Pine

STRUCTURAL INTEREST

Evergreen
Effective landscape height: 12 feet
Effective landscape spread: 18 feet
Zone 5
Pinaceae (Pine Family)
Garden origin

This Pine is recommended because its shape is unique and very useful design-wise. Tanyosho Pine is always multi-trunked and flat-topped. The trunks rise from a single point at ground level and fan out to give a wedge-shaped silhouette. The very dense foliage is composed of yellow-green needles 3–5 inches long, and usually disappears from the trunks as the plant matures, leaving a horizontal band of green at the top. The stems are basically greenish-brown but exfoliate copiously, revealing an orangey-brown undercoat which is extremely attractive with the foliage color. The foliage is highlighted during the winter and early spring with highly ornamental, brownish, new-growth buds, and at an early age the plant sets copious cones of a slightly darker color.

The form of the plant is that of a rather regular inverted cone in younger stages, becoming more distinctive and irregular as the plant reaches maturity. Because of the contrast of horizontal and angled lines, Tanyosho Pine has design qualities reminiscent of a good piece of sculpture. On the other hand, its umbrella-like quality makes it highly valuable for keeping the eye focused downward on some important detail such as a collection of gem-like bulbous plants or a diminutive sculpture. The contrasting color and textural qualities of bark and needles impart a delightful richness to any garden setting in which it is used. Darker greens and bronzy tones in companion plants help to show it off to good advantage.

A bronzy background of three *Ilex aquifolium* 'Ciliata Major' might be used to show off a single specimen of *Pinus densiflora* 'Umbraculifera' in a bed of the spiky, dark green ivy *Hedera helix* 'Conglomerata Erecta.' Or the background might be three bronzy-leaved, red-berried Willowleaf Cotoneasters (*Cotoneaster salicifolia* 'Flocossa') with a ground cover of Bowles Periwinkle (*Vinca minor* 'Bowles'). In the former case, the background forms are cones, in this case pendulous globes. A lighter treatment might use deciduous shrubs with green twigs as companion plants. For instance, a specimen Tanyosho Pine might be planted in a sea of the low, green-twigged *Genista sylvestris* 'Lydia'; backed by a planting of eight or ten bronze-leaved Leucothoë *(Leucothoë fontanesiana)*; and this backed by three plants of the green-twigged, yellow-fruited Hardyorange *(Poncirus trifoliata)*. The green twigs and bronze of the Leucothoë would provide strong winter interest; the butter-yellow blossoms of the *Genista* would carry the show in June; and the ornamental oranges of the *Poncirus* would steal the show during the early fall months.

The typical species of the Japanese Red Pine, *Pinus densiflora*, has little to recommend it as a garden plant. This interesting variant in the form of an inverted cone, however, is definitely noteworthy. It was "discovered" by the German horticulturist

Pinus densiflora 'Umbraculifera'

Heinrich Mayer in 1888 and first described in 1890. For many years it was cultivated under the later but descriptive name of 'Tabulaeformis,' and was long grown in Japan as a variety 'Tanyosho.'

32

STRUCTURAL INTEREST

Deciduous
Effective landscape height: 12-15 feet
Effective landscape spread: 18 feet
Zone 5
Rosaceae (Rose Family)
Commercial origin

Prunus cerasifera 'Thundercloud'
'Thundercloud' Plum, Redleaf Plum

There is no finer plant than 'Thundercloud' Plum for attractive, lively, plum-red foliage which remains so over a long time period. Whereas the ubiquitous "Japanese Red Maples" turn dull, bronzy shades (and some become dirty green) by midsummer, this plant puts on a fine show all season. A small, compact tree, the new foliage is bronzy-pink and the new stem growth is pinkish, making a rich but subtle contrast with the duller maroon of older foliage.

One of the unfortunate prejudices common in American horticulture is the dictum that plants with colored foliage are in poor taste. In my opinion, such plants have often been used unwisely and it does take greater thought to use them effectively; this does not mean, however, that they are not extremely valuable garden plants when properly sited!

During the six months of the year when it sports its showy foliage, 'Thundercloud' Plum is a highly valuable "designer's" plant. The solid mass of colored foliage makes this an excellent foil and enricher for a wide variety of color combinations, a real "anchor" plant for almost any situation! Generally its most effective use is as a background plant; however, since it makes an excellent hedge or "cut-back" shrub (3-5 feet in height), it may well come into its own in the middle ground.

In late May or early June its "plum-iness," when seen with the rich orange blossoms of the Ghent Azalea 'Coccinea Speciosa' (*Rhododendron* x *gandavense* 'Coccinea Speciosa') is downright exciting. A happy combination might feature ten to fifteen of the Azaleas in a grove of three well-spaced 'Thundercloud' Plums—all backed by four or five yellow-green Spreading Junipers such as the lively *Juniperus chinensis* 'Armstrong.'

The foliage color is an extremely valuable complement to the old-fashioned Shrub Roses which bloom in June, because 'Thundercloud' Plum's foliage contains just about every shade of rose and lavender in its own makeup. The pink of *Rosa* 'Jacques Cartier' and the light lavender of *Rosa* 'Tour de Malakoff' are examples of colors that look especially good with 'Thundercloud' Plum. Four or five plants of each of these roses might be underplanted with the pink-flowered perennial *Centranthus ruber* and masses of deep purple Heliotrope—all featured against a clipped hedge of *Prunus cerasifera* 'Thundercloud.' The velvety, deep maroon-purple blossoms of *Rosa* 'Tuscany' are another case in point. Six or seven plants of this Rose combined with a single Fountain Buddleia *(Buddleia alternifolia)*, three cut-back 'Thundercloud' Plums, and a large massing of the feathery blue blossoms of the herbaceous *Amsonia tabernaemontana* would need only the accent of three or four clumps of *Lilium martagon* or Foxtail-lily *(Eremurus)* hybrids to make a breathtaking spectacle.

In midsummer there is no finer picture than the pink-flowered *Tamarix* 'Pink Cascade' featured against 'Thundercloud' Plum foliage. The needly, blue-green foliage of *Tamarix* provides a refreshing contrast against the broadleaf Plum foliage even when blossoms are not present. A planting of three *Tamarix* backed by four Plums could, in a large area, feature a foreground planting of eight or ten of the native meadow plants called Iron Weed *(Vernonia novaboracensis)*, with its royal purple flowers; this might be accented with one Plume Grass *(Erianthis ravennae)*, with its 8-foot skyrocket-like spikes

Prunus cerasifera 'Thundercloud'

of silvery fluff. There would be nothing dull about this summer scene!

In late September and early October the tawny pink of Eulalia grass *(Miscanthus sinensis)* is at its most striking when seen against the very deep, plum-red of this *Prunus.* An attractive plan might be to feature three *Miscanthus* in a sea of the broad-foliaged *Sedum spectabile* 'Indian Chief,' then covered with its rusty red flower heads—all against a planting of six to eight lavender-fruited Japanese Beautyberries *(Callicarpa japonica)* backed by four staggered *Prunus cerasifera* 'Thundercloud.'

'Thundercloud' Plum is no exception to the rule that plants grown for their colorful foliage are most effective when in full sun and rich soil. As its foliage color is best when in active growth, a good watering and feeding program is recommended. The natural form of the tree may need some help in the pruning department since it has the bad habit of cross-branching.

Prunus cerasifera, native from the Caucasus Mountains to Afghanistan and Turkey, has been grown in Europe since the sixteenth century. A red-leaved form long known as *Prunus pissardi* was brought there from Persia about 1880 and arrived in this country soon afterward. There have been several red-foliaged forms on the market, but 'Thundercloud,' introduced by Housewearts Nursery of Woodburn, Oregon, in 1937, is the finest of them all.

33

Oxydendrum arboreum

Sourwood, Sorrel Tree

SEASONAL INTEREST

Deciduous
Effective landscape height: 25 feet
Effective landscape spread: 12-15 feet
Zone 6
Ericaceae (Heath Family)
Native range: United States—Pennsylvania to Louisiana

There is a quality of excellence about this Rhododendron-related tree that definitely puts it in the category, "an aristocrat of the garden." It puts on a brilliant performance in July and again in the fall and has a habit of growth that is enchanting all year. Generally round-headed in form, this is the only quality that is common to most Sourwood trees—and there are exceptions to *that* rule of thumb. Sourwoods are extremely irregular growers: some single-stemmed, some multistemmed, some with lower branches intact, some very high-headed, some broad and spreading, and others extremely columnar. Individual branches are often quite twisted, the bark in older trees considerably fissured. Each plant is a distinct character and in this fact lies much of the charm. The flowers are white and pendulous, very similar to those of its relative, Japanese Andromeda *(Pieris japonica)*. The total inflorescence is approximately 12 inches long and often contains as many as thirteen sprays with up to twenty-six tiny buds on a spray. There is a slight upcurve at the bottom of each spray which adds to the grace of the bloom. These blossoms appear in July and are seen against the lustrous leathery, apple-green foliage. Individual leaves (approximately 7 inches long) are pointed, oblong ovals, resembling Sour Gum leaves. These have a pleasant acid taste, to which the common name refers. The form of the flower is maintained in the fruiting stage in a green-white coloration. As the summer progresses, the foliage often takes on a bronzy, plum coloration, and in October we are treated to absolutely breathtaking, glossy red leaves.

Oxydendrum arboreum

Because of the distinct "character" of *Oxydendrum* and its all-season interest, it makes an excellent specimen plant around which to build a garden. The irregular form is well dramatized by contrasting it with the horizontal line of an evergreen hedge. For example, the richness of Red Sourwood leaves as seen against the pendulous, gray form of Deodar Cedar *(Cedrus deodara)* and contrasted with a companion planting of yellow-fruited Hardy-oranges *(Poncirus trifoliata)* could well do with the structuring effect of a clipped hedge of the shiny, dark-green-leaved Japanese Holly, *Ilex crenata* 'Compacta,' in the foreground.

Another such combination might break the tall vertical silhouette of a single Sourwood by a background planting of three horizontally branching Burning-Bush *(Euonymous alatus)*. Their forms could be repeated with more strength and finer texture in a foreground planting consisting of three or four clumps of Maiden Grass (*Miscanthus sinensis* 'Gracillimus') for vertical strength, fronted with a hedge of the compact dark green Helleri Dwarf Japanese Holly (*Ilex crenata* 'Helleri'), providing a horizontal contrast.

A fine summer picture might well consist of backing a Sourwood planting with the fine-textured Golden-larch *(Pseudolarix amabilis)*; massing eight or ten Glossy Abelia *(Abelia* x *grandiflora)*, with its white, Arbutus-like flowers and bronzy flower parts, about their base; and planting the lavender-to blue-flowered Lilyturf (*Liriope muscari* 'Big Blue') in mass in the foreground.

Because of its natural inclination to grow in bottomland and the valid design gimmick of using pendulous-branched or pendulous-flowered plants near water, Sourwood makes an excellent subject with which to landscape a pond. The contrasting fine-foliaged, vertical form of Pond Cypress *(Taxodium ascendens)* and masses of the femininely rounded *Viburnum nudum* would be appropriate companions to dramatize the Sourwood. The Viburnum berries go through spectacular color changes—from green to white to pink to blue—during the same time that the Sourwood is progressing through its delightful summer and early fall foliage sequence.

Where space permits, it would be a marvelous indulgence to plant a whole grove of *Oxydendrum*. A bit of elegant sophistication would further come from adding a ground cover of the spiky, dark green Shrub Ivy, *Hedera helix* 'Conglomerata Erecta' and providing a background planting of the needly, yellow-green Juniper, *Juniperus chinensis* 'Armstrong.'

Although related to the Rhododendrons, a tribe generally preferring acid soil, *Oxydendrum* seems to do well under either neutral or acid conditions as long as the soil is of good quality and contains plenty of organic matter. In nature it inhabits rich woodlands but is definitely its ornamental best in full sun. The roots are fibrous, making it an easy transplanter, assuming a ball of earth is provided.

This American native was introduced into England in 1747 and was grown enthusiastically there by 1752. It has received a series of awards from the Royal Horticultural Society during the current century: Award of Garden Merit, 1947; Award of Merit, 1951, 1957.

34

Salix elaeagnos
Hoary Willow, Elaeagnos Willow

This shrubby, narrow-leafed willow has the same exciting textural magic (on a larger scale) as Rosemary *(Rosmarinus officinalis)* or Lavender *(Lavandula angustifolia)*, previously known as *L. vera*. A round-headed shrub, *Salix elaeagnos* produces slender reddish-brown branches (2 feet or more per year) clothed with gray, linear foliage (only ¼ inch wide to the 2¼-inch length). The newer growth shoots and leaves are white-gray, the older foliage is greenish with white undersides. The leaves are produced very thickly on the wand-like stems, giving a total effect of feathery blue-grayness.

Salix elaeagnos is an extremely valuable structural plant, providing much textural and color interest. Used with red-foliaged plants such as 'Thundercloud' Plum (*Prunus cerasifera* 'Thundercloud'), Redleaf Barberry (*Berberis thunbergii* 'Atropurpurea'), River's Purple Beech (*Fagus sylvatica* 'Riversi'), or Redleaf Smoke-Tree (*Cotinus coggygria* 'Foliis Purpureis'), it successfully brings out the very best in these summer foliage colors and enriches any mix of these with such blue-lavender-

STRUCTURAL INTEREST

Deciduous
Effective landscape height: 25 feet
Effective landscape spread: 20 feet
Zone 5
Salicaceae (Willow Family)
Native range: southern Europe and Asia Minor

pink flowering companions as Butterfly-Bush (*Buddleia davidii* varieties), Chaste-Tree (*Vitex agnus-castus* 'Latifolia'), *Caryopteris* x *clandonensis* 'Blue Mist,' *Tamarix* 'Pink Cascade,' Blue Althaea (*Hibiscus syriacus* 'Blue Bird'), Pink Althaea (*Hibiscus syriacus* 'Woodbridge'), Crape-myrtle *(Lagerstroemia indica),* Mimosa *(Albizia julibrissin* 'Rosea'), and Blue Plumbago *(Ceratostigma plumbaginoides).*

On the other hand, *Salix elaeagnos* is equally useful as a companion for cheery yellow-orange combinations such as the soft Yellow Day-lily, *Hemerocallis* x 'Hyperion,' and Butterfly Weed *(Asclepias tuberosa),* or the soft yellow Meadow-rue *(Thalictrum glaucum)* and the bright orange Maltese Cross Plant *(Lychnis chalcedonica),* or yellow Mullein (*Verbascum* sp.) and the orange Trumpet-vine (*Campsis* x *tagliabuana* 'Madame Galen'), or the Dwarf Golden Variegated Bamboo *(Arundinaria viridistriata)* and the annual, orange-flowered *Tithonia rotundifolia* 'Torch.'

Any good gray plant immediately brings to mind that wonderful "room" in V. Sackville-West's garden at Sissinghurst (Cranbrook, Kent, England) where grays and whites are blended most subtly with here and there a touch of very dark green. *Salix elaeagnos, Yucca glauca,* Woolly Lamb's Ear *(Stachys olympica), Artemesia stelleriana, Artemesia albula*, and the architectural thistles, *Onopordum* spp., would provide such a rich gray palette. White flowers might include Fragrant Mock-orange *(Philadelphus coronarius), Clematis lanuginosa* x 'Henryi,' White Althaea (*Hibiscus syriacus* 'W. R. Smith'), White Spider-plant (*Cleome spinosa* 'Helen Campbell'), and those incomparable Shrub Roses: *Rosa* 'Alba' and *Rosa* 'Mme. LeGrays.' These should be balanced with just the right amount of dark green using such treasures as the Shrub Ivy (*Hedera helix* 'Conglomerata Erecta'), Roundleaf Osmanthus *(Osmanthus rotundifolius),* Hollyleaf Osmanthus (*Osmanthus heterophyllus* 'Gulftide'), and the Curlyleaf Privet (*Ligustrum japonicum* 'Rotundifolium').

Salix elaeagnos has the drawbacks of most Wil-

Salix elaeagnos

lows. Its roots will seek out water and can clog drains. It is weak-wooded and can break up in storms, but this is a minimal disadvantage as it responds promptly with abundant new growth.

Salix elaeagnos came to us from the mountains of central and southern Europe and Asia Minor. It was introduced to this country sometime prior to 1850 but has never been used to the extent justified by its virtues.

35

Stewartia koreana
Korean Stewartia

Stewartia koreana is a delicate little gem of a flowering tree. The habit is fastidious, dense, and pyramidal. It is sometimes single-stemmed, sometimes multistemmed. The ascendant branches have a rhythmic zigzag from leaf bud to leaf bud. The new growth is reddish; the bark on older trunks is flaking and varicolored, resembling that of a miniature Sycamore. All this adds up to a striking winter picture made all the more charming when gilded with fresh snow.

June finds *Stewartia koreana* clothed with attractive apple-green leaves, slender pointed ovals up to 3 inches wide and 4 inches long. Late in the month the flowers, each on a short stalk, appear both in the leaf axils and terminally. Imagine 3-inch white, camellia-like blossoms, each with an attractive center cluster of yellow stamens! Although not terribly outstanding from a distance, close up the spectacle is absolutely enthralling, and completely justifies the Japanese vernacular name, which means "snow cups." I think part of the charm is the total design quality of the plant; every detail seems in perfect proportion and balance with the rest of the plant. If one had designed a "structure" to display

SEASONAL INTEREST

Deciduous
Effective landscape height: 25 feet
Effective landscape spread: 15–18 feet
Zone 6
Theaceae (Tea Family)
Native range: Korea

"camellia blossoms," one couldn't have done better!

In the fall the orange-red foliage color is outstanding as well.

Because of the design delicacy of Korean Stewartia, it is important to plant it where it will not get lost among coarse-textured companions. Because it branches (and flowers) well to the ground, it is used to fullest advantage where other shrubs will not crowd in upon it. For these reasons it might well be featured against the fine texture of a clipped Hemlock hedge *(Tsuga canadensis)* and underplanted with drifts of low-growing blooming companions such as White Astilbe, chartreuse Meadow-rue (*Thallictrum rugosum*, also known as *T. glaucum*) and purple Salvia (*Salvia* 'East Friesland'); or the Blueleaved Plantain-lily (*Hosta sieboldiana*, also known as *H. glauca*), the compact, pink-flowered ground cover *Spirea japonica alpina*, and blue and lavender forms of Japanese Iris *(Iris kaempferi).*

Stewartias do best in good bottomland soil, on the moist side. Copious amounts of organic matter are beneficial. As all of their flowers suggest, *Stewartia, Camellia*, and *Franklinia* are closely related. *S. koreana* was introduced into this country from Korea by Ernest H. Wilson in 1917.

Stewartia koreana

SEASONAL INTEREST
Deciduous
Effective landscape height: 25 feet
Effective landscape spread: 12 feet
Zone 5
Oleaceae (Olive Family)
Native range: Japan

36

Syringa reticulata

Japanese Tree Lilac

Huge creamy white plumes (10–18 inches long) decorate this tree-like shrub at a time in mid-June when all other Lilacs and most "spring" flowers have gone, and "summer" flowers have not yet started. The pyramidal, Rhubarb-like blossoms seem even larger because of the relatively small size of the plant on which they are borne. The yellow-green leaves are pointed, oval, approximately 4½ inches long. They fortunately provide rather sparse clothing to the tree, thus revealing the rather rugged black-barked branching habit. The green seed pods which follow the flowers are not unattractive, and the dark bark with its horizontal white lenticels is interesting in the winter. However, the primary value of the Japanese Tree Lilac is in the great floral show it puts on around the middle of June.

The form of Japanese Tree Lilac is sufficiently interesting and the flowers spectacular enough that it can be featured alone. One appropriate spot would be against a hot wall. The show will be particularly attractive if the wall is dark in color and the Potentillas 'White Gold' (soft yellow) and 'Katharine Dykes' (bright yellow) are planted in drifts beneath its branches.

Mid-June is also the time of year when the old-fashioned Shrub Roses are putting on their big show. I should like to try a planting of pink cabbage roses and great quantities of the blue perennial *Amsonia tabernaemontana* with the white of *Syringa amurensis* var. *japonica* and, if I could be so lucky, establish a rose-colored Beech (*Fagus sylvatica* 'Rosea Marginata') as background. The broadleaf, broad-petaled textures would be relieved by the froth of the Lilac blossoms and the delicacy of the *Amsonia*. The pinks and blues should relate to each other and feature the white of the Lilac.

Syringa reticulata does best in full sun, in ordinary well-drained garden soil. Pruning is limited to removal of dead wood and old flower and seed stalks. Gardeners with great sensitivity to scent should plant this Lilac at a distance from outdoor living areas as the flower fragrance is not particularly pleasant, resembling a strong privet odor.

Japanese Tree Lilac was introduced into this country in 1876 by W. L. Clark via the Arnold Arboretum. In England this plant received a First Class Certificate of the Royal Horticultural Society in 1887.

Syringa reticulata

37

SEASONAL INTEREST

Deciduous
Effective landscape height: indefinite, depending on support available
Effective landscape spread: indefinite, depending on support available
Zone 5
Leguminosae (Pea Family)
Native range: Japan

Wisteria floribunda

Japanese Wisteria

This rampant vine can be a fabulously rewarding plant for any gardener who can take pleasure in providing it with sympathetic discipline. I call it rampant because it will frequently grow as much as 6 feet in one year. On the other hand, it also qualifies as one of the most delightfully lush and voluptuous plants in the world. The 11-inch-long, coarse compound leaves are composed of anywhere from eleven to nineteen clean, blue-green leaflets. The seeds are contrastingly smooth and bean-like and the trunks are smooth, muscle-like, and occasionally gnarly. No other adjective describes the flowers as well as "spectacular." The trusses are pendulous, generally ranging from 18–30 inches in length (although they have been reported up to 5 feet, 4 inches long), and have a color range from white through pink and shades of blue and lavender. A number of garden varieties have been selected and named, especially by the Japanese. Some of the better known ones are: 'Alba,' 'Macrobotrys' ('Multijuga'), 'Rosea,' 'Violacea-plena,' 'Beni-Fuji,' 'Issai,' 'Mrs. McCullough,' 'Penn Valley,' 'Royal Purple,' 'Sierra Madre,' 'Kyashaku,' 'Murasaki Noda,' and 'Naga Noda.'

There is a very famous plant (of 'Macrobotrys') at Kameido, Japan, according to W. J. Bean (1951), which has often been illustrated and described by travelers. It forms a huge arbor, extending partly over a body of water spanned by a semicircular Japanese bridge. With its thousands of slender, pendulous racemes 3 to 4 feet long, crowded with lilac blossoms "odorous of honey and buzzing with bees," it makes, no doubt, one of the most remarkable floral exhibitions on the globe.

When grown as an arbor plant, Wisteria can also be handsomely featured, in a more Western manner, midst solid color blocks of tulips, the ground covered with the light blue of *Phlox divaricata* and the wine-foliaged, dark blue-flowered *Ajuga reptans* 'Metallica Crispa.'

In addition to its possible use as an arbor plant, Wisteria can also be trained as a tree with a central stem and one, two, or three whorls of branches. Such a plant might be featured in the austere setting of a sculptural contemporary building using only a moss-like ground cover and cut-granite edging to complete the picture. (Because the trunks even when young give a feeling of great age, Wisteria seems to relate well to the timelessness of stone in any form.) Trained as a tree it also comes across extremely well with the moundy forms of its blooming mates the Kurume Azaleas contrastingly underplanted with Hayscented Fern *(Dennstaedtia punctilobula)* and light blue *Scilla campanulata.*

I cannot emphasize enough the importance of making a real commitment to disciplining the plant, if you decide to grow it. The growth is rank and twining and grasping. Strong structures must be provided whether the plant is grown in tree or arbor forms. It will quickly destroy weak ones. I use 3-inch pipes, 8 feet tall, set in concrete for tree training. Once a basic shape is established, heavy pruning must be done in late June or early July, cutting all new growth back to two eyes (the first two buds on the new growth). This must be followed by light bimonthly pruning to remove any late growth that occurs. In addition, the plants often sucker (when young) from below ground, and these shoots must be removed until they are totally discouraged. When the stem has been wounded in any way, rot frequently develops in the center. Generally, as long as grooves can be cut in the trunk in such a way as to drain water from these wounded spots, no harm is done. The outer bark or skin remains

Wisteria floribunda

as strong as a piece of metal pipe. Plants grown from seed *may* never flower. For this reason and because of the great investment in time that will go into training the plant, it is most important to start with a named clone which will have been grafted or grown from cuttings. The intensity of effort that goes into this sort of plant training is very much akin to that of a sculptor. Each year is a new challenge, however, as old branches may die and new ones may have to be trained in their place; or the foliage may become dense, and artistic decisions may have to be made about removing leafage to expose attractive sections of trunk. All in all, shaping a Wisteria can be a most satisfying sort of experience, with pruning shears and saw as the sculptor's tools.

Wisteria floribunda is a Chinese plant, cultivated for centuries by the Japanese. It was described by Englebert Kaempfer in the late 1600's, and Carl Peter Thunberg brought back samples of it before 1760. It was first grown in England about 1816, as an espaliered subject. That plant was reported in 1840 to have a branch spread of 100 feet on each side of its trunk. In 1862, George R. Hall, M.D., sent it from Japan to the United States, where it was grown and introduced by the Samuel B. Parsons Nursery of Flushing, New York.

III
SHRUBS

Compared to both large and small trees, there is a great abundance and variety of shrubs available to the landscape planner. Partly because of this, and partly because of my own personal preferences, I have included fifty here, making it the largest single category of plants in the book. Besides such classic shrub types as Azaleas (about which there is a special introductory note on pages 142-4) and Lilac, this section also includes more unusual varieties such as *Chimonanthus praecox* (Wintersweet) and *Stranvaesia davidiana* var. *undulata* (Chinese Stranvaesia), three dwarf trees, and two ornamental grasses. Again, entries are distinguished according to their primary use—for garden structure or for seasonal interest—though of course many serve both functions.

38

SEASONAL INTEREST

Semi-evergreen
Effective landscape height: 5 feet
Effective landscape spread: 5 feet
Zone 6
Caprifoliaceae (Honeysuckle Family)
Hybrid origin

Abelia × *grandiflora*

Glossy Abelia

Abelia x *grandiflora* has a long blooming season (July, August, September), making this neat, moundy shrub a favorite of butterflies and a gardener's delight! The Arbutus or bell-like white blossoms protrude gracefully from delicate pinky-bronze cross-like flower parts. This color is reinforced by the pinkish stems of the new growth and contrasts happily with the dark olive-green of the 1-inch glossy, pointed leaves. The softness of the new growth and the graceful qualities of the flowers conceal a rather stiff branching habit. The foliage turns shades of bronze and purple in the fall and is often reasonably attractive until after Christmas.

Because of its semi-evergreen qualities and broad-leaf texture, Glossy Abelia can be a lively feature among a planting of needle evergreens such as *Taxus adpressa* 'Fowles Variety' or *Taxus cuspidata* 'Nana.' Thinking of Abelia strictly as a summer flowerer, one could well mass nine or ten Abelias in a sunny location with a structure of perhaps three narrow-leaved grasses (*Miscanthus sinensis* 'Gracillimus'), tie them together with a ground-cover planting of the yellow-green *Sedum kamtschaticum*, and perhaps provide an accent with one clump of the yellow-flowered Day-lily, *Hemerocallis* x 'Hyperion.'

I find that Abelia is probably at its very best in sun but still performs reasonably well in light shade. A well-drained location with good soil seems to minimize winter damage to tip growth. Certainly protection from the sweep of winter wind leaves the plant in better condition in the spring, although Abelia always seems to make a fast recovery from the winter damage it occasionally experiences.

Except for removal of damaged wood, the only pruning that is recommended is occasional removal of heavy wood to encourage a more graceful shape. It is certainly a grave mistake to shear the plant and destroy its natural habit.

This hybrid of two Chinese parents, *A. chinensis* and *A. uniflora*, was raised by the nurseryman Carlo Rovelli and his brother at Pallanza, Italy, on Lake Maggiore sometime before 1880. Since the cross may have occurred subsequently in other gardens it is not known whether the plants grown today are really from Rovelli or not. As with many hybrids, *Abelia* x *grandiflora* is of a sturdier, more vigorous constitution than either parent.

Abelia x *grandiflora* received the Award of Garden Merit from England's Royal Horticultural Society in 1962.

39

Acer palmatum var. *dissectum* (*A. palmatum* 'Viride,' *A. palmatum palmatifidum*)

Green Cutleaf Japanese Maple

STRUCTURAL INTEREST

Deciduous
Effective landscape height: 6 feet
Effective landscape spread: 15 feet
Zone 6
Aceraceae (Maple Family)
Native range: China, Korea, and Japan

This dwarf, mound-shaped Maple is a distinguished garden jewel both because of its sculptural branching habit and because of its summer cloak of light green, fern-like foliage. The heavy, often twisted stem supports horizontal to pendulous branches, which terminate in fine finger-like twigs. These characteristics, combined with a natural tendency of the outermost branches to conform to a mushroom-headed form, give it a distinctly bonsai-like quality. The 2–4-inch-long leaves are divided into seven to eleven lobes, each deeply cut and each division finely toothed. The light green color of these leaves is downright refreshing in its contrast to the duller green of other plants with which it is likely to be associated. The green variety is distinctly to be preferred to the red forms more commonly marketed. The overuse of red-foliaged Maples as specimen plants has produced many discordant landscape pictures in this country. The green form is a more subtle beauty blending well with most other plant material.

Keeping in mind that the average American's life style is neither ascetic nor contemplative in the Japanese sense, it would be unfortunate to conclude that the best use of this plant requires all the accompanying trappings of a Japanese garden. To be sure the fine features of the plant would be lost in any kind of mass shrub planting and we can follow the essence of the Japanese discipline in using this Maple as a gem-like focal or accent point, free from competitive distractions.

The stark simplicity of materials used in much of our contemporary architecture provides the perfect foil for the Cutleaf Maple's complex beauty. And, as a matter of fact, we frequently see it used in such settings with a simple ground cover as the only accompaniment. Rectilinear forms such as wooden plant boxes, paths edged in cut granite or crisp, broadleaf, evergreen hedges provide satisfactory elements for emphasizing the "naturalistic" form of the plant. It is important to select and limit the number of complimentary materials to such "naturals" as aged-looking rocks or pebbles and moss or moss-like ground covers such as Moss Sandwort *(Areneria verna caespitosa)*, Corsican Pearlwort *(Sagina subulata)*, Common Thrift *(Armeria maritima)*, or fine-foliaged Sedums. These efforts will go farther toward making this plant communicate it own message in American gardens than attempting to copy the foreign culture.

This Maple is slow-growing, and each individual has a distinct character. Consequently we should expect to pay for and cherish such a plant just as we would a fine piece of jewelry or a good painting.

Japanese Maples prefer perfectly drained soil, not necessarily highly fertile but rich in organic matter.

Acer palmatum var. dissectum

Acer palmatum var. *dissectum* is usually grown in the sun; however, it is perfectly tolerant of partial shade, for in Japan, where it is prized for its glowing fall foliage, it is an understory tree.

There is confusion about the correct botanical name of this plant. The one given above is its current "sales name" in the United States. There are literally hundreds of variants of *Acer palmatum* which the Japanese had been cherishing and naming for many years prior to the first introduction of the species into Holland about 1750 by Dutch East Indies sea captains. The outstanding merits of *Acer palmatum* var. *dissectum* were recognized in an Award of Garden Merit from Britain's Royal Horticultural Society in 1956.

40

Arundo donax
Giant Reed

STRUCTURAL INTEREST

Herbaceous
Effective landscape height: 12-18 feet
Effective landscape spread: indefinite
Zones 7-8
Gramineae (Grass Family)
Native range: Mediterranean region

The extreme size and striking foliage arrangement of this bamboo-like grass make it a real show stealer in the late-summer garden. Thick, fresh shoots start late each spring from the heavy rhizome-like roots and often climb skyward in excess of 15 feet, giving it the children's name of Jack-and-the-Beanstalk Plant. Two-foot silvery panicles top the foliage in September. By far its most entrancing quality, however, is the dramatic spacing of the 18-inch gray-green leaf blades. The overall effect is that of a cross between bamboo and corn but with a captivating grace which is best appreciated as the breezes move the foliage.

Because of its coarseness and grace, Arundo is definitely a plant for a relaxed, informal—in fact exotic, erotic—situation. In some settings it needs other grasses and grass-like foliage such as Giant

Arundo donax

Eulalia (*Miscanthus sinensis* 'Giganteus'), Fountain Grass *(Pennisetum alopecuroides)*, Day-lilies *(Hemerocallis)*, and Siberian Iris *(Iris siberica)*, to dissipate its impact. Contrasting foliages should be equally bold; for example, Yucca *(Yucca smalliana)*, Angel's Trumpet *(Datura meteloides)*, Devil's Walking Stick *Aralia spinosa)*, Plume-poppy *(Macleaya cordata)*, Cutleaf Sumac (*Rhus typhina* 'Laciniata'), and *Helianthus salicifolia*. Large ground-cover masses of Fountain Grass *(Pennisetum alopecuroides)* and *Rudbeckia fulgida* var. *sullivantii* 'Goldsturm' are very effective companions.

Full sun and rich soil on the moist side are its preferences. It will, however, freeze out in winter if drainage is not adequate. (M. L. Hockenberry says that it needs winter protection and rarely flowers above Zone 6.) It spreads by rhizomes. Plants should be divided every two years if the lushest canes and largest flower heads are to be enjoyed.

This plant is a native of the Mediterranean region and has become well-established in the southern United States, particularly from Arkansas and Texas to southern California. It is a frequenter of stream banks and irrigation ditches and is used for mats and screens as well as in the construction of adobe huts. The tough rind of the culm is used to make reeds for musical instruments. The thicker bottom part of the canes make the best reeds for bassoons, clarinets, and saxophones, while the smaller top parts are considered first-rate for English horn, oboe d'amore, and oboe reeds. Its cultivation for this purpose is a tradition in southern France around Cagolin and Frejus. An oboe player for the Baltimore Symphony makes annual trips to that area to select his own canes because he considers American cane of poorer quality.

Arundo's blossom, cut at its peak and dried, is a significant addition to winter arrangements.

41 *Berberis wisleyensis* (frequently sold inaccurately as *B. triacanthophora*)

Threespine Barberry

Technically a *broadleaf* evergreen, Threespine Barberry is extremely valuable as a texture plant, reading, interestingly enough, of as *fine* a texture as most needle evergreens. The very narrow, linear leaves are 1 to 2 inches long and arranged in whorl-like groups 1 inch apart along the stems. Each whorl contains approximately five larger leaves and five smaller leaves as well as the prominent ⅝-inch-long three-part spine. The newer yellow-green foliage contrasts well with the older apple-green foliage; the new stems are bright green, the older stems brown. The flowers appear in May, are whitish, tinged with red, about ¼ inch in diameter, and while not a major attraction are certainly charming. In the fall and winter a delightful scattering of reds and yellows persists among the leaves. Although there is a dense, almost impenetrable body to the plant, the branch extensions are irregular and give it a definitely "soft" character.

Threespine Barberry is usually known as a 2½–3-foot plant and certainly can be kept in this often more usable size range by occasionally removing some old branches from near the base. It is frequently considered the most hardy of the evergreen barberries and is completely happy where we garden in Zone 7. *Berberis wisleyensis* is one of the ten species determined to be resistant to black-stem rust of wheat. It grows well in full sun or very light shade and like all barberries is undemanding as to soil quality.

The overall fine texture and chartreuse-like color provide a marvelous contrast to dark broad-leaved evergreens. A most satisfying combination might

STRUCTURAL INTEREST

Evergreen
Effective landscape height: 4 feet
Effective landscape spread: 4 feet
Zone 6
Berberidaceae (Barberry Family)
Native range: central China

contain three plants of the black-green *Ilex* x 'Nellie R. Stevens,' seven of *Berberis wisleyensis*, a ground cover of Baltic Ivy, and a clump of three *Bergenia cordifolia*, with its cabbage-like foliage, for a little spice.

All in all, Threespine Barberry is an excellent textural asset to the designer and a most undemanding and satisfactory performer. Ernest H. Wilson collected it on his third plant-collecting trip to China, sending it to the Arnold Arboretum in 1904. The Arboretum was responsible for its introduction into cultivation in 1907.

42

SEASONAL INTEREST

Deciduous
Effective landscape height: 8 feet
Effective landscape spread: 8 feet
Zone 6
Loganiaceae (Logania Family)
Native range: central and western China

Buddleia davidii 'Princeton Purple'
Purple-flowered Butterfly-Bush,
Summer-lilac

This "one-season" flowering shrub is a cheerful and valuable addition to the summer garden. Starting in early August the 12-inch rich purple blossom spikes nod gracefully on the end of succulent branches produced during the same season. Absolutely "as advertised," the flowers attract quantities of butterflies by day and in addition are a great source of interest to moths at night. A close look reveals bright orange throats in the individual florets making up the spike. In summers with a reasonable amount of moisture I have had continuous blossoming into October. The length of the blooming season is definitely extended by keeping the old flowers cut off.

There is one cultural practice that I feel is absolutely essential to satisfactory performance: the entire plant must be cut back to within 6 inches of ground level every spring before new growth starts.

This encourages fresh, lush stems well-clothed with leaves and gives an attractive form to the bush. Otherwise the shrub has a thickety character with foliage of varying size and blossoms of varying quality. Good soil is desirable; in fact, the better the soil the better the blossoms. Growth should not, however, be forced by heavy feeding. Butterfly-Bushes tend to seed themselves easily about the garden. In fact, they have become widely naturalized in parts of Europe, and often appeared in the rubble of bombed-out areas. This was particularly evident after World War I in Verdun, where it was called the "Flower of the Ruins." This same quality has made it a key subject for plant breeders, who have selected and named many color variants from seedling populations. 'Princeton Purple' was selected and named by William Flemer III at Princeton Nurseries in Princeton, New Jersey. There are 35 to 40 other clones now grown by American nurseries. Other particularly good ones are 'Black Knight,' 'Empire Blue,' 'Fortune,' 'Magnifica,' 'Royal Red,' and 'White Profusion'—all of which have received awards in England from the Royal Horticultural Society. I also like 'Charming,' 'DuBonnet,' and 'Fascination.'

I have always been intrigued by the addition of motion and activity to any garden scene, as with doves, peacocks, or ornamental fish in a pond. Certainly plants that attract butterflies are a great asset. In addition to *Buddleia davidii* clones, Glossy Abelia (*Abelia* x *grandiflora*), *Caryopteris* x *clandonensis* 'Blue Mist,' Butterfly Weed *(Asclepias tuberosa)*, Joe Pye Weed *(Eupatorium purpureum)*, Goldenrod *(Solidago* sp.), and Adam's Needle *(Yucca smalliana)* should be included where butterfly attraction is the objective.

I like to place *Buddleia*s with plenty of open space around them and, if possible, uphill of the viewer so that the blossoms and their attendant butterfly activity can be seen against the sky. The rich purple blossoms of *Buddleia davidii* 'Princeton Purple' show off well in either a setting of grays or yellow-greens. Gray ground-cover massings of *Artemesia stelleriana*, Mouse's Ear *(Cerastium tomentosum)*, and Lav-

Buddleia davidii 'Princeton Purple'

ender (*Lavandula angustifolia*, previously known as *L. vera*) can be given a little height variation by the taller *Artemesia albula*, the large woolly-leaved *Salvia argentea*, and the blue-flowered, silver-foliaged *Eryngium plenum*. If a background must be used, the fine texture of the narrow gray-leaved Willow, *Salix elaeagnos*, or the needled texture of Deodar Cedar *(Cedrus deodara)* would complete the picture. If you prefer a yellow-green color scheme, plant ground-cover massings of 'Buttercup' Ivy (*Hedera helix* 'Buttercup'), Hayscented Fern *(Dennstaedtia punctilobula)*, the dwarf striped Bamboo, *Arundinaria viridistriata*, and Variegated Lilyturf (*Liriope muscari* 'Variegata') using the yellow-green Juniper, *J. chinensis* 'Armstrong,' or the golden-foliaged False-cypress, *Chamaecyparis pisifera* 'Filifera Aurea Nana,' if background is required. These two combinations would provide continuing interest at least as long as the *Buddleia* blossom season. *Buddleia davidii* 'Princeton Purple' is also useful as a combination plant for the shorter flowering seasons of pink Crape-myrtle *(Lagerstroemia indica)*, Althaea 'Blue Bird' (*Hibiscus syriacus* 'Blue Bird'), *Hydrangea paniculata grandiflora*, and *Vitex agnus-castus* 'Latifolia'.

Buddleia davidii was found near Ichang in China about 1887 by Dr. Augustine Henry and named by the French botanist-collector Adrien Franchet for the French Jesuit missionary and plant collector Abbé Armand David, who had been the first to discover the plant some twenty years before. Alice Coats (1965) quoted Farrar as saying, "Its thickets on the banks of the Satani River in its native country are . . . 'famous harborage for leopards.'" Its first importation via St. Petersburg was a poor form. A better variety was raised by the French firm of Vilmorin et Cie from seed sent by another missionary-botanist, Père Jean André Soulie, in 1893. It remained, however, for Ernest H. Wilson to search the moist river banks of northwestern Hupeh province for the much more decorative variety *magnifica*, which he brought back to the British nursery, Messrs.

Veitch, in April, 1901. Most if not all of our modern selections are believed to have come from this re-introduction of the species.

43

Calycanthus floridus
Sweet Shrub, Carolina Allspice

SEASONAL INTEREST

Deciduous
Effective landscape height: 8 feet
Effective landscape spread: 10 feet
Zone 5
Calycanthaceae (Calycanthus Family)
Native range: United States—Virginia to Florida

A shrub of suckering, rather vertical branching habit—this plant would hardly receive a second glance but for the fascinating dark rusty-brown flowers, which at first impression appear to be some sort of seed pod. While the blossom itself is more of a cone-like curiosity, its fragrance is a thing of great beauty. This, to me, resembles a cross between bananas and strawberries, but as with all fragrances, is variously described by different sniffers. According to Alice Coats (1965), "Bowles described the flowers as having a strong scent of pineapple when newly opened and of grapefruit later, with an alcoholic fragrance like that of cider as they fade." The shiny green leaves are also aromatic when crushed, and turn a cheerful yellow in the fall.

There should be a plant of *Calycanthus* near the entrance to every house, as this fragrance is a very important part of the voluptuousness with which early May assaults our shrunken winter senses. One "shrub blossom" carried in a lady's pocketbook or worn in a man's lapel will cast its spell for several hours.

I feel we should allow ourselves to enjoy scented flowers more often as dooryard plants. *Chimonanthus praecox* (Wintersweet), *Viburnum fragrans* 'Nana' (Fragrant Viburnum), *Viburnum carlesii* (Spice Viburnum), *Poncirus trifoliata* (Hardy-orange), *Calycanthus floridus* (Sweet Shrub), *Rho-*

dodendron canescens, Magnolia virginiana (Swamp Magnolia), *Rhododendron arborescens*, and *Elaeagnus pungens* 'Fruitlandii' (Fragrant Elaeagnus) can provide fragrance sequentially from January through October. For landscape effect *Calycanthus* has little to offer other than a mound of clean green foliage which is a good background for more spectacular material.

Because a form with practically no fragrance has gotten into the nursery trade in the United States, it is advisable to try to obtain a sucker (divisions transplant readily) from an old plant known to have good fragrance. In our area practically every farmyard has one. It is interesting that in nearly 250 years of cultivation no superior garden forms have evolved.

Calycanthus grows easily in any ordinary garden soil. The quantity of blossoms is probably greater and the habit of the plant a little more civilized if one-third of the old canes are cut to the ground each year after flowering.

Writing about the plant in 1768, Phillip Miller of Chelsea, England, noted: "This shrub grows naturally in America. Mr. [Mark] Catesby, who first introduced it into English gardens [in 1726], procured it from the continent, some hundred miles on the back of Charles Town, in Carolina." Peter Collinson, who was one of the foremost plantsmen among English merchants to introduce American plants, made a fresh importation in 1757.

44

SEASONAL INTEREST

Deciduous
Effective landscape height: 18 feet
Effective landscape spread: 20 feet
Zone 2
Leguminosae (Pea Family)
Garden origin

Caragana arborescens forma *Lorbergii*
Lorberg's Siberian Pea-Tree

This fine-foliaged form of a very tough Asiatic shrub is of great landscape value for the airy quality of its foliage. In addition, for a brief period in mid-May, it is covered with yellow blossoms. The plant has an upright branching structure. Its rounded crown is composed of small branches which curl at the tip, very irregularly, some sideways, some downward, and some upward, giving a frothy fountain-like effect. The stems are a dark yellowish-green with darker horizontal markings. The yellow-green needly foliage is actually compound leaves whose very narrow opposite leaflets resemble the ultimate divisions of a fennel leaf. The leaves are clustered on fat, spine-like stalks, ½–1½ inches long. The butter-yellow pea-like blossoms are produced singly on their stalks, each flower being ⅝–⅞ inch long.

Caragana arborescens forma *Lorbergii* is of great value for its textural interest being a "lightener" for broadleaf plantings. It works equally well with the dark green of the shelter-loving broadleaf combination of 'Otto Luykens' Cherry-laurel (*Prunus laurocerasus* 'Otto Luykens'), Roundleaf Osmanthus *(Osmanthus rotundifolius)* and *Hedera helix* 'Conglomerata Erecta,' as it does with the tough, wind-resistant combination of Inkberry Holly (*Ilex glabra* 'Densa') Adam's Needle *(Yucca smalliana)*, and Prickly-pear *(Opuntia compressa)*. For blossom effect it is handsome for a very few days in combination with the white-flowered Doublefile Viburnum *(Viburnum plicatum forma tomentosum)*. The flat heads and broad flower petals of the Viburnum are a striking background or foil for the delicately shaped, intense yellow blossoms of the *Caragana*. The two foliages offer a handsome contrast: the Viburnum very bold and broad; the *Caragana* very fern-like. It is not always easy to arrange, but a ground carpeting of the deep lavender Johnny-Jump-up *(Viola tricolor)* is spectacular with the *Caragana* blossoms, both colors being of an equal intensity.

Caragana is very hardy. The wild form of the species is used for shelter belts and windbreaks in Canada. By training to a single leader it may be encouraged to take the form of a small tree. *Caragana arborescens*, a native of Siberia and Manchuria, was introduced into the Imperial Botanic Garden, St. Petersburg (now Leningrad), by Johann Ammann

Caragana arborescens

(1707–1741), or one of his collectors, early in the 1730's. It was known to Carolus Linnaeus in Sweden by 1750, and in 1752 was grown in Germany. Soon it was grown in much of western Europe, and came to America early in the 1800's. The clone described here was selected by a German nurseryman named Lorberg, and introduced there about 1905. Emil Koehne named and described it late in 1906. It was growing in America by 1912.

45

Caryopteris × *clandonensis* 'Blue Mist'
Blue Spirea

SEASONAL INTEREST

Deciduous
Effective landscape height: 3 feet
Effective landscape spread: 3 feet
Zone 6
Verbenaceae (Vervain Family)
Hybrid origin

A small, gray-foliaged ball of a plant, with leaves narrow and lance-like with cut edges, this plant is constructed of twigs sprouting vertically from the central base and leaning out fan-like on the sides. Its outstanding feature is its beautiful true blue blossoms, appearing in clusters among the stems in mid-August—a time when few other shrubs are in bloom. Some writers have commented on its sweet aromatic fragrance (which has not struck me as what one might call prominent). Because the flowers are not large and appear among the gray foliage, they must be seen close up to be appreciated.

It is a valuable plant for a small-scale situation, often being used with herbaceous plants. Three or four plants of *Caryopteris* featured in a mass planting of the evergreen, white-flowered ground cover, *Liriope muscari* 'Monroi #1,' is a favorite combination of mine. The strong character of the white, spike-like flowers against the strap-shaped evergreen foliage is an excellent contrast for the pale blue and gray froth of the *Caryopteris*.

Caryopteris performs best for me if it is cut back to within 3–4 inches of the ground every spring after danger of hard frost. The fresh new shoots are much more graceful than would be obtained otherwise. This plant likes a sunny location and rich, well-drained soil. It will occasionally kill out in severe winters; it is my observation that this is a problem primarily when the soil is very clayey.

The history of this hybrid is illustrative of the thin thread of chance by which we have received many of our garden plants. *Caryopteris incana (Mastacanthus)* was sent to England by Robert Fortune from the environs of Canton in 1844, but it was lost within a few years and not re-introduced until Charles Maries obtained it for the British nursery firm of Messrs. Veitch in 1880. The other parent *Caryopteris mongholica* was introduced from Mongolia in 1831, given its name by von Bunge in 1834; then the stock at St. Petersburg was lost, and re-introduced by Abbé Armand David in 1866. Attractive self-sown seedlings presumed to be crosses between these two were discovered under a bush of *Caryopteris mongholica* in the garden of Arthur Simmonds (later secretary of the Royal Horticultural Society) near Guildford, England, in 1930. The seedlings of this parentage were outstanding but variable. It is not clear whether 'Blue Mist' was from the original chance cross or from subsequent breeding activity, but it is a seedling selected and named by John Gruellemanns, formerly of Wayside Gardens in Mentor, Ohio.

Caryopteris x *clandonensis* 'Blue Mist'

46

Chamaecyparis obtusa 'Nana Gracilis'
Dwarf Hinoki Cypress

This dense, conical, slow-growing conifer is of great value for its textural effect. It is certainly unusual because of the arrangement and coloration of its

STRUCTURAL INTEREST

Evergreen
Effective landscape height: 7 feet
Effective landscape spread: 4-5 feet
Zones 3-4
Cupressaceae (Cypress Family)
Garden origin

Chamaecyparis obtusa 'Nana Gracilis'

short, scale-like leaves. These are grouped in flat fans which are basically horizontal in orientation; their outer edges curl upward, however, and resemble a funnel or a spiral. The new growth originates from the center of these and is more open and twisted. The older growth is blacker green; the newer growth lighter; the color holds well during the burn of winter. The total effect is not only cheerful and fascinating, but when well-placed this crinkly alien literally stops the viewer dead in his tracks.

Any gardener fond of textural interest would love to use this plant because there are literally an infinite number of combinations in which it might be placed. Generally speaking, it ends up being *the* feature, whether singly or in a group, in any combination in which it is used. One possibility might be a single Dwarf Hinoki Cypress with background drifts of 'Crimson Pygmy' Barberry (*Berberis thunbergii* 'Crimson Pygmy') and *Genista sylvestris* 'Lydia'; foreground planting of the broad, oval, red-foliaged *Ajuga reptans* 'Metallica Crispa.' The broad leaves of the Barberry and *Ajuga* would contrast with the finer foliage of the *Genista* and *Chamaecyparis*. All these companion plants would provide horizontal-line contrasts for the verticality of the Hinoki. Seasonal interest would come from the butter-yellow flowers of the *Genista* in June and the blue flowers of the *Ajuga* in May. Another grouping could be a single Dwarf Hinoki Cypress with three plants of the shiny, broad-leaved pincushion-like Dwarf Chinese Holly (*Ilex cornuta* 'Rotunda'), surrounded by a ground-cover planting of the chartreuse-foliaged Thyme, *Thymus serpyllum citridorus,* all backed by a planting of five yellow-foliaged Barberries, *Berberis thunbergii* 'Aurea.' The Hinoki's dark green would be dramatized by the lighter green of the Holly, the yellow-green of the Barberry and Thyme, and the broadleaf texture of the Barberries and Holly, an extraordinary combination.

Three Dwarf Hinoki Cypress could be featured against a background planting of four gray-foliaged Fragrant Elaeagnus (*Elaeagnus pungens* 'Fruitlandii'), backed by three Japanese Black Pine *(Pinus thunbergii)*; the foreground planted with the woolly gray foliage of Lamb's Ear *(Stachys olympica)*, accented by a single clump of the blue-gray, succulent foliage of *Euphorbia Myrsinites*. In this case the Japanese Black Pines echo the color and texture of the Hinoki, but in a very different way. The other companion plants all provide gray broadleaf contrast for the Hinoki.

Chamaecyparis obtusa is a valuable timber tree in Japan, growing to 120 feet. The species has produced many interesting variants, most of them dwarf or at least slower-growing than *Chamaecyparis obtusa*. *Hillier's Manual of Trees and Shrubs* (1972) lists thirty-nine; H. J. Welch in *Dwarf Conifers* (1966) lists thirty-one; P. den Ouden and Dr. B. K. Boom in *Manual of Cultivated Conifers* (1965) list fifty-six.

Several different variants are sold as Dwarf Hinoki Cypress. The plant described here is given the name *Chamaecyparis obtusa* 'Nana Gracilis' by den Ouden and Boom and is in my opinion a superior garden plant to the even slower-growing *Chamaecyparis obtusa* 'Nana,' which is a poorer green in color and too slow-growing for the practical uses described here. *Chamaecyparis obtusa* 'Nana Gracilis' performs in a more compact manner when grafted, a more open manner when grown from cuttings. A very hardy plant, it performs best in moist soil free of lime.

This handsome plant is an interesting example of a garden form of a species being as valuable ornamentally as the type is valuable for timber.

47

Chimonanthus praecox
Wintersweet

SEASONAL INTEREST

Deciduous
Effective landscape height: 8 feet
Effective landscape spread: 8 feet
Zone 7
Calycanthaceae (Calycanthus Family)
Native range: China

Gardeners would never look twice at this sparse, rangy, leggy shrub if it were not for the fact that it produces delightfully scented blossoms in the middle of winter. In Delaware it is frequently in bloom by Christmas time although it may be as late starting as mid-February, depending on the season and the hardiness zone where grown. The stems are dotted with fat, round buds which open to charming, 1-inch, waxy-yellow, red-throated blossoms whenever the weather is sufficiently moderate. I have gotten up on a January morning to find open flowers, buds, and twigs all completely encased in glimmering ice. This performance may be repeated several times during the same blooming season with no real detriment to the effectiveness of the bloom. On bright warm days more buds open; on cold dull days the picture holds its status quo. The fragrance is so special that admirers have written superlative descriptions since it was first known. The famous British horticulturist E. A. Bowles was moved to say that *Chimonanthus* should be grown in any garden large enough to hold two plants—the other being *Iris unguicularis*.

Special effort is certainly required to give it a worthy setting. Because it is of borderline hardiness north of Philadelphia, a protected, sunny spot is required, sheltered from the north and west winds. I like to put it near a window where the blossoms can be seen in comfort and the viewer tempted outside for a winter sniff. The long pageant of unfolding blossoms is made even more entrancing by the fact that juncos and other small winter birds sometimes pause to partake of the flower nectar. The delicate tracery of the rangy twigs is beautiful, and I have often wished that I might feature this plant and its yellow blossom against a light blue wall. The British frequently do treat it as an espalier. In a mixed planting its form would contrast well with the stockiness of Chinese Holly *(Ilex cornuta)* and its legginess be minimized by a ground-cover planting of the graceful English Weeping Yew (*Taxus baccata* 'Repandens').

Chimonanthus should be provided with fertile, well-drained soil. Annual pruning is required to remove both dead twigs and an occasional heavy stem, encouraging renewal growth from the base. Any pruning should be done early in the spring to allow the longest possible period of time for the production of the new shoots on which the next year's flowers will occur. If espaliered, this shrub will often go higher than 8 feet and requires annual pruning and tying up of its new shoots. There are other garden forms with larger flowers and without the deep center; however, none is so strongly scented as this type.

In a sense, it is the Chinese counterpart of our native Carolina Allspice *(Calycanthus floridus)*, in which family it is placed botanically. "It has long been the custom," Alice Coats (1965) states, "for Chinese ladies to use the scented flowers to decorate their hair. The wood, too, is aromatic and housewives both in China and Japan are said to tie the twigs and prunings into bundles to scent their linen cupboards and clothes closets." It has been domesticated since early in the Sung Dynasty (A.D. 960–1279) and was first described botanically by Englebert Kaempfer as early as 1712, and by Carolus Linnaeus in 1762.

It was introduced into England in 1766, when a specimen was sent to Lord Coventry at Croome in Worcestershire. There it was planted in a conservatory and by 1779 had grown into a shrub, 15 feet high and 10 feet wide, whose fragrance when in bloom could be smelled 50 yards away from the building (see *Curtis Bot. Mag.*, Vol. 13, plate 466, 1799). In 1928 the Royal Horticultural Society Award of Merit was given to this plant.

Wintersweet is *not* a hardy, well-formed, maintenance-free plant. It is, however, a delightful treasure for the gardener who is willing to take his rewards in charming subtleties.

48

SEASONAL INTEREST

Deciduous
Effective landscape height: 7 feet
Effective landscape spread: indefinite
Zone 2
Cornaceae (Dogwood Family)
Native range: North America — Newfoundland to Kentucky

Cornus sericea (Cornus stolonifera)
Redtwig Dogwood, Redstem Dogwood, Red Osier

This hardy native shrub is an extremely valuable landscape plant because of its winter interest. It is thickety in nature, spreading by underground stems. The branches are thin and rise straight from the ground at angles not far from the vertical. The bark, particularly on the young twigs, is a wonderful shiny, light-reflective red.

Red Osier's summer character is moundy, with leaves that are darker green on top and whitish underneath. The flowers are small and white, in loose clusters 2½ –3½ inches in diameter, and are followed by white fruit. There is a burst of bloom in late May and intermittent blossoming throughout the summer. Although the flowers are interesting and the fruit is attractive to birds, certainly the overriding reason for growing the plant should be the winter interest of its bark. There is, also, a form with bright yellow bark, *Cornus sericea* 'Flaviramea,' which is every bit as attractive and useful (both red and yellow forms are shown in the photograph).

Redtwig Dogwood occurs naturally throughout northeastern North America in sunny, damp places. Because of its stoloniferous habit, it is excellent for holding banks. Excessive moisture is not, however, essential to its happy performance as a garden plant — sun is. Good rich topsoil is important. It is recommended that once the plants are established, old wood be cut back to the ground every spring in order to encourage the growth of copious young shoots. These have the brightest colored bark. Old branches are occasionally subject to scale, another reason for eliminating them. The scale is manageable with dormant oil sprays.

For a rather naturalistic effect, there is no finer winter scene than a mixed thicket of the Redtwig and Yellowtwig Dogwoods backed with a planting of the very horizontally branching Corkbark Euonymous *(Euonymous alatus)*, accented with one or more of the very vertical, native Red-cedars *(Juniperus virginiana)*. In a more refined situation the moundy, bronzy-foliaged Willowleaf Cotoneaster *(Cotoneaster salicifolia* 'Flocossa') might be used as background for a grouping of spiky Redtwig Dogwoods. Three plants of the needly, very horizontal Bird's Nest Spruce *(Picea abies* 'Nidiformis') in the foreground would add a trim note. By contrast of form these would emphasize the verticality of the Dogwood. It might be advisable to use one Yellowtwig Dogwood among the reds to highlight the entire scene.

Acer palmatum 'Senkaki' is an intriguing red-twigged form of Japanese Maple. The irregular to horizontal form of this plant makes it an interesting companion for Yellowtwig Dogwood. Such an association might feature a single Maple amongst a group of the mounded Dwarf Chinese Hollies *(Ilex cornuta* 'Rotunda'), backed with four or five Yellowtwig Dogwoods and three needly, horizontally branching, dark green Japanese Yews *(Taxus cuspidata)*.

The American Indians used the bark of *Cornus sericea* to make the Kinnikinnik which they smoked. The plant is of even greater importance today as an ornamental addition to the winter landscapes.

Cornus sericea

49

Corylopsis glabrescens

Fragrant Winterhazel

SEASONAL INTEREST

Deciduous
Effective landscape height: 18 feet
Effective landscape spread: 12 feet
Zone 6
Hamamelidaceae (Witch-hazel Family)
Native range: Japan

Pendulous, fragrant, delicate, cool yellow flowers appearing in March just before Forsythia are the great charm of this large shrub. The blossoms when they first open are brushed with chartreuse, a subtlety of great charm at that season. Everything about the plant is delicate: fine twigs, wiry branching habit, intriguing detail to the flowers, and delicate, pale green, paper-thin leaves with a saw-tooth edge. For this reason it is best used *en masse* and careful attention given to its associates. I like it with dark green and white. Take a black-green background such as several Canadian Hemlocks *(Tsuga canadensis)*, plant three of the white-flowered *Magnolia denudata*, surround with six to eight *Corylopsis*, underplant with English Weeping Yew (*Taxus baccata* 'Repandens') and quantities of the white forms of the bulbous *Chionodoxa*, and you will have a fine early-spring picture.

That master gardener H. F. du Pont, creator of the gardens at his Winterthur estate near Wilmington, Delaware, studied *Corylopsis* for many years and discovered the stimulating effect of combining its cool yellow with the warm lavender of *Rhododendron mucronulatum*. He added *Prinsepia uniflora* for its "spring green" foliage and carpeted the ground with *Primula abschasica* (whose flowers are an amazing match for *Rhododendron mucronulatum*), *Helleborus* in wine-colored variety, and *Corydalis densiflora* with its delicate lavender blossoms, making an unforgettable picture!

There are a number of good kinds of *Corylopsis* with flowers longer than the 1–1½-inch blossoms of *Corylopsis glabrescens*, but this one is most reliable for bud hardiness in northern parts of the United States. *Corylopsis platypetala* has done consistently well at Winterthur and is the favorite there. *Corylopsis spicata* is good there most years. Because of the time of flowering, the blossoms of all kinds are potential victims of frost damage. They prefer sun or light shade and moist, well-drained loam.

Corylopsis glabrescens was introduced into Europe from Japan in 1905, but did not get into the American trade until after World War I. It became popular in England in the early 1920's and has been the recipient of three awards from the Royal Horticultural Society: Award of Merit 1960, First Class Certificate 1968, Award of Garden Merit 1969.

50

Cytisus × praecox 'Luteus'
Dwarf Warminster Broom

The vertical rich green stems of this shrub have a dramatic spike-like quality which can add great richness to many garden scenes. Because the gray-green foliage is sparse and small, the summer effect is every bit as good as the winter character. In addition, a beautiful, soft, sulphur-yellow blossom effect occurs in May, when the stems are covered with bicolor, yellow and white pea-like flowers. It is best to plant these shrubs at some distance from living areas because the fragrance of the blossoms is musty and should be avoided.

To dramatize Warminster Broom's charming verticality, some horizontal growing companions offer an advantage. A rich scene might include six to eight Warminster Brooms surrounded by a ground-cover sea of Wilton's Creeping Juniper (*Juniperus horizontalis* 'Wiltonii') or pink, summer-blooming Heather, *Erica vagans* 'Mrs. Maxwell,' all planted

STRUCTURAL INTEREST

Deciduous
Effective landscape height: 6 feet
Effective landscape spread: 6 feet
Zone 6
Leguminosae (Pea Family)
Hybrid origin

Cytisus x *praecox* 'Luteus'

against a background grouping of Corkbark Euonymous *(Euonymous alatus)* or Black Haw Viburnum *(Viburnum prunifolium)*.

Its flower color and flowering date make it an attractive blooming companion for the chartreuse-white-flowered *Viburnum macrocephalum forma macrocephalum*, the warm pink and apricot shades of Mollis Azaleas *(Rhododendron* x 'Kosterianum'), and the lavender shades of some German Iris clones.

The precursors of this plant hail from southern Europe and North Africa. Like its ancestors, Warminster Broom thrives in abundant sunshine and good but not rich, well-drained soil. It is a vigorous grower whose chief disadvantage is that it should be dug out and replaced every six to seven years. After that time, it often becomes leggy and winter-damaged. Since its vigorous verticality is the reason for its use, it is best to plan on setting in fresh, young plants whenever decline sets in.

Cytisus x *praecox* 'Luteus' was an insect-pollinated, chance hybrid seedling of *Cytisus purgans* x *Cytisus multiflorus* which occurred in the Wheeler Nurseries in Warminster, England, about 1867. The Royal Horticultural Society bestowed an Award of Garden Merit upon Warminster Broom in 1933.

51

STRUCTURAL INTEREST

Evergreen
Effective landscape height: 8 feet
Effective landscape spread: 16 feet
Zone 7
Elaeagnaceae (Oleaster Family)
Garden origin

Elaeagnus pungens 'Fruitlandii'
Fragrant Elaeagnus

While the shiny, broad, olive-green leaves of this sprawling evergreen make it an excellent background for other plantings, the gardenia-like fragrance of its inconspicuous blossoms subtly permeates the garden every October. Either one of these qualities make it well worth growing. New shoots and fresh spring foliage coat the mound-like shape of Fragrant Elaeagnus annually with a silvery sheen. Upon closer inspection, as when the plant is used as an espalier, the underside of the leaves holds its silver character year round, contrasting attractively with the rusty brown color of the younger branches and the silvery white, pendulous, bell-shaped blossoms. Except when featured close up, it has a valuable neutral quality which contrasts well with dark green conifers such as Japanese Black Pine *(Pinus thunbergii)*, Incense-cedar *(Calocedrus decurrens)*, and Hinoki Cypress (*Chamaecyparis obtusa* 'Nana Compacta').

This member of the olive family will thrive in full sun in well-drained, moderate-quality soil, and it will also tolerate partial shade. In late winter some years and in windier locations every year, the newer growth may turn the color of a paper bag. This disappears, of course, when the new growth appears.

This form of Thorny Elaeagnus *(Elaeagnus pungens)* was introduced by Fruitland Nurseries of Augusta, Georgia, about 1926. There are other forms, the most noteworthy of which, *Elaeagnus pungens* 'Maculata,' has darker green leaves the centers of which are attractively variegated with splotches of gold and chartreuse. Fragrant Elaeagnus is a fine garden plant for winter interest if planted in a protected location.

Elaeagnus pungens 'Fruitlandii'

52

Forsythia × intermedia 'Spectabilis'

Forsythia, Goldenbells,
Showy Border Forsythia

Golden-yellow, bell-shaped flowers thickly coat the stems of this sun-loving shrub in a manner so lush and brassy as to be positively sensuous. The 2-inch flowers, appearing as they do in early April, are the

SEASONAL INTEREST

Deciduous
Effective landscape height: 10 feet
Effective landscape spread: 10 feet
Zone 6
Oleaceae (Olive Family)
Hybrid origin

first truly spectacular spring flowers and have very few blooming companions. For this reason Forsythia should be planted in bold positive masses of at least 6–8 plants—not pristinely and distractingly about the landscape. Forsythia can stand on its own among the bright green of spring grass or be surrounded with large drifts of trumpet *Narcissus*, such as 'Beersheba' or 'King Alfred.' An even more dramatic effect can be achieved by featuring Forsythia with White Birch clumps against a dark needly background such as Canadian Hemlock *(Tsuga canadensis)* or Oriental Spruce *(Picea orientalis)*.

Forsythia x *intermedia* 'Spectabilis'

The form of this plant when properly pruned is gracefully fan-shaped, reaching 10 feet in height. Each year after blooming the heaviest canes should be cut back to 6 inches above ground level, thus encouraging long graceful new shoots to develop. Forsythia is unfortunately too often sheared into a round ball, totally destroying its natural attractive character. Gardeners preferring less bold color should try a variety called 'Spring Glory'; in addition to having lighter colored flowers it has the distinct advantage that the blossoms are less of an ugly butter-yellow at the end of the flowering period than *Forsythia* 'Spectabilis.'

Forsythia is probably the most popular flowering shrub in the United States. It is easily established, ships well as a bare root shrub, will tolerate sitting around in a grocery store package for weeks before being planted, and is not demanding as to site or soil. This is an excellent example of an alien shrub that has greatly enriched our lives.

The parents of this hybrid are both from China, have flowers of inferior quality, and are very distinct from one another in habit: *Forsythia suspensa* is very graceful and pendulous in habit and *Forsythia viridissima*, on the other hand, is upright. *Forsythia* x *intermedia* 'Spectabilis' was introduced by the Berlin nurseryman F. Ludwig Spaeth in 1906.

The shrub has dubiously immortalized the name of William Forsyth, gardener to King George III of England. Forsyth, A. W. Anderson (1966) explains, came from a small village in the north of Scotland, rising to become curator of the Chelsea Physic Garden in 1771 and director of His Majesty's Gardens at Kensington Palace in 1784. He is primarily remembered, however, for having bluffed Parliament into awarding him £1,500 in recognition of his claim to having originated "Forsyth's Plaister"—a mixture of cow dung, old plaster, wood ashes, river sand, urine, and soap suds, which he claimed was capable of healing wounds and reconditioning dead trees.

This hybrid has received three awards from the Royal Horticultural Society: the Award of Merit 1915, the Award of Garden Merit 1923, and a First Class Certificate 1935.

53

Hamamelis × *intermedia* 'Jelena'
Orange-flowered Chinese Witch-hazel

SEASONAL INTEREST

Deciduous
Effective landscape height: 8 feet
Effective landscape spread: 10 feet
Zone 6
Hamamelidaceae (Witch-hazel Family)
Hybrid origin

This hybrid Witch-hazel with rusty, orange-yellow flowers is one of the finest members of a tribe renowned for its excellent winter-flowering characteristics. Some years, depending on the weather, the spidery blossoms appear as early as January. Because they uncurl on warm days and curl up and rest in cooler weather, the blooming period is often extended over three or four weeks. Seen close up the blossoms are composed of four narrow ($\frac{1}{16}$-inch) petals, $\frac{5}{8}$ inch or more long. These are tightly spaced along the angular branches, emphasizing their attractive form. Large, rather heart-shaped leaves clothe this open, vase-shaped or spreading shrub in the summer months and turn an attractive yellow in the fall.

Because of the highly attractive, spidery texture of the flowers, I feel they show to best advantage when planted against a background of broadleaf

Hamamelis x *intermedia* 'Jelena'

evergreens. An attractive winter scene might feature this plant with a mass of the dark green Cherry-laurel (*Prunus laurocerasus* 'Otto Luykens') and *Osmanthus rotundifolius.* Background structure could be provided by three plants of the bright green Incense-cedar *(Calocedrus decurrens)* or the blacker green Red-cedar *(Juniperus virginiana).* I might also carpet the foreground with masses of the bulbous Winter Aconite *(Eranthis hyemalis),* whose cheerful, ground-hugging, yellow blossoms would occur with the Witch-hazel most years. Overplanting the bulbs with the creeping Periwinkle (*Vinca minor* 'Bowles') would probably be a tidy and attractive maintenance aid, since *Eranthis* has little to offer the balance of the year.

If you have the space, a large grouping of Witch-hazels spanning the entire color range is a great treat. I like *Hamamelis mollis* 'Pallida' (soft yellow and very fragrant), *Hamamelis mollis* (butter-yellow), and *Hamamelis* x *intermedia* 'Diane' (wine-red), all of which bloom at the same time as *Hamamelis* x *intermedia* 'Jelena.'

These plants are perfectly hardy in my garden. They grow easily in any good loam, preferring sun or just a little light shade. Reputedly, all Witch-hazels are tolerant of smoke, dust, and dry air, thus making them desirable to try under city conditions. Some years there is the annoying problem that the foliage, instead of falling off, turns brown and hangs on the bush, interfering with a complete showing of the blossoms. This seems to be related to an early fall frost coming after a warm spell—without a gradual hardening off. An annual maintenance chore with named varieties of Witch-hazel is removal of the quantities of suckers which come up from the roots. This problem is a consequence of the generally accepted practice of using the American *Hamamelis virginiana* (with its vigorous root system) for the understock of these grafted Witch-hazels. Failure to remove these shoots can result in the less desirable *H. virginiana* taking over and crowding out the superior variety. If suckers are removed with careful persistence for a few years, the tendency to put forth shoots will eventually cease.

This particular hybrid originated in Belgium at what is now known as Kalmthout Arboretum. This property had previously been a nursery operated by a plant-lover named Kort. When the deBelder family converted the nursery to an arboretum, there were already a number of Witch-hazels growing there. Among these were a number of seedlings with an outstanding range of flower color. These had come up under a bush of *Hamamelis japonica* 'Flavopurpurascens.' Robert deBelder selected *H.* x *intermedia* 'Jelena' from these, the name chosen being that of his wife. *Hamamelis mollis* was suspected as the other parent in this match, and this fact was essentially confirmed by subsequently making the same cross, which produced seedlings with the same color and character range as the seedlings in question. *Hamamelis japonica* and its varieties are not, in my opinion, outstanding garden plants, and seedlings of straight *H. mollis* are quite variable. Hence, this is a good example of the possibility of enriching our gardens by crossing varieties which themselves may not have much to offer. Most of the good hybrids we have are *Hamamelis* x *intermedia*—that is, crosses between *Hamamelis mollis* and *Hamamelis japonica* (which flowers later). Further hybridization including the even earlier flowering American *Hamamelis vernalis* would seem to offer promise for the future.

The history of *Hamamelis mollis* offers another good example of how a plant was almost lost and shows the importance of careful plant observation by both amateurs and professionals. Charles Maries discovered *Hamamelis mollis* in the Kiukiang district of China while collecting for the British nursery firm of Messrs. Veitch in 1879. The plant was ignored in their Coombe Wood Nursery for over twenty years. In 1900 or 1901, George Nicholson, keeper of the Royal Gardens at Kew, spotted it on a tour of inspection and called attention to the fact that it was a valuable species. It was promptly propagated, marketed the following year, and received the Royal Horticultural Society's First Class Certificate in 1918 and Award of Garden Merit in 1922.

Hamamelis x *intermedia* 'Jelena' received the Royal Horticultural Society's Award of Merit in 1955.

54

Hydrangea quercifolia
Oakleaf Hydrangea

SEASONAL INTEREST

Deciduous
Effective landscape height: 6 feet
Effective landscape spread: 6 feet
Zone 6
Saxifragaceae (Saxifrage Family)
Native range: United States—Georgia, Tennessee, Florida, and west

This aristocrat of the shrubs—a native American—has four outstanding seasons of interest. Yet it is little used because inexperienced gardeners have associated the name "Hydrangea" with the ubiquitous blue and pink florists' hydrangeas.

The 11-inch-long, cone-shaped blossom heads appear in mid-June. These are composed of two kinds of white blossoms arranged as if by a master jeweler's hand. The outer flowers are fewer, larger (1½ inches), and sterile. The inner flowers are more numerous, only ⅛ inch across, densely crowded, and fertile. The large heads terminate the branches, their weight causing a mildly pendulous effect. The leaves are large (9 inches x 9 inches), five-lobed, medium green on top and white on the underside. The handsome blossoms as seen against this dramatic foliage make an elegant picture.

During July these flower heads mature to marvelous shades of green and chartreuse. Against the attractive foliage these make a subtle and intriguing picture.

In the fall the larger outer flowers turn a whitish-tan, the inner fertile flowers a rich rust color. At the same time the foliage takes on pink and maroon shades while the leaf veins remain green. This charming picture is dramatically accented by new stem growth, which is a beautiful pubescent pinkish-white.

Winter is not without interest either, as the branching habit is attractively "irregular" if not "erratic." These qualities are only enhanced by the rust and tan shadings of the curly, exfoliating bark.

This stoloniferous shrub is happiest in moist, fairly rich soil. Contrary to what you might expect, *Hydrangea quercifolia* does not perform well in heavy shade. It prefers a sheltered but not too dark position. Full sun is perfectly acceptable, especially if the plants are kept mulched.

A planting that is attractive all year can be made with two of Oakleaf Hydrangea's June blooming companions: Korean Stewartia *(Stewartia koreana)* and Adam's Needle *(Yucca smalliana)*. The *Stewartia*, a small tree, bears white, *Camellia*-like blossoms and the Yucca produces 8-foot spikes of white, bell-like florets. The bark of the Stewartia exfoliates like a Sycamore and is of a color very close to the Hydrangea bark during the winter months. The Yucca has, of course, a foliage equally as strong as the Hydrangea and of contrasting shape. With a planting of, say, three Stewartias, six Hydrangeas, and an accent group of seven Yuccas, I would add a ground cover tie-in of *Liriope muscari* 'Big Blue,' with its blue blossoms (August) and narrow, strap-shaped, evergreen leaves.

William Bartram discovered Oakleaf Hydrangea during his travels in Carolina, Georgia, and Florida in 1773–1778; he commented on the fact that the flower heads were "truly permanent, remaining on the plant for years, 'til they dry or decay." Professor Joseph C. McDaniels of the University of Illinois has noted extreme variation in the quality of flowers in the wild and has selected and named garden varieties which he feels are superior. These include 'Harmony' and 'Roanoke.' Judging entirely from photographs, they do not appear to me to be superior to the fine conical-shaped blossoms of the form currently "in the trade" in the mid-Atlantic states; a clone being asexually reproduced.

In England the species received an Award of Merit from the Royal Horticultural Society in 1928.

55

STRUCTURAL INTEREST

Evergreen
Effective landscape height: 10 feet
Effective landscape spread: 10 feet
Zones 6–7
Aquifoliaceae (Holly Family)
Native range: eastern China, Korea

Ilex cornuta
Chinese Holly

Glossy, exaggeratedly "horned," yellow-green leaves set this Holly apart as uniquely attractive and distinct from any other Holly variety. One and a half to 5 inches long and narrower in width, the typical leaf has five spines. Three are grouped at the tip—the other two at the rear with the leaf stem. All leaves are generally downward-curving, causing the upper surface of the leaf to have a quadrangular shape, which is very dramatic in its light-reflective qualities. Exercising a little imagination, one can see, as W. J. Bean suggests, that the shape resembles a flying bat. The berries are fat (⅜–½ inch in diameter) and shiny red and are clustered in groups of five to eight along the stem. The plant is more of a shrub than a tree, sometimes pyramidal in form, sometimes nearly boxy.

Because of its denseness and positive reaction to hard pruning, it makes an excellent hedge or espalier. Because of its form, it does not make a particularly striking "specimen." It works exceedingly well, however, as part of a shrub or screening planting. The black-green of Oriental Spruce *(Picea orientalis)* or Japanese Black Pine *(Pinus thunbergii)* is just right to show it off to good advantage. The green stems of *Kerria japonica*, Warminster Broom (*Cytisus* x *praecox* 'Luteus'), or Hardy-orange *(Poncirus trifoliata)* make a charming subtlety with Chinese Holly during the winter months. For ground-cover or foreground plants in such situations I would use needly black-greens again, such as English Weeping Yew (*Taxus baccata* 'Repandens') or *Pachistima canbyi.*

My favorite use of Chinese Holly is in a situation

where the high design quality of the leaves and berries can be easily seen close up. This might be as an espalier near the entrance to a house or as part of a shrub grouping near a path or doorway. Whereas the above groupings emphasize textural contrasts involving needle evergreens, I have used it in a dooryard situation happily associated with the broadleaf companions Threespine Barberry *(Berberis triacanthophora)*, with its narrow, lighter green leaves, and the Shrub Ivy, *Hedera helix* 'Conglomerata Erecta,' with its striking, dark green, arrowhead-shaped foliage.

It is difficult to pinpoint the northern limit of hardiness of this plant; certainly it thrives on much of Long Island and north to Boston and Cape Cod. It is hardier much farther north if given shelter from the wind than where such protection does not exist. It will withstand much lower winter temperatures once the roots are well-established than as a young plant newly established.

Ilex cornuta

I consider *Ilex cornuta* a "fussy transplanter" in our area, and therefore recommend starting with a container-grown plant. Because a long season is needed for the fruit to color, I prefer to use it in a hot, sunny location. *Ilex cornuta* will set fruit without a male pollinator present but the quantity is not usually great and the lasting quality poorer than when a pollinator is present. There is an attractive dwarf form, *Ilex cornuta* 'Rotunda,' which much resembles a large, dense pincushion.

Chinese Holly was sent from eastern China to the firm of Standish and Noble in England by Robert Fortune in 1846 and was first named and described (with a color plate) by John Lindley in 1850. The Chinese had for centuries made medicine from the foliage gathered in spring and winter. The potion was prescribed for fever with cough, pain in the back and knees, dizziness, and ringing in the ears!

56

STRUCTURAL INTEREST

Evergreen
Effective landscape height: 8 feet
Effective landscape spread: 8 feet
Zone 6
Aquifoliaceae (Holly Family)
Native range: Japan

Ilex crenata 'Microphylla'
Littleleaf Japanese Holly

Ilex crenata 'Microphylla' is a real workhorse for any garden designer. It is one of the hardiest broadleaf evergreens available for our area. It is easy to grow. It has narrow, dark green, boxwood-like foliage. Untrimmed it makes a dense shrub or handsome, irregularly shaped small tree. It responds well to pruning, making an excellent hedge, topiary, pleach, or espalier. Examples of its usefulness are legion.

I have taken old plants, removed the lower branches, and used them as small, irregular multi-stemmed trees. A pair of these uplighted from underground fixtures on either side of a path to a house make a welcome feature at any time of the year. The black-green of the foliage makes it perfectly suited for use as background material to show off White Birch trunks or feature a golden-needled plant such as *Chamaecyparis pisifera* 'Filifera Aurea Nana.' Littleleaf Japanese Holly provides a welcome evergreen foliage texture with the needly, white-flowered *Spirea thunbergii* and yellow trumpet Narcissus in April. As a formal hedge anywhere from 2½ to 8 feet there are few substitutes.

Ilex crenata 'Microphylla' has been in the Philadelphia trade for at least forty years, and in the American trade since 1910. Other garden varieties of *Ilex crenata* (introduced to Europe in 1864) have been on the market since 1867, when the Dutch-introduced variety *latifolia* was marketed under the name *Ilex fortunei*. The list of excellent varieties includes 'Helleri,' 'Compacta,' and 'Green Island,' but none of these is so hardy or of such general usefulness as *Ilex crenata* 'Microphylla.'

57

Ilex glabra 'Densa'

Inkberry

This mound-like shrub with large, dark green, lustrous, boxwood-like leaves is extremely hardy. It is another example of a native plant—much ignored—which has become a great asset to landscape designers. The stems of the plant are rather thin and willowy. The branches therefore move easily in the wind and it has none of the stiffness of comparably shaped plants of Japanese Holly. In the wild populations of *Ilex glabra* there is great variation in growth rate, leaf size, winter color, and berry size and color. This selection is relatively dense in habit (being "self-branching"), broad in leaf shape, darker green in winter color, and has ¼-inch black fruit. Various other forms have been selected for even slower growth habit, narrower leaves, more of a purple winter color, and white berries.

Natively it is usually found from Nova Scotia to Florida and west to Missouri, in damp places with full sun. It is stoloniferous in habit. Inkberry is, however, extremely flexible as to site, being quite tolerant of both shady and dry, windy locations. As with many stoloniferous plants, it can be cut back to the ground in the spring and will send up enough bushy growth to constitute a "new plant" the same growing season. Although the variety 'Densa' usually remains compact, its response to severe pruning is a helpful fact to know in the event branches are broken out or the plant becomes rangy and rejuvenation seems desirable. As with all Hollies, the color of the foliage is greatly enhanced by the addition of well-balanced fertilizer. It transplants readily in almost any stage of growth or in its dormant condition.

STRUCTURAL INTEREST

Evergreen
Effective landscape height: 8 feet
Effective landscape spread: 7½ feet
Zones 3-4
Aquifoliaceae (Holly Family)
Native range: North America—Nova Scotia to Florida and Missouri

I use *Ilex glabra* 'Densa' primarily when I need a broadleaf evergreen that is *tougher* than those I would rank higher in appearance, such as variants of *Ilex crenata* or of *Osmanthus*, or as *Prunus laurocerasus* 'Otto Luykens.' Therefore, the plants to be associated with it must be equally tough. The mounded form and lighter green foliage contrasts well with the dark green, irregular form of Japanese Black Pine *(Pinus thunbergii)*, and these two associated with the spiky habit of *Yucca smalliana* make a very handsome picture. An interesting "silhouette" planting to be associated with a contemporary building might include a clump of Yellowgroove Bamboo *(Phyllostachys aureosulcata)*, a continuous mound of six to eight plants of *Ilex glabra* 'Densa,' and a fairly extensive tie-in with interlocking sweeps of water-worn pebbles and the gray-green Sargent's Juniper *(Juniperus chinensis* 'Sargentii').

The 'Densa' form of *Ilex glabra* is a selection made by Bert Flemer at F and F Nurseries and one which I have used and admired for nearly twenty years. In 1938, five hundred *Ilex glabra* seedlings were planted and as they matured the five best were selected. Subsequently four of these were discarded when this plant was determined to be the best of the lot!

58

SEASONAL INTEREST

Deciduous
Effective landscape height: 9 feet
Effective landscape spread: 9 feet
Zones 3-4
Aquifoliaceae (Holly Family)
Native range: North America—Canada to Florida and Missouri

Ilex verticillata

Winterberry, Black-alder, Coonberry

This deciduous American Holly ranks higher for winter interest, in my judgment, than any other plant. The very fact that its summer appearance—a mound of small, bright green leaves—is innocuous adds to the drama of its fall activities. With the coming of frost, the leaves turn yellow and fall off revealing a truly wonderful winter spectacle. Black stems, clustered together at the base, fan out in an ascendant manner supporting fine horizontal to ascendant twig growth. Small (¼-inch) sparkling red berries cover almost the entire frame in generous clusters. There is a luster and lusciousness about these fruits that is very special and lasts until severely low temperatures combined with high-velocity winds take their toll.

Usually the fruits are in fine condition well through Christmas and as such rank as the very best red berry for Christmas decorations. We would all do well to consider this desirable quality when selecting plants for our gardens. There are many good garden plants which can contribute rich and exciting materials for live Christmas decorations. Most other plants which have red fruit (in good condition at Christmas time) also possess evergreen foliage of one sort or another. (*Ilex pedunculosa, Ilex aquifolium, Cotoneaster salicifolia* 'Flocossa,' *Stranvaesia davidiana* var. *undulata*, and *Ilex cornuta* are examples.) Although any one of these may be attractive in itself, the presence of the foliage limits the way in which it can be used. *Ilex verticillata*, on the other hand, presents its berries on bare black stems, leaving us free to combine it with dark green, narrow-leaf textures such as Umbrella-pine *(Sciadopitys verticillata)*, Dwarf Japanese Yew (*Taxus cuspidata* 'Nana'), Scotch Broom *(Cytisus scoparius)*, and Canaert's Red-cedar (*Juniperus virginiana* 'Canaertii'); dark green, broadleaf textures such as English Boxwood (*Buxus sempervirens* 'Suffruticosa'), Roundleaf Ligustrum (*Ligustrum japonicum* 'Rotundifolium'), and *Magnolia grandiflora*; blue-green colorations such as Blue Atlas Cedar (*Cedrus atlantica* 'Glauca'), Arizona Cypress *(Cupressus arizonica)*, Limber Pine *(Pinus flexilis)*, and Leatherleaf Mahonia *(Mahonia bealei)*; bronzy foliages such as *Ilex aquifolium* 'Ciliata Major' and Leucothoë *(Leucothoë fontanesiana)*; and accents of pure gold such as the Cripp's goldenform of Hinoki Cypress (*Chamaecyparis obtusa* 'Crippsii') and the golden-variegated broadleaf *Elaeagnus pungens* 'Maculata,' whose dark green leaves have an irregular, light yellow blotch

Ilex verticillata

surrounded by irregular borders of chartreuse in their centers.

The value of *Ilex verticillata* as a garden plant is almost without limit because of the wonderful sparkle of its berries at what is really a long, drab time of year. It might be featured as a two- or three-plant clump amidst drifts of the gray-green, broadleaf *Yucca smalliana* and the pendulous, dark green, needle evergreen, English Weeping Yew (*Taxus baccata* 'Repandens'). These companions in addition to providing texture and color interest to the winter picture guarantee a planting with strong interest the balance of the year, especially when the *Ilex* is least attractive—the Yucca sends up dramatic spikes of white blossoms in June.

Very dark green plants and those with golden highlights seem to combine in a most elegant manner with the intensity and light-reflective quality of the Winterberry red. Three possible combinations come to mind. For a wet spot, Winterberry with the deciduous Yellowtwig Dogwood (*Cornus sericea* 'Flaviramea') and the roundleaf, black-berried evergreen shrub, Inkberry (*Ilex glabra* 'Compacta'); in normal garden soil, Winterberry with the dark, broadleaf evergreen shrub 'Otto Luykens' Cherry-laurel (*Prunus laurocerasus* 'Otto Luykens') and the golden, needly, vertical, Cripp's goldenform of Hinoki Cypress (*Chamaecyparis obtusa* 'Crippsii'); or, reversing the texture of the companions, Winterberry with the golden broadleaf (mentioned earlier) *Elaeagnus pungens* 'Maculata' and the dark green, fine-needled conifer Oriental Spruce *(Picea orientalis)*.

Bird-lovers are strong Winterberry fans because of the high favor in which songbirds hold the fruit of this shrub. As a bird attractor *Ilex verticillata* ranks with such other old reliable garden plants as American Holly *(Ilex opaca)*, Dogwood *(Cornus florida)*, Chokeberry *(Aronia arbutifolia* 'Brilliantissima'), Bush-honeysuckle *(Lonicera tatarica)*, Spice-Bush *(Lindera benzoin)*, Bayberry *(Myrica pensylvanica)*, and Black Haw Viburnum *(Viburnum prunifolium)*.

In its wide range in the eastern United States *Ilex verticillata* is frequently found in swamps and adjacent to water. As a garden subject, it thrives in deep topsoil, regardless of site, and requires—as do most Hollies—that a male plant be present as pollinator for every eight or ten berry-bearing plants used. Farmers have recognized the ornamental value of *Ilex verticillata* for years, bringing the berry-laden branches to market at Christmas time—in our area under the name "Coonberry." Only just recently have nurserymen begun to acknowledge the virtues of the plant for landscape work. A fine berry-bearing form of *Ilex verticillata* has been selected and put on the market by Gulf Stream Nursery under the name *Ilex verticillata* 'Xmas Cheer.' The berries are large and abundant and remain on the plant late in the season. In addition, Dr. Elwin Orton of Rutgers University has crossed Winterberry with its Asiatic counterpart, *Ilex serrata*, selected two of the progeny for their compact growth habit and abundance of small red fruits, and introduced them as *Ilex* x 'Harvest Red' and *Ilex* x 'Autumn Glow.' The National Arboretum has recently introduced an outstanding hybrid from the same parentage, *Ilex* x 'Sparkleberry,' which is pictured here.

The British gave well-deserved recognition to Winterberry's virtue in 1962 with an Award of Merit from the Royal Horticultural Society.

59

Kerria japonica

Kerria, Single Orangeblossom

This little-used single form of the old-fashioned dooryard shrub is a real garden asset at two distinct seasons of the year. Its stoloniferous habit causes the slender, vertical, bright green twigs to be produced very close together in a ground-cover-like

SEASONAL INTEREST

Deciduous
Effective landscape height: 4 feet
Effective landscape spread: indefinite
Zone 5
Rosaceae (Rose Family)
Native range: China

fashion that gives a cheerful sparkle to any winter landscape scene. Later, in mid-May, single, butter-yellow blossoms resembling those of the orange tree appear in great profusion—at a time when nature's palette is dominated by other hues. The flowers are effective at a distance; the twigs at closer range.

For winter effect I would like to develop a planting using bronzes and purples with green Kerria twigs as the spice in the pudding. This would be achieved by structuring a mass of six to eight apple-green- and red-leaved, red-berried Stranvaesia (*Stranvaesia davidiana* var. *undulata*) with the purple, needly foliage of the vertical *Thuja orientalis* 'Juniperoides.' The *Kerria japonica* (perhaps three of them) would be featured in the foreground with five or six bronzy-leaved *Leucothoë fontanesiana* and a needly ground cover of the purple-hued Andorra Juniper (*Juniperus horizontalis* 'Plumosa').

As a May feature, a single Kerria plant against a background of the billowy, lavender-flowered Chinese Lilac (*Syringa* x *chinensis*) would make quite a splash. The picture could be enriched by a foreground planting of the red-foliaged *Berberis thunbergii* 'Crimson Pygmy' and a drift of herbaceous material such as Forget-me-nots *(Myosotis)*, 'Queen of the Night' Tulips, and the wine-purple Honesty *(Lunaria annua)*. An extremely attractive alternative combination I have seen at that season is the white form of Redbud *(Cercis canadensis forma alba)* planted with a ground cover of *Kerria japonica* below.

In both seasons it is obvious that Kerria is a "designer's plant," and its placement must be thought out carefully. Site selection is equally important from a cultural viewpoint, as bud kill and twig damage can be significant in a severe winter if it is grown in a cold, windy place. In fact, pruning out dead wood is its only maintenance requirement, assuming it has been placed in rich, well-drained loam. I grow it happily in a sunny situation; it will, however, do equally well in quite heavy shade.

It is curious to me that the more complex, double-flowered form, *Kerria japonica* 'Floreplena,' was

Kerria japonica

both the first one introduced for garden use and has been the most popular and widely used. The single-flowered *Kerria japonica*, which is, in my opinion, the superior plant from a landscape viewpoint, was introduced into England in 1835 by John Russell Reeves, who sent it to the Royal Horticultural Society from garden-grown material found in Canton. The double form had been sent to England in 1805 by William Kerr, after whom it was named—also collected from garden stocks in the Canton area. This is, of course, a matter of pure chance. That the single form has been so much less used than the double is appalling to me and a sad commentary on the taste which rates as higher that which is bigger, brighter, and more complex.

Kerria japonica received an Award of Garden Merit from the Royal Horticultural Society in 1928.

60

Kolkwitzia amabilis

Beauty-Bush

SEASONAL INTEREST

Deciduous
Effective landscape height: 12 feet
Effective landscape spread: 8 feet
Zone 5
Caprifoliaceae (Honeysuckle Family)
Native range: central China

This large, sturdy Asiatic shrub has been unjustifiably slow in gaining popularity with American gardeners. The tan, exfoliating branches, clustered lightly together at ground level, rise at first vertically and then gradually spread outward to form a mounded umbrella shape. Foliage of the softest gray-green clothes this graceful form, the individual leaves being broad ovals tapering to points, 2½ inches long. The blossoms appear in late May as lush cascades of small (½-inch), pink, bell-like flowers. Close examination reveals that each pink floret has a yellow throat and the new leaf growth, at that moment, has a bronzy hue. Some observers feel that this foliage color detracts from the floral display. However, after the sharper contrasts of the mid-May cornucopia of blossoms, I find these rich subtleties most welcome and at a time when we can spend more time out of doors. Attractive, brown, bristly seed pods follow the blossoms; the foliage takes on a reddish hue in the autumn.

In a large-scale situation, masses of pink-flowering *Kolkwitzia* and a few plants of Redleaf Plum (*Prunus cerasifera* 'Thundercloud') can make a perfect foil for the spectacular lavender blossoms of an Empress-Tree *(Paulownia tomentosa).* In a smaller-scale garden, a single Beauty-Bush might serve as background plant, along with perhaps four Redleaf Barberries (*Berberis thunbergii* 'Atropurpurea') for six or eight large clumps of a light blue Siberian Iris and a ground cover of the shiny red-leaved *Ajuga reptans* 'Metallica Crispa.'

Beauty-Bush is thoroughly reliable and thrives in any average, well-drained garden soil in full sun or very light shade. It takes a few years to reach its graceful mature shape and full blossoming potential. Pruning should be limited therefore to removal of dead wood, for any more severe action will definitely delay its development.

Kolkwitzia has twice been found in the wild: first by the Italian Missionary Giuseppe Giraldi, who worked in Shensi, China, from 1890 to 1895; second by Ernest H. Wilson, who collected it among the rocks at 9,000–10,000 feet in northern Hupeh province. Wilson's seed went to the British nurseryman Veitch in 1901, and plants first flowered in cultivation at the Veitch Coombe Wood Nursery in 1910. In the United States it did not become well known until 1922, when an enterprising nursery decided to distribute it as "new." Large numbers were propagated, and according to Dr. Donald Wyman (1971 *a*), "an expensive advertising campaign made the plant popular almost overnight." It is still, however, not used so often as is justified by its beauty. W. J. Bean suggests that this may well be due to the fact that seedlings with small, poorly colored flowers may have been distributed in the trade. For this reason, home gardeners should be encouraged to search out and demand one of the named garden varieties such

Kolkwitzia amabilis

as 'Rosea' (originated in Holland) or 'Pink Cloud' (from England).

In 1923 *Kolkwitzia amabilis* received an Award of Merit from the Royal Horticultural Society in England.

61

Leucothoë fontanesiana (L. catesbaeii)

Leucothoë, Drooping Leucothoë

This pendulous member of the Heath clan is more valued for its foliage than its flowers. Three-inch-long racemes of white, waxy, bell-shaped blossoms do line the underside of the branches for 12 to 18 inches of their length in early June each year. However, since they are hard to see (because of their positioning) and there are so many other plants with better quality bloom available at the same time, its blossoms must be rated as insignificant.

The foliage, on the other hand, is a great garden asset. The leaves are glossy, apple-green, pointed ovals, 5–7 inches long. The alternate arrangement of this foliage gives an interesting zigzag character to the stems. The stems themselves rise from the ground to about two-thirds their length and then arch over very gracefully.

Leucothoë will grow well in either sun or shade. In winter the plants receiving the most sun turn a marvelous bronze color, while those in full shade remain a rich green. Leucothoë is generally a more compact grower in the sun than elsewhere; in shade, in its native Great Smoky Mountain region, it can reach 6 feet in height. Farther north at Longwood Gardens in Kennett Square, Pennsylvania, where it grows among handsome ancient Hemlock trunks, it reaches 5 feet in height.

Because Leucothoë spreads by underground stems,

STRUCTURAL INTEREST

Evergreen
Effective landscape height: 4 feet
Effective landscape spread: 6 feet
Zone 5
Ericaceae (Heath Family)
Native range: United States—Virginia to Georgia to Tennessee

it tends to grow in thickets. It is most effective if older canes are periodically cut to the ground in the spring. This encourages regeneration with fresh young growth from the base. Leucothoë prefers acid soil with plenty of peat. It transplants well in the spring when dug with a ball of earth.

Because Leucothoë is used mainly as a foliage plant, it is important to select companions that, by contrast, emphasize its excellent features. In semishade or on the north side of a building, two contrastingly needled companions might be chosen: Dwarf Japanese Yew (*Taxus cuspidata* 'Nana') as the taller part of the composition and Pachistima *(Pachistima canbyi)* as the ground cover. In a sunnier spot the green stems of *Kerria japonica* and the arrow-shaped, dark green foliage of Shrub Ivy (*Hedera helix* 'Conglomerata Erecta') would emphasize the charming reddish-bronze winter color of the Leucothoë. Or, in a larger area a background planting of Willowleaf Cotoneaster (*Cotoneaster salicifolia* 'Flocossa') might feature a single specimen Weeping Hemlock (*Tsuga canadensis* 'Pendula') in a mass planting composed partly of Leucothoë and partly of Lilyturf (*Liriope muscari* 'Big Blue'). The leathery, willow-shaped leaves of the Cotoneaster take on the same bronze character as the Leucothoë in winter. Both would contrast with the finer texture and winter green of the Hemlock needles and strap-like leaf shape of the *Liriope*. All four plants have pendulous characteristics, thus making similarity of form the subtle but exciting tie-together of this relationship.

62

Lonicera fragrantissima

Fragrant Honeysuckle, Winter
Honeysuckle, Breath of Spring

During the growing season this vigorous, easy to
grow, medium-sized shrub is covered with attractive
oval leaves that are dark green above, bluish-green
below. This is a one-season plant grown soiely for
its inconspicuous but delightfully fragrant cream-
colored blossoms. Flowers may open in February in
a warm corner or not until April in an exposed location. In any case, the fragrance will continue to
pervade the garden for nearly a month and, coming
on the heels of winter, is most welcome. The season
can be further extended by cutting a branch early in
the spring and forcing it to open by taking it into the
heat of the house. The young stems are reddish and
the attractive oval leaves personify "health and
vigor."

Fragrant Honeysuckle is not usually a shrub to be
featured, being more useful in background plantings.
It is a must for any garden emphasizing fragrance.
I have used it successfully in dooryard plantings
featuring scent with Sweet Shrub *(Calycanthus floridus)*, Wintersweet *(Chimonanthus praecox)*, Spice
Viburnum *(Viburnum carlesii)*, Clove Currant
(Ribes odoratum), Sweet Mock-Orange *(Philadelphus coronarius)*, Fragrant Elaeagnus *(Elaeagnus
pungens* 'Fruitlandii'), Fragrant Viburnum, *(Viburnum fragrans)*, Lavender *(Lavandula angustifolia)*,
Royal Azalea *(Rhododendron schlippenbachii)*, and
Slender Deutzia *(Deutzia gracilis)*. I see no reason,
however, why it couldn't be featured successfully
amongst a mass of early-spring-flowering bulbs in

SEASONAL INTEREST

Deciduous in the North, semi-evergreen in the South
Effective landscape height: 7 feet
Effective landscape spread: 7 feet
Zone 6
Caprifoliaceae (Honeysuckle Family)
Native range: China

white and blue shades, such as *Chionodoxa, Scilla siberica, Iris reticulata*, and *Crocus*.

Because the blossoms are borne on wood grown the previous year it should not be pruned in the late autumn or early spring or flower buds will be cut off. It is vigorous and easy to grow.

It was collected from cultivated material near Shanghai, China, by Robert Fortune in 1845 and first flowered in England in 1852, at which time John Lindley of the Royal Horticultural Society published an article on it, with a color plate and brief historical account (in Paxton's *Flower Garden*, Vol. 3).

63

STRUCTURAL INTEREST

Evergreen
Effective landscape height: 6 feet
Effective landscape spread: 6 feet
Zone 7
Berberidaceae (Barberry Family)
Native range: China

Mahonia bealei

Leatherleaf Mahonia

This vigorous, evergreen, multistemmed shrub is striking because of its coarse, compound blue-green foliage. Each leaf may be up to 18 inches in length and composed of as many as fifteen individual Holly-shaped leaflets. In addition, pyramidal clusters of beautiful, fragrant, lemon-yellow flowers terminate the stems in April. These are followed by frosty blue berries, maturing in June.

The extremely large scale of its foliage creates an exotic effect and makes it both a great asset (in garden design) and a challenging subject to use well. As a single specimen in a small garden, it is best to allow it to be the center of attention as it will certainly diminish the importance of any other garden "features." In a larger-scale situation involving masses of blending foliage, a grouping of these Mahonias can provide the strength to give structure to the whole picture. Wherever it is used, it is well to include some other foliages in the picture, such as the blue-leaved *Hosta sieboldiana* (also known as *H. glauca)* or gray-foliaged Japanese Silver Fern *(Athyrium goeringianum pictum)*, which reinforce the coloration of its foliage. Likewise it may be desirable to balance the scale of its foliage with other coarse foliages such as Oakleaf Hydrangea *(Hydrangea quercifolia)* or *Bergenia cordifolia*, with its cabbage-like foliage rosettes. The texture of a fieldstone wall is an unusually fine background for this handsome plant.

Mahonia bealei is a tough member of the Barberry family and will grow in sun under fairly rugged conditions. It is, however, at its best on the north side of a building or where provided with shade or semishade from nearby trees and where the soil is good and moisture is adequate. It is lime-tolerant.

In 1848, during his second trip to China, the plant explorer Robert Fortune found this plant in the Huychow area of Chekiang. It was growing in a neglected garden and according to Alice Coats (1965), Fortune described it as an upright flowered shrub "surpassing in beauty all the known species of Mahonia." Five small plants stored in the Shanghai garden of Thomas Clay Beale, consul from Portugal, were subsequently dispatched to the Standish and Noble Nursery in Sunningdale, England, which put the plant into commerce in 1858. Fortune described and named this garden favorite in 1850, honoring the plant's Shanghai host in its name. Britain's Royal Horticultural Society presented *Mahonia bealei* with an Award of Garden Merit in 1916.

64

STRUCTURAL INTEREST

Effective landscape height: 6 feet
Effective landscape spread: indefinite
Zone 6
Gramineae (Grass Family)
Native range: Japan and China

Miscanthus sinensus 'Gracillimus'
Maiden Grass

This plant is the epitome of what a good ornamental grass should be. Its very narrow foliage (never much wider than ¼ inch) and wiry stems (³⁄₁₆ inch) provide the details that, without any possible question, read "grass." In addition, it is neat in habit, and makes a feathery, uniform mound of foliage 6 feet tall. It dresses itself well to the ground on all sides and never shows any browned or dried-out stems. The texture and the dark, yellow-green color make the beholder feel cool and suggest visually that water may be nearby. Actually Maiden Grass is undemanding as to site, flourishing in either moist or dry locations. Reddish-pink blossoms appear in September and subsequently become seed heads that go through shades of pink and beige and eventually take on the color of corn husks. This obviously adds a valuable element of interest to the garden at a season when interest is low. Unlike some grasses, it is amazingly resistant to wind and rain damage, and is effective until heavy snows have crushed its stems out of shape.

Whereas many newly planted shrubs are not really effective for three to five years, the grasses are valuable in providing immediate effect. Maiden Grass should be planted in the spring as a dormant division and can be planted later if obtained in containers. With adequate attention to watering, this grass will be an effective part of the landscape the same fall. Average soil enriched with a good supply of organic matter and some fertilizer is desirable. The foliage *can* be cut back any time after winter damage occurs and must be removed before new growth starts in the spring.

Miscanthus is definitely a designer's plant. Exciting textural combinations can result from planting it next to large broadleaf foliages. In a dry site any one of the Mulleins (*Verbascum* sp.) might be chosen. In a wet site the round, purplish foliage of Bigleaf Golden-ray, *Ligularia clivorum* 'Desdemona,' or the even larger foliage of the Japanese Butterbur *(Petasites japonica)* would pack a real wallop. With average garden moisture a bit of fun can be had by treating ordinary Rhubarb *(Rheum rhaponticum)* as an ornamental and as *Miscanthus'* texture mate.

All the grasses are prime candidates when the object is to create a tropical effect. In addition to the companions discussed above, such a setting might include Devil's Walking Stick *(Aralia spinosa)*, with its enormous compound foliage, the Hardy-orange *(Poncirus trifoliata)*, and Staghorn Sumac *(Rhus typhina)* and its ferny-leaved variant, *R. typhina* 'Laciniata.'

An intriguing mood can also be set by developing an entire garden with grass-like foliages. In addition to such grasses as *Miscanthus sinensis* 'Gracillimus,' its taller (10–12-foot) cousin *Miscanthus sinensis* 'Giganteus,' and the Giant Reed *(Arundo donax)*, one might include two Bamboos: Yellowgroove, *Phyllostachys aureosulcata*, and the variegated ground cover, *Arundinaria viridistriata*, a selection of Irises, Brooms *(Cytisus), Genistas, Yuccas*, Daylilies *(Hemerocallis)*, Lilyturfs *(Liriope)*, and the very ancient Horsetail Reed *(Equisetum hyemale)*.

65

Myrica pensylvanica
Northern Bayberry

Bayberry is a native plant of extremely subtle beauty valued almost entirely for its winter effect. This mounded shrub has a very vertical branching habit

SEASONAL INTEREST

Deciduous
Effective landscape height: 9 feet
Effective landscape spread: 9 feet
Zone 2
Myricaceae (Sweet Gale Family)
Native range: North America—Newfoundland to western New York, south to Maryland

Myrica pensylvanica, close-up of fruit

which is covered with broad, dull, somewhat leathery, olive-green leaves all summer and fall. The foliage may persist in a bronzed-green form throughout the winter in very wind-free places. Generally, however, the leaves are literally blown off by winter gales revealing fully the shrub's angular twigginess and, most important, the thick clusters of light, waxy gray berries (1/16 inch). These usually persist throughout the bitterest part of the winter until migrations of tree swallows, myrtle warblers, catbirds, and Baltimore orioles clean them off in early spring.

Because these fruits are present during the bleakest part of the gardening year, *Myrica* is important ornamentally. The gray of the fruits is, when closely studied, composed of white, red, and purple. Other plants possessing these colors bring out the subtle liveliness of *Myrica* berries. For instance, three of the fine, purply-foliaged conifers, *Thuja orientalis* 'Juniperoides,' spotted among a group of six or eight *Myrica* create a light purple haze, against which a single Redtwig Dogwood *(Cornus sericea)* can act as a very effective accent.

Against a background of dark green Nordmann's Fir *(Abies nordmanniana)* a sizable grouping of Bayberries and the spreading, but spiky, dark green Dwarf Japanese Yew (*Taxus cuspidata* 'Nana') might be planted. In the foreground of this dark green and gray combination a single plant of one of the White-stem Raspberries (*Rubus leucodermis, R. biflorus,* or *R. cockburnianus*) would add the final touch. The arching stems of the *Rubus*, covered with a milky-white bloom, would capture the eye of the viewer and cause him to feel, even more, the white qualities of the *Myrica* berries.

Another approach might be to feature a single plant of *Myrica* in a sea of low, purple-foliaged Andorra Juniper (*Juniperis horizontalis* 'Plumosa') and back it with a planting of five dark green English Weeping Yews (*Taxus baccata* 'Repandens') and three Bronzeleaf English Hollies (*Ilex aquifolium* 'Ciliata Major'). The Holly and Juniper foliage colors would repeat colors from the *Myrica* fruit while the dark green by contrast would emphasize its quality of whiteness.

Myrica pensylvanica should not be confused with the other native, *Myrica cerifera*, which retains its foliage in winter but has less spectacular, less aromatic berries. (The wax from the berries of *Myrica pensylvanica* has been used since colonial times to make candles, although today the demand for candles is so great that usually only enough is added to scent candles made of commercial wax.) *Myrica pensylvanica* is an amazingly adaptable native, occurring both in swamps and on sand dunes. It adapts itself perfectly well to inland sites away from its natural range. It is a thickety plant in nature and should be planted where it need not be disturbed by cultivating and pruning and where it can be allowed to develop its natural mound-like character. Because male and female flowers occur on separate plants, it is desirable to use a majority of female or berry-bearing plants, making sure to have one male for every ten females. To date, no enterprising nurseryman has offered the sexes for sale separately. Therefore buyers would be well-advised to select the plants themselves during the fruiting season.

Because of its tough characteristics and particularly its ability to hold soil on gravelly slopes, Bayberry has been widely used in recent years for highway plantings. Bayberry has not been widely used in home gardens, however, where its subtle enrichment of the winter scene can be most fully appreciated.

Myrica pensylvanica

66

SEASONAL INTEREST

Deciduous
Effective landscape height: 6 feet
Effective landscape spread: 8 feet
Zone 6
Paeoniaceae (Peony Family)
Hybrid origin

Paeonia × 'Black Pirate'
Saunder's Hybrid Tree Peony
'Black Pirate'

This handsome woody shrub is one hybrid of a group of plants (the Tree Peonies) that have intrigued sophisticated gardeners for centuries. From fat buds on rather vertical stems, reddish new growth begins unfolding in April. This develops quickly into large (18-inch) leaves composed of three or more deeply cut leaflets. These eventually turn a dark yellow-green; however, at the time the blossoms occur they have a fresh bluish cast. The flowers (one to a stem) open in late May, are 8–10 inches in diameter, single to semi-double, a beautiful black-maroon with a yellow center. Words cannot describe the richness of the visual experience. There is a sheen to the petals which does the quietest magic with light reflection and literally stops the viewer dead in his tracks. The season of bloom is short, usually not lasting more than ten days, but the experience is so rich that even if the plant had nothing else to offer, one would be justified in giving it a place of honor in the garden. The plant does have more to offer, however, in terms of its foliage texture which, although coarse, is eye-catching and has great character.

'Black Pirate' blossoms with Columbine, *Achillea tomentosa* 'Flowers of Sulphur,' and the tall bearded German Iris. The *Iris germanica* varieties 'Chivalry' (blue), 'Black Hills' (deep purple), and 'Dream Castle' (lavender-pink) make a particularly good color combination with it. The foliage makes it an excellent anchor plant in any herbaceous garden for the rest of the season.

'Black Pirate' is equally delightful in a grouping

of woody plants. 'Thundercloud' Plums (*Prunus cerasifera* 'Thundercloud') and a partially over-lapping sweep of Beauty-Bush *(Kolkwitzia amabilis)* make a handsome background for a planting of seven to nine 'Black Pirate' Tree Peonies. The Plum foliage is a good repeat of the flower color, while the Beauty-Bush flower color provides a good contrast. Both the Plum and Beauty-Bush foliage shapes are a good foil for the dramatic Peony leaves.

This hybrid, as well as any other you fancy, is best obtained from a Tree Peony specialist and preferably growing on its own roots. Mid-October is the recommended time for transplanting and good soil preparation is very important. Tree Peonies like an alkaline soil, high in organic matter. They demand good drainage and the blossoms last longer if there is a little shade (but no more than half shade). In my own garden, I dig a pit 2½ feet deep and 3 feet in diameter. First I put in 6 inches of 2b crushed stone to assure good drainage. Then I fill the hole with a mixture of half topsoil and half well-rotted manure. A couple of handfuls of crushed limestone is added to the mix to bring the pH up to 6.5 to 7. This may seem like a lot of work. However, it should be looked upon as a long-range investment because under these conditions the plants will persist for years, with the flowers seeming to be finer every season.

If the plants you buy are grafted, it is important to set the plant so that the graft union is covered with six inches of soil. This will encourage the development of "own roots" and will also tend to develop a bushier plant. Since the plants grow natively in mountain forests, they are quite tolerant of drought. Therefore, watering is not generally a burdensome necessity. Rabbits are very fond of the young shoots, and it is important to protect new plantings from them. After the plants are well-established, the rabbits are less attracted by them; also, the plants, if nibbled off, will sprout abundant new stems the following spring. This characteristic of the plant is useful to know about should you ever have an infestation of carpenter bees which seem to fancy the Tree Peony wood. In the event of such a calamity,

Paeonia x 'Black Pirate'

cut and burn the stems in the late fall and a new plant will grow without any trouble the following spring.

The chief disease problem is gray mold blight *(Botrytis paeoniae)*, which attacks the new shoots and foliage. It can be controlled by spraying with standard-strength solution of fermate or benolate. This disease seems to be particularly prevalent in wet springs and in situations where air circulation is poor and there is too much shade. Feeding with high-nitrogen fertilizers is to be discouraged as it forces lush growth, which is particularly susceptible to *Botrytis*. A deep mulch probably accentuates the problem by harboring spores.

'Black Pirate' is an "all-American" plant in that unlike many of our garden favorites, it is the result of strictly American breeding efforts. A. P. Saunders (1869–1953), a professor at Hamilton College, Clinton, New York, became interested in the Tree Peony hybrids developed in France around the time of World War I. He procured plants of the species *Paeonia delavayi* and *Paeonia lutea* and went to work crossing them with the single and semi-double Japanese Moutan varieties *(Paeonia suffruticosa)*. These crosses were made by saving the pollen of the Moutan varieties and putting it on the later-blooming *Paeonia lutea* and *Paeonia delavayi*. An astonishingly beautiful race was the result, and 'Black Pirate' is one of the finest. Whereas the older Moutan varieties were often double, heavy, and hung their heads under the foliage, the newer varieties are single and semi-double and hold their heads up. Whereas the old Moutan color range was white, pink, rose-red, vermilion, crimson, maroon-purple, magenta, and lilac-rose, the new race featured yellow, yellow-suffused reddish, reddish with yellow undertones, crimson to black-maroon, ivories, and suffused mauves.

This is a real success story, in that Professor Saunders inspired William Gratwick of Pavilion, New York, to such an extent that he has carried on the work. Gratwick's crosses have been made with the aid of a New York artist-friend, Nassos Daphius, who makes a pilgrimage to Pavilion during the blooming season each spring. Their work has resulted in a new second-generation hybrid race with tremendous vigor, large size and good form to the flowers, and exceptionally strong stems. Some of the problems encountered by this determined pair are well-described in the excellent book by John C. Wister, *The Peonies* (published by the American Horticultural Society in 1962).

The Moutan Peonies *(Paeonia suffruticosa)* have been garden plants in China and Japan for centuries— early references go back at least as far as A.D. 536. Marco Polo was ridiculed for having described these flowers accurately as "roses as large as cabbages." They were imported into Europe first from China in 1789 and then from Japan in 1844 and became a real craze there during the 1800's. Prices soared and a Belgian amateur who produced a seedling so magnificent that he called it 'Gloria Belgarum' would only allow his closest friends to see it, refused to share propagations from it, and reportedly had it guarded night and day by two enormous dogs!

Paeonia delavayi and *Paeonia lutea*, on the other hand, were not discovered until 1883–1884 when Père Jean Marie Delavay found them in the Chinese province of Yunnan. They first bloomed in the Jardin des Plantes at the Museum National d'Histoire Naturelle in Paris in 1891–1892.

Subsequent explorers have brought back superior forms of *Paeonia lutea* and *Paeonia delavayi* which vary in color and foliage characteristics. In 1914, Reginald Farrar found that *Paeonia suffruticosa* was always white in the province of Kansu but magenta farther north. It was his opinion that further exploration in China would reveal wild types in other colors. Improved political relations with China with the possibility of pursuing quests such as these, combined with the success of breeding programs like those of Saunders and Gratwick, give hope for even finer hybrids in years to come. In the meantime, varieties like 'Black Pirate' live up to the Chinese epithet for the Moutan Peony, "king of the flowers."

67

Deciduous
Effective landscape height: 9 feet
Effective landscape spread: 12 feet
Zone 5
Saxifragaceae (Saxifrage Family)
Native range: southeastern Europe and Asia Minor

Philadelphus coronarius
Sweet Mock-orange,
Fragrant Mock-orange

This old-fashioned garden plant is, most justifiably, still a favorite. Its cascades of fragrant white flowers are a major contribution to the ebullience of early June gardens. The flowers are single, feature pretty yellow stamens in their centers, and are attractive to butterflies. It is basically an upright shrub, but older branches bend over to the ground giving it a very graceful form.

Fountain Buddleia *(Buddleia alternifolia)*, with its pendulous branches lined with rosettes of lavender blossoms, and 'Thundercloud' Plum (*Prunus cerasifera* 'Thundercloud'), with its wine- to plum-colored foliage, make colorful companions for Fragrant Mock-orange. Actually, I find *Philadelphus coronarius* particularly attractive as part of a green and white scheme. Five plants of *Philadelphus* would make an attractive foreground planting for a specimen Korean Dogwood *(Cornus kousa)* featured against a couple of dark green Oriental Spruces *(Picea orientalis)* or Canadian Hemlocks *(Tsuga canadensis)*. The *Philadelphus* might be "dressed down" with dark green Dwarf Japanese Yew (*Taxus cuspidata* 'Nana') and the whole planting accented by an off-center clump of *Yucca smalliana*, with its spikes of white blossoms.

Philadelphus coronarius is tough. It will thrive in full sun or partial shade. Any good garden soil will do and it will tolerate drier conditions than most shrubs. Very little pruning is required. Should thinning seem necessary, this is best done immediately after the flowering period so that vigorous flowering wood for the following season will have a chance to form during the summer months.

This plant was introduced to Europe in 1562, when Ogier Ghiselin de Beesberg, ambassador from the Emperor Ferdinand to Soleimin the Magnificent, brought it back to Vienna from Turkey along with the Lilac. It reached England in 1597 and the United States in very early colonial times.

For many years it was known only as a garden plant. Because it became naturalized throughout Europe, there was great confusion about its true source. However, wild specimens were subsequently found growing in mountain thickets in the hinterland of Bulgaria, and its true place of origin is now considered to be southeastern Europe and Asia Minor.

In Germany and the Scandinavian countries *Philadelphus* is known as the "pipe shrub." This refers to the fact that the stems of long pipes used in Turkey and the Near East are made from young, hollowed-out *Philadelphus* stems. The pith of the older stems is very large in diameter and for the last century or more has been used as a "holder" (the soft medium kept in alcohol) when making thin hand-cut sections of tissue for microscopic examination.

Native from eastern China to the Balkans, about twenty-five species of the genus are cultivated. During the first half of the twentieth century, plant breeders produced from them a large number of Mock-orange hybrids. The flowers of many of these are desirable because of increased size, doubleness, and so on. Where the large size of *Philadelphus coronarius* presents a garden problem, its smaller offspring *Philadelphus* x 'Mont Blanc' (*Philadelphus macrophyllus* x *P. coronarius*) may prove useful. This hybrid was developed by the French nurseryman Victor Lemoine, is smaller-leaved, smaller-flowered, almost as fragrant, and only 5 feet in height. Generally speaking, however, I prefer *Philadelphus coronarius* to any of the hybrids because of its tough character, reliable performance, and most important, its rich and heady fragrance.

Philadelphus coronarius

68

SEASONAL INTEREST

Deciduous
Effective landscape height: 13 feet
Effective landscape spread: 15 feet (to 35 feet in the South)
Zones 6-7
Rutaceae (Rue Family)
Native range: northern China, Korea

Poncirus trifoliata

Hardy-orange, Japanese Bitter-orange

This hardy member of the Orange tribe is of interest as an ornamental at all seasons of the year. In late April its green twigs are covered with fat, white buds which open to 2-inch, single, white, sweetly scented Orange blossoms. Clean dark green leaves carried in groups of three clothe the plant all summer, turning various shades of yellow and yellow-green in the fall. The small (1½–2-inch) lemon-colored fruits turn color with the leaves from late September to early October and are most ornamental after the leaves have fallen, when they are seen in clusters against the green twigs. The winter silhouette of this plant is charming. It is irregular in branching habit and the angularity of its bright green stems is dramatized by the 4-inch thorns.

Unlike other Oranges, the fruit of Hardy-orange is of no practical use because of its extremely bitter flavor. In the South, because of its relative hardiness, it is used commercially as grafting understock for commercial oranges. The stout thorns make it extremely desirable as a barrier planting, being much resented by small boys as well as the nursery crews who must dig and plant the shrubs.

It is an extremely valuable ornamental. For best fruiting effect, allow it to grow naturally with several plants in a group. It could be backed with a specimen tree of the wholly unrelated Osage-orange *(Maclura pomifera)*, which carries huge bright green fruits at the same season, and dressed down in the foreground with a grouping of dwarf, needly, dark green Yews (*Taxus cuspidata* 'Nana'). Hardy-orange's spring blossoms open with the orange and white

Narcissus x 'Cheerfulness,' the clear blue blossoms of *Phlox stolonifera* 'Blue Ridge,' and the bright pink of *Bergenia cordifolia*. This combination is very cheerful in a cacophonic sort of way. For winter effect, feature a single untrimmed specimen against a background of six to eight Redtwig Dogwoods *(Cornus sericea)* and three red-berried American Hollies *(Ilex opaca).*

Other fall companions might include Beautyberry *(Callicarpa dichotoma)*, with its small purple fruit, *Viburnum setigerum*, with its pendulous red fruit, and the yellow-flowered bulb, *Sternbergia lutea.*

Poncirus responds well to various kinds of pruning, making it a good subject for clipped hedges, formal espaliers, or topiaries. Although it requires high maintenance, a single espalier or topiary can be a dramatic feature of any garden and over the years can be a very satisfying form of sculpture. Espaliers are relatively popular these days, but topiaries deserve more attention. In addition to Hardy-orange, Pyramidal Japanese Yew *(Taxus cuspidata* 'Capitata'), Downy Hawthorn *(Crataegus mollis)*, American Holly *(Ilex opaca)*, and Pyramidal Arborvitae *(Thuja ocidentalis* 'Nigra') are good subjects for topiaries.

Poncirus trifoliata prefers acid soil. Aside from this requirement, it seems to be undemanding and will flourish once it is established. It seems to be completely hardy as far north as Philadelphia and will do well in sheltered locations as far north as Boston. If used in a clipped form, it is desirable to delay pruning until after the spring blossoms appear. Alice Coats (1965) writes of a curious botanical observation about this plant by E. A. Bowles: " . . . the first flowers to open usually had stamens, but no stigma; then a few perfect (hermaphrodite) flowers appeared, and the last buds had stigmas but no stamens. If for any reason the female flowers were delayed till the pollen ones had fallen, no fruit was borne that season."

The plant was first discovered in Japan circa 1690–1692 by the Dutchman Engelbert Kaempfer,

Poncirus trifoliata

who wrote its botanical description from cultivated specimens. It is actually a native of northern China and Korea, and was introduced into England from China by Robert Fortune in 1850.

A NOTE ON AZALEAS

Azaleas deserve a special note because of the wealth of horticultural variation found in the group. Frederick P. Lee, in his excellent *Azalea Book* (1965), lists in excess of 2,500 different species and varieties. These with all the other many species of the genus Rhododendron form the most conspicuous group of woody plants grown for ornamental purposes.

The geographical distribution of Azaleas is a fascinating subject in itself. They occur naturally in two primary areas—the eastern United States and eastern China. In each country they form narrow longitudinal strips up and down the continents, separated by 7,000 miles and the earth's largest ocean. The exception is the Pontic Azalea *(Rhododendron flavum)* from the Caucasus and our own West Coast Azalea *(Rhododendron occidentale)* from Oregon and California. All are in the Northern Hemisphere and all in the temperate zone, except for the spillover of a few species into southern Asiatic areas just below the Tropic of Cancer.

Botanists have grouped most of the plants we know as Azaleas in the "Series Azalea" of the genus *Rhododendron* (hence, the confusing system of calling all Azaleas by the botanical name *Rhododendron*). The Series Azalea is then subdivided by earlier botanists into six subseries, grouping together those species supposedly most closely allied in the process of evolution. Dr. George Lawrence, one of the most eminent botanists today, feels that these groupings are arbitrary and capricious.

It is of interest that some eastern American Azaleas are more closely allied to some eastern Chinese Azaleas than they are to other eastern American

Azaleas. Interestingly enough, we find this sort of relationship occurring in a number of other plant families, with North American species having very similar Chinese relatives, namely the Fringe-Trees: *Chionanthus virginicus* and *Chionanthus retusus*; and the Devil's Walking Sticks, *Aralia spinosa* and *Aralia elata.*

The fact that counterpart species occur has been explained, according to Flemer (1972), by the existence of a flora (called "tertiary flora"), "which once encircled the Northern Hemisphere before the great cycle of glaciation." This flora was wiped out in areas where the mountain ranges run east and west as in Europe. As the glaciers moved south, the flora was "largely exterminated because its retreat was cut off by the ranges lying across the path to safety." In regions like the United States and eastern China, where the ranges run north and south, "the vegetation simply retreated south also, only to recolonize much of its former habitat when the ice withdrew." It is possible to postulate that the wealth of Azalea species we enjoy now and their occasional similarity, even though geographically separated, is a rich inheritance of tertiary flora and its subsequent successful variation and adaptation to geologic and climatic change.

The Azaleas available for our gardens today may be *species, varieties* of species (caused by natural variation in minor characteristics, usually on a geographic basis), or *forms* of varieties (natural local or sporadic variations of flower color or habit), or they may be *hybrids* (crosses between parents from different species, varieties, or forms, or between progeny of different hybrid groups); or, they may be and very often are *clones* selected from plants in any one of these categories. A clone is a particularly desirable individual plant whose qualities are maintained via asexual propagation—that is, by cuttings, grafts, or layers—and whose descendants are all asexually propagated, ensuring that all retain an identical genetic makeup.

Of the six Azaleas that I discuss here, three are deciduous and three are evergreen.

One of the deciduous Azaleas, *Rhododendron* x *gandavense* 'Daviesii,' is a clone of a hybrid group (the Ghent hybrids); one is an Asiatic species, *Rhododendron shlippenbachii*; one is an American species, *Rhododendron vaseyi*.

All three of the evergreen Azaleas are hybrids. 'Pink Pearl' is a Kurume hybrid. 'Herbert' and 'Stewartstonian' are Gable hybrids.

I have included no true Rhododendrons, as distinguished from Azaleas, among my selections in this book because I feel their landscape value is not sufficiently outstanding to warrant meeting what are very demanding requirements in our climatic area.

69

SEASONAL INTEREST

Evergreen
Effective landscape height: 6 feet
Effective landscape spread: 6 feet
Zone 7
Ericaceae (Heath Family)
Hybrid origin

Rhododendron × *gable* 'Herbert'

Gable Azalea 'Herbert'

70

Rhododendron × *gable* 'Stewartstonian'

Gable Azalea 'Stewartstonian'

These two newer, hybrid, evergreen Azaleas are the result of a very responsible breeding program started in 1927 and carried on by that very modest Pennsylvania nurseryman Joseph B. Gable (1886–1972).

'Herbert' is spreading, and of low to medium height. It is covered annually with handsome, clear, orchid-purple flowers blotched with darker purple. These flowers are single, frilled, of the hose-in-hose type, and about 1¾ inches in size. As with its parent *R. poukanense*, it loses all or most of the leaves in the winter.

'Stewartstonian' is of slightly more upright habit and is likewise reliably covered with blooms every year. The flowers are bright, clear red, in the brick-red direction, without any of the muddy purple found in the red of the popular 'Hinodegiri' or 'Hino-Crimson' varieties. The winter foliage is wine-red. The plant is named for Stewartstown, Pennsylvania, the village where Gable lived and did his outstanding work.

These two with Kurume 'Pink Pearl' (see page 148) form an excellent color trio with which to structure a cheerful display of "evergreen" Azaleas.

Among the evergreen Azaleas the choice of named plants and shades available is, of course, overwhelming. (Lee lists 89 of the older Kurumes, 47 Gables, and 443 Glenndales alone.) Starting with these three as a core, one might experiment with some of the newer ones after carefully observing them on a comparative basis in such plantings as that at the U.S. National Arboretum in Washington, D.C. Practically all of the colors mix well together, especially if white is omitted.

The Gable hybrids should be studied especially by those gardeners in harsher climates. They have already achieved wide acceptance in many areas in the Northeast and Midwest. In the group are plants of every habit known to the Azalea subseries Obtusum. Flower color ranges from orange-red to purple. Flowers are mostly singles, a few semi-doubles or doubles, and many hose-in-hoses. Some are frilled. Gable made hardiness one of his prime objectives, relying heavily on the Korean Azalea *(R. poukanense)* as one parent to boost this quality. The latter is one of the hardiest of the evergreen Azaleas, and comes from central and southern Korea and the Japanese island of Tsushima off the southern coast of Korea; it is hardy in Zone 5 in this country. *R. poukanense* was crossed with *R. kaempferi* among others and frequently the progeny were found to be hardier than either parent. The parentage of 'Herbert' is *R. poukanense* x *R.* x *sander* 'Hexe.'

Rhododendron x *gable* 'Herbert'

Rhododendron x *gable* 'Stewartstonian'

71

Rhododendron × *gandavense* 'Daviesii'
Ghent Azalea 'Daviesii'

SEASONAL INTEREST

Deciduous
Effective landscape height: 6-10 feet
Effective landscape spread: 6 feet
Zone 5
Ericaceae (Heath Family)
Hybrid origin

This sturdy, upright shrub is a favorite garden subject because of its fragrant, creamy blossoms, attractive furry foliage, and general all-around adaptability and reliability. The blossoms come late in May, are single, 2¼ inches across, and are pale yellow to white with a yellow throat. The fragrance, which presumably comes from the American Swamp Azalea *(R. viscosum)* in its parentage, makes it a desirable plant to have near an entrance to the house.

Because 'Daviesii' is tall and narrow and consequently a bit leggy it needs lower shrubs around it. I once featured a group near the doorway of a horizontal-lined, contemporary house, enclosed, as in a jewel box, with a low, 12-inch hedge of clipped Dwarf Japanese Yew (*Taxus cuspidata* 'Nana') and underplanted them with the crinkly, slower-growing, evergreen Ivy *Hedera helix* 'Shamrock.' This provided enough winter green and horizontal line to show off the verticality of the Azalea stems and provided an extremely happy setting for the late-May spectacle.

The breeding of 'Daviesii' is part of a fascinating story. By 1800 most of the native American Azaleas were being grown in European gardens as well as our own. In 1792 seeds had been sent to England of the eastern European Pontic Azalea *(Rhododendron flavum)*. During the first two decades of the new century the Chinese Azalea *(R. molle)* was brought to England on the ships of the East India Company and made its way into European gardens by 1836. This set the stage for a most exciting period in Azalea breeding, as the Chinese Azalea had large, more open flowers than the narrower, longer-tubed

American and Pontic types and provided another source of yellow. Hybridizing began in Ghent around 1820, when the baker P. Mortier crossed the two Americans, *R. calendulaceum* x *R. nudiflorum* (one can speculate that he may have used the heat from his ovens to get the late flowerer to bloom with the early flowerer). Subsequently, J. R. Gowen, gardener to the Earl of Caernarvon in Wales, crossed two Americans: *R. calendulaceum* and *R. viscosum*, with the Pontic Azalea and, later, *R. viscosum* with *R. molle*, the newly arrived Chinese Azalea. This later cross was also made by Isaac Davies of Ormskirk, England, around 1840, producing the clone here considered, which bears his name. These and other crosses made during the same period were culled over by Verschaffelt of Ghent, who named over one hundred of them. The whole hybrid group is known as the "Ghent hybrids" and those of Gowen and Davies, using the *viscosum-molle* parentage, as "Viscosepalum hybrids." In my experience 'Daviesii' is one of the most satisfactory performers of the whole complex.

72

Rhododendron x *kurume* 'Pink Pearl' (*R.* x *kurume* 'Azuma-Kagami')

'Pink Pearl' Azalea

It would be difficult to imagine a present-day American garden center or housing development without the color of evergreen Azaleas, particularly red ones: either *Rhododendron* x *kurume* 'Hinodigiri' or one of its so-called "improved" forms. However, for the discriminating gardener, there are also many forms in shades of pink, red, and purple, as well as white.

SEASONAL INTEREST

Evergreen
Effective landscape height: 6 feet
Effective landscape spread: 6 feet
Zone 7
Ericaceae (Heath Family)
Hybrid origin

The Kurume variety 'Pink Pearl' is one of the best. It is the only evergreen variety hardy in my area which is a true *soft* pink. Various writers list it as clear pink (Domoto), salmon-rose with a lighter center (Bobbink and Atkins), deep pink (E. H. Wilson), violet-pink (or phlox-pink) flushed with a darker pink (F. P. Lee). Such descriptions are often misleading because they are made by looking at a single flower *close up*, shortly after it opens. The *overall* effect of 'Pink Pearl' as seen in a landscape setting during the full two-week period it is effective is of the sort of soft pink one finds inside the ear of a white rabbit! As such, it is a marvelous "blender."

With the exciting palette of vivid Azalea colors that are available, it is a natural temptation to want to combine some of the shades. White is often recommended as a blender when this is done. I cannot agree! Look at a mass of many-colored Azaleas with some whites included, and your eye goes immediately to the whites; they poke holes in the whole picture. Remove them and the eye feels satisfied with a rich and harmonious blend, particularly if some of the soft pink of 'Pink Pearl' is included.

As with most Kurumes, 'Pink Pearl' blooms early in the Azalea season, early to mid-May. Its flowers are single, sometimes semi-double, 2 inches in diameter, and always hose-in-hose. Its chief drawback is limited hardiness, sometimes giving trouble in my area. I have observed that protection from wind, planting in a situation with light evergreen shade or at least protection from early morning sun, and placing in a setting where it dries out and hardens off early in the fall, all help to guarantee glossy foliage and fat buds in good condition in May.

The interest of Americans in highly colored evergreen Azaleas dates only from 1915. That year at the Panama-Pacific Exposition in San Francisco, the nurseryman Kojiro Akashi from the town of Kurume, on the Japanese island of Kyushu, exhibited thirty Azalea plants in a dozen varieties. He received a gold medal. The California nursery of Domoto Brothers began an importation program from Japan,

Rhododendron x *kurume* 'Pink Pearl'

which was later aided and abetted by Ernest Wilson of the Arnold Arboretum, Bobbink and Atkins Nurseries of Rutherford, New Jersey, and Henry A. Dreer Company of Riverton, New Jersey. The private estates of John S. Ames in Massachusetts and Henry F. du Pont at Winterthur, Delaware, were among the first to recognize the outstanding virtues of the group and acquire collections. According to Akashi, the Kurume hybrids originated a century before with Motozo Sakamoto, who had raised and selected seedlings of Azaleas growing on the sacred mountain Kirishima, near Kurume.

There has been much speculation as to exactly what parentage is involved in this group. Although *R. obtusum* was long assumed to be the principal parent, Dr. John Creech, director of the National Arboretum in Washington, D.C., now feels that *R. kaempferi*, *R. kiusianum*, and *R. sataense* are of more significance. *R. kaempferi* and *R. kiusianum* grow on Mt. Kirishima today and although *R. sataense* does not, it is elsewhere on the island of Kyushu and several of its unique characteristics appear in the Kurume group.

'Pink Pearl' was apparently the same plant listed as 'Azuma-Kagami' by Domoto Brothers, as the two names are used synonymously by Bobbink and Atkins in their catalogs for 1922–1929 and by Ernest Wilson in listing his 1919 selection of fifty "best" varieties (Cox, 1961).

Interest stimulated by the introduction of the Kurumes triggered further Azalea introduction and breeding, particularly with an eye to producing hardier varieties. Thus, Akashi's exhibit was responsible for a greater proliferation of plant varieties in the United States than has occurred in any other plant group, with the probable exception of Roses. Unfortunately, among the newer, hardier selections there is none with flowers of as good a soft pink as 'Pink Pearl.'

73

SEASONAL INTEREST

Deciduous
Effective landscape height: 6 feet
Effective landscape spread: 6 feet
Zone 5
Ericaceae (Heath Family)
Native range: Korea, Manchuria

Rhododendron schlippenbachii
Royal Azalea

The handsome form and foliage, hardiness, and constantly reliable performance of Royal Azalea, combined with its outstanding bloom characteristics, make it a true garden aristocrat. Since the plants are customarily grown from seed, the funnel-shaped flowers appearing in late April may vary in color and size. Being generally 2–4 inches in diameter, they are white, flushed violet-red to rose-pink; the throat is dotted with brown. They have a faint fragrance. Certainly there is nothing finer than the deeper pink forms, and these should be selected and propagated asexually as clones. The leaves are large, wedge-shaped, and carried in handsome whorls of five at the end of the stem. Suffused in early spring with purplish-red, the leaves glow with tints of orange in the autumn and are the largest and most striking among Azaleas. The plant is compact in form and generally nearly as broad as it is tall. In addition, it has a special quality of sturdiness that is particularly attractive. The branches are thick but graceful and in happy proportion with the fat winter buds.

Royal Azaleas should not be crowded. They are better spaced as individuals so that the "gem setting" growth habit with which the handsome blooms are displayed can be clearly seen in the spring. For a strictly "one-season" impact of great charm there is nothing finer than a planting of Royal Azalea and Shadblow *(Amelanchier canadensis)* underplanted with blue Grape-hyacinths *(Muscari armeniacum)*. The delicacy of the white *Amelanchier* blossoms is a marvelous contrast with the boldness of the *Rhododendron schlippenbachii* flowers. The carpet of blue brings out the richer pink tones in the *R. schlippenbachii* blossoms.

The practice of lightening an all-evergreen planting by the addition of a few deciduous shrubs is highly recommended, and Royal Azalea is an ideal plant for the purpose. The tan twigs and buds of six to eight Royal Azaleas silhouetted against a group of three or four Hemlocks and surrounded with clumps of *Liriope muscari* 'Big Blue' make a winter picture with fine textural interest and a most attractive promise of things to come. The abundant, large pink blossoms in May would find a rich setting midst the contrasting textures and greens of the companion plants. Although in the setting described the eye-catching foliage of Royal Azalea combined with the needly Hemlock would be reward enough in the summer, the blue flower spikes of *Liriope* (seen above strap-shaped leaves) would definitely enliven the scene.

Good, well-drained soil with plenty of organic matter is all that is needed to make this plant happy. The late Peter Van Melle believed it needs less acidity than most Azaleas. When the soil acidity gets higher, it does respond to extra feeding. It comes easily from seed for any gardener who can be that patient for his reward.

Royal Azalea was discovered in Korea in 1854 by Baron A. von Schlippenbach of the Russian navy. It was introduced into Europe in 1893, and into this country by the Arnold Arboretum in 1905 from seed sent from Korea by its renowned propagator John George Jack; then re-introduced by seeds from Japan between 1930 and 1936 by the Plant Introduction section of the United States Department of Agriculture.

This plant has been the recipient of three awards. From the Royal Horticultural Society in England it received an Award of Merit in 1896, a First Class Certificate in 1944, and an Award of Garden Merit in 1969.

Rhododendron schlippenbachii

74

Rhododendron vaseyi

'Pink Shell' Azalea

SEASONAL INTEREST

Deciduous
Effective landscape height: 6-9 feet
Effective landscape spread: 5-8 feet
Zone 5
Ericaceae (Heath Family)
Native range: United States—mountains of western North Carolina

It is hard to believe that such superb delicacy and grace can exist in a woody plant as is the case with 'Pink Shell' Azalea. This plant is upright in habit, has very slender twigs, and is the exemplification of the sympodial habit, for which deciduous Azaleas and Dogwoods are known. The flower buds are fat in contrast to the slender twigs, and open to single Tyrian-rose-colored flowers in May before the leaves appear. The throat of the flower is green; it is charmingly winged with orange dots at the base of the upper petals. The overall effect is airy and most refreshing. The foliage turns crimson to purple in the autumn.

Rhododendron vaseyi has a preference for moist, acid soils. It seems to do equally well in sun or light shade. There is a pond near my home, the banks of which are planted with clumps of *Rhododendron vaseyi* backed by a large group of Doublefile Viburnum *(Viburnum plicatum forma tomentosum)*. Not every year is the season such that they bloom together—the Viburnum sometimes being later—but when they do it is a combination of unforgettable beauty. Another nearby lightly wooded stream valley is a Jackson Pollock splatter of ferns, Spring Beauties, emerging May-apples, Dogwoods, and clumps of 'Pink Shell' Azaleas every year. This Azalea is pretty much a one-season plant but a real gem!

Rhododendron vaseyi was discovered on Balsam Mountain in North Carolina by George L. Vasey in 1878. It is placed in the subseries Canadense composed of the two North American species *R. vaseyi* and *R. canadense* and the Japanese species *R. pentaphyllum* and *R. albrechtii*. Interestingly enough, this subseries does not include any of the other American deciduous Azaleas such as *R. viscosum, R. nudiflorum, R. canescens, R. arborescens, R. calendulaceum, R. speciosium, R. roseum, R. serrulatum,* and *R. atlanticum.*

England's Royal Horticultural Society gave *Rhododendron vaseyi* an Award of Garden Merit in 1927.

75

Ribes odoratum
Nutmeg-Bush, Clove Currant,
Missouri or Buffalo Currant

The absolutely charming, fragrant yellow flowers provide the chief reason for growing this shrub. The sharp yellow, tubular blossoms are clustered, five to ten together, in a pendant fashion, and each is flushed reddish at the base. Born at the same time the new foliage appears in late April, they literally cover the plant. There is no better shrub for spring fragrance. It is an old-time garden favorite and has been called Nutmeg-Bush or Clove Currant, depending on how the inhaler interpreted the fragrance.

Its habit is what some persons might call "lax" and can variously be described as pendulous or even awkward. It is always open, never dense, and has attractively shaped, shiny grayish-green leaves, which turn more or less red in the fall—a western exposure favoring greater coloration.

Because of its intriguing blossoms, Clove Currant is a nice detail among details. There is no more charming picture than this plant amongst drifts of blue Grape-hyacinths *(Muscari armeniacum)* and Guinea-hen-flowers *(Frittilaria meleagris).* Because of its pendulous nature, *Ribes odoratum* is very effective seen hanging over a stone wall. It likewise

SEASONAL INTEREST

Deciduous
Effective landscape height: 6 feet
Effective landscape spread: 6 feet
Zone 5
Saxifragaceae (Saxifrage Family)
Native range: United States—Great Plains area

makes a happy combination with the verticality of our native Red-cedar *(Juniperus virginiana)*, with foliage rich in both yellow-greens and black-greens, and the horizontality of a hedge of the broadleaf Dwarf Japanese Holly (*Ilex crenata* 'Helleri').

The reason Clove Currant is not seen in more gardens today is largely because most nurserymen have given up growing it. The nurserymen have been discouraged by the United States Department of Agriculture restrictions on interstate shipment of the plant, which are in effect in twenty-five states. Like many Currants *(Ribes)*, it is the alternate host for White Pine blister rust, a disease affecting all five-needled pines. Therefore, it is a plant for gardens without five-needled pines nearby and for gardeners who would enjoy the challenge of searching it out from old local gardens.

Propagation is relatively easy. In Yorkshire, Alice Coats (1965) tells us, "the tradition was that it must always be grown in a bottle. Cuttings taken in the spring were inserted in a bottle of water on a window sill, and when they had developed roots the bottle was smashed and the slips planted out." Frankly, it is such a heady treasure as to be worth a great deal of effort.

Ribes odoratum has long been cultivated in British and American gardens as *Ribes aureum* and called the "Golden" Currant. Both are American plants, but the latter has much smaller flowers and is generally less ornamental. *Ribes odoratum* comes from the Great Plains.

76

Rhus typhina 'Laciniata'
Cutleaf Sumac,
Staghorn Sumac

STRUCTURAL INTEREST

Deciduous
Effective landscape height: 10 feet
Effective landscape spread: indefinite
Zones 3-4
Anacardiaceae (Cashew Family)
Native range: eastern North America

The yellow-green, cutleaf foliage of this suckering shrub makes it a valuable garden plant where space permits. In summer the 18-inch compound leaves with their deeply incised (4½-inch) leaflets have much the same quality as the cymbotium fern used for church wedding decorations. Because of their great size, the leaves provide a strong horizontal note. These leaves turn rich shades of red and orange in the fall. Greenish female flowers born in June and July produce erect, conical clusters of hairy, crimson-russet fruits in late summer. In winter the appropriateness of the common name of the type, Staghorn Sumac, is most apparent due to the velvety covering of reddish hairs on the newer growth. The total character of the plant at this time of year is open, irregular, and upright, almost completely the opposite of its summer effect.

Untended it makes a wide-spreading, sparsely branched shrub. Where its use justifies the effort, suckers can persistently be removed to encourage the formation of a small specimen tree of gaunt, muscled structure. When handled in this manner, a tropical, or at least exotic, effect is created, which makes it a rich and appropriate companion for the purer forms of contemporary architecture. I have seen it used most effectively in a raised planter with its dramatic foliage silhouette against the weathered rough-sawn siding of a contemporary shopping center.

It can also be handled as a cut-back shrub in situations where its foliage is valuable but its height is undesirable. To do this, the stems are cut almost to the ground each year; when new shoots appear, all but one or two are eliminated. Assuming adequate fertilizer and moisture are applied, erect stems, 5–6 feet high, will be produced with leaves 3 feet long— the leaflets correspondingly large.

Cutleaf Sumac's fine-textured foliage has a definite cooling and lightening effect in the summer landscape, when we depend more heavily on the effect of foliage contrasts than in the spring and fall. Also, the light green color of its foliage seems to produce a synergistic effect of great impact when used with red- and purple-foliaged plants. This is enhanced further by the shades of orange that often creep into the Sumac foliage during late summer.

In a large-scale situation, a heavy bank of *Rhus typhina* 'Laciniata' planted in front of a grouping of three or four Redleaf Beeches (*Fagus sylvatica* 'Riversi') can be extremely effective. Space permitting, a foreground sweep of Redleaf Barberry (*Berberis thunbergii* 'Atropurpurea') accented with a large clump of the blue-green, fig-like foliage of Plume-poppy *(Macleaya cordata)* would further enrich the picture.

In smaller quarters, Cutleaf Sumac can play a most significant role as part of a textural potpourri that spells lushness and refreshment. The background here might be a clump of the extremely vertical, fine-foliaged Yellowgroove Bamboo *(Phyllostachys aureosulcata)* and a sprawling specimen of the broad-foliaged Purpleleaf Smoke-Tree (*Cotinus coggygria* 'Foliis Purpureis'). The horizontality of the Cutleaf Sumac would contrast richly with these plants. In the foreground a broadleaf ground cover of either the cabbage-like *Bergenia cordifolia* or the garden Blackeyed Susan, *Rudbeckia fulgida* var. *sullivanti* 'Goldsturm,' would repeat the broad texture of the Smoke-Tree and might be accented with a single clump of a Redleaf Canna. There are innumerable variations which might be made on this theme. The spiky foliage of Siberian Iris *(Iris siberica)* might be substituted for the Canna, the even broader foliage of *Clerodendron trichotomum* for the Smoke-Tree, and if greater space was available, the fine-textured foliage of Dawn-redwood *(Metasequoia glyptostroboides)* or Golden-larch *(Pseudolarix amabilis)* for the Bamboo.

Natively, Sumac is most often found growing in dry upland positions, making it a valuable plant for adverse conditions. On a poor, dry soil it will outshine most other shrubs, and it also appears to be quite resistant to air pollution. The bark and leaves are rich in tannic acid and, according to W. J. Bean (1951), its juice is one of the best possible marking inks, being indelible on linen.

The English, always quick to recognize the ornamental value of native plants we Americans take for granted, have used *Rhus typhina* in their gardens since the reign of James I. Their Royal Horticultural Society has given *Rhus typhina* 'Laciniata' two awards: Award of Merit in 1910 and Award of Garden Merit in 1969.

77

Salix repens var. *argentea*
Creeping Miniature Pussy Willow

Whereas the commonly grown Pussy Willow *(Salix caprea)* is a somewhat gross and rangy plant, *Salix repens* var. *argentea* is a neat, diminutive little gem. Never exceeding 4 feet in height, this shrub spreads by means of creeping underground stems, making an excellent ground-cover shrub. The tiny silvery catkins (¼–¾ inch long) appear in April and thickly coat the thin, vertical branches. During the summer the glaucous gray foliage is also extremely attractive. Leaves are narrow ovals, ¼–¾ inch long, bluegray above and lighter gray below. The spiky new tip growth is lighter and very silky. The overall effect is rich, spiky gray, multidirectional—much

SEASONAL INTEREST

Deciduous
Effective landscape height: 4 feet
Effective landscape spread: indefinite
Zone 5
Salicaceae (Willow Family)
Native range: Europe and northern Asia

Salix repens var. argentea

like a terrier's hair. The appearance is equally charming during the winter because of the stem coloration, which is reddish-brown highlighted with purple.

Salix repens var. *argentea* performs best in poor soil of average to high moisture conditions similar to its native habitat along the Atlantic coasts of Europe. Rich soil causes it to overgrow, losing much of its natural beauty and making it more subject to fungus diseases.

Under moist conditions a most attractive grouping might feature a single Redtwig Dogwood *(Cornus sericea)* against a grouping of six to eight of the native, evergreen Inkberry Hollies *(Ilex glabra* 'Densa') backed by a mixture of, say, three Alders *(Alnus incana)* and three large catkined Pussy Willows *(Salix gracilistyla)*. The planting would be completed by a ground-cover planting of *Salix repens* var. *argentea* in the foreground. In April the catkins of the Willows and Alders in a variety of sizes and colors would make a happy symphony. The fine details of the red twigs of *Cornus sericea* and miniature catkins of *Salix repens* var. *argentea* would be dramatized by the evergreen background provided by the *Ilex glabra* 'Densa.'

Under drier conditions, another fine spring picture could be painted using a single specimen plant of the horizontal branching, Yellow-Flowered Dogwood, *Cornus officinalis*, in a mass planting of ten or twelve of the *Salix*. In the foreground three plants of the fragrant, purple-flowered Daphne, *D. mezereum rubrum*, could be planted midst a sea of diminutive April-flowering bulbs, including yellow-flowered Winter Aconite *(Eranthis hyemalis)*, white-flowered *Leucojum vernum*, and the rich blue *Iris reticulata* 'Royal Blue.' It is important that this grouping be intimately visible from a window of the house. Because of the diminutive scale of all of the blossoms and catkins, the charm would be very much decreased if seen from a greater distance. A rich color experience would result from the play of the blues, purples, and grays of the Iris, Daphne, and Pussy Willow against the yellows and whites of the Dogwood, Winter Aconite, and *Leucojum.*

In a larger-scale situation, the vertical lines of *Salix repens* var. *argentea* (used as a ground cover) might be contrasted against the rounded form of Redleaf Barberry (*Berberis thunbergii* 'Atropurpurea') in the middle ground and the horizontal form of Corkbark Euonymous *(Euonymous alatus)* in the background. The gray foliage of the Willow would make a handsome contrast with the red of the Barberry all summer and the flame of the Euonymous come fall.

Salix repens var. *argentea* was introduced into this country in colonial times but apparently must wait for greater maturity on the part of the gardening public to be widely appreciated. It is not, unfortunately, much used at present.

78

Stranvaesia davidiana var. *undulata*
Chinese Stranvaesia

This broad, sprawling Chinese evergreen has attractive foliage all year and provides some very special interest during the winter months and on into early spring. It has narrow leaves (½–1¼ inches), anywhere from 1½–3½ inches long, sometimes having slightly wavy margins. These leaves are a rich, glossy, apple-green during the summer, turning darker green in the winter—even bronze and sometimes red when the plant is grown in full sun. The leaves make the perfect setting for the large, pendulous clusters of ¼-inch, bright scarlet-red berries which persist the entire winter. The quality of the berry color and texture is perfectly balanced with the quality of the foliage color and texture. The stems of the fruit are a wine color as are the stems of the leaves. The red of the fruit is not just red; there is a "Day-Glo" quality about it that has great

SEASONAL INTEREST

Evergreen
Effective landscape height: 8 feet
Effective landscape spread: 15 feet
Zone 7
Rosaceae (Rose Family)
Native range: western China

Stranvaesia davidiana var. undulata

impact. The foliage-fruit combination, seen in the midst of a bleak winter landscape, has a quality of real magic about it. The visual impression stays with one a long time.

The new growth is an attractive bronze-red and comes early in the spring. In fact, in this area, it is often nip and tuck as to whether late frost will catch the Stranvaesia sprouts. Small white flowers come in terminal clusters in late May but fall quickly.

Stranvaesia is an excellent material to cut for Christmas decorations. The plant also lends itself very well to training on a wall as an informal espalier. Plenty of space must be allowed if it is to develop into its natural shrub form.

The strength of dark green and gold companion plants balances well with the intensely rich qualities of Stranvaesia. The dark green needly texture of six English Weeping Yews (*Taxus baccata* 'Repandens') and one Oriental Spruce *(Picea orientalis)*, the former in front of a grouping of four Stranvaesia and the latter behind, would provide just the textural contrast needed. The whole combination could be highlighted by one plant of Yellowtwig Dogwood (*Cornus sericea* 'Flaviramea') among the Yews and a foreground planting of Periwinkle (*Vinca minor* 'Bowles') and the early-spring-blooming Adonis *(Adonis amurensis)*, a low, tuberous plant with ferny foliage and yellow flowers.

This theme could be varied in a larger-scale situation by planting three tall, narrow Incense-cedars *(Calocedrus decurrens)* with a mass grouping of nine Stranvaesias, using the spiky, broadleaf Ivy *Hedera helix* 'Conglomerata Erecta,' as a ground cover with a foreground accent of one dwarfish Golden Thread Cypress (*Chamaecyparis pisifera* 'Filifera Aurea Nana'). The bright green needles of the Incense-cedars and the dark green, arrow-shaped foliage of the Ivy would provide exciting textural contrast to the Stranvaesias. The Golden Cypress would accent the whole scene with the same electric quality as the Stranvaesia berries.

Another, more relaxed version of this theme might include three Japanese Black Pines *(Pinus thun-*

bergii) with a grouping of four Stranvaesias as well
as featuring three untrimmed Dwarf Japanese Yews
(*Taxus cuspidata* 'Nana') in a sea of chartreuse-
foliaged Variegated Liriope (*Liriope muscari* 'Variegata') in the foreground. The informal habit, needly texture, and black-green of the pines and yews
would provide a structure and a contrast that would
feature the Stranvaesia nicely. The color of the
narrow, strap-shaped foliage on the Liriope would
have the same lively quality as the Stranvaesia
berries.

Because this Stranvaesia shows no signs of winter
injury here in Zone 6, I speculate that it must be
hardy farther north. I have no confirming information on this, however. The foliage does seem to
remain in its best condition all winter when protected from strong wind.

Forms of *Stranvaesia davidiana* were collected in
Yunnan, China, about 1900 by Ernest H. Wilson,
then collecting for James Veitch & Sons of England.
S. davidiana var. *undulata* is the best selection. In
1922 it received both an Award of Merit and an
Award of Garden Merit from the Royal Horticultural Society. The earliest collections of the species
were made in western China in the early 1870's by
the Jesuit missionary-explorer Abbé Armand David
(1826–1900). So far as is known, none of David's
material came back to France alive (only as dried
specimens).

79

Syringa × *chinensis*
Chinese Lilac, Rouen Lilac

This is a delightful, mounded, billowy shrub covered
with foamy purple flower heads at tulip time, early
to mid-May. Although there are many Lilac hybrids

SEASONAL INTEREST

Deciduous
Effective landscape height: 6 feet
Effective landscape spread: 8 feet
Zone 6
Oleaceae (Olive Family)
Garden origin

and clonal selections that have larger, more spectacular blossoms, none in my opinion can equal this plant for overall landscape effect. The fan-shaped branching habit leaves no ugly stems revealed; the fine, narrow leaves are a comfortable texture to associate with other plants; the blossoms more fully cover the entire plant than do those of traditional French hybrid Lilacs; and the fine twigs enable the blossoms and foliage to move gracefully in the breeze.

It is a perfect foil for the many riotous color associations of mid-May and is an easy plant to use from a design standpoint. One of my favorite combinations is to back it with *Viburnum macrocephalum forma macrocephalum*, with its enormous white blossoms, featuring an accent of one or three soft yellow Warminster Brooms (*Cytisus* x *praecox* 'Luteus') in the foreground surrounded by tulips in many shades and underplanted with the light blue *Phlox divaricata*.

It is easy to grow in full sun and good loam and practically never needs any pruning, save to remove dead or damaged wood.

Syringa x *chinensis* is believed to be a hybrid of *S.* x *persica* x *S. vulgaris*, first raised in the Botanic Garden at Rouen about 1777. It is often mistakenly sold in the nursery trade as *Syringa* x *persica*, but the latter is less desirable, with its smaller flowers of a paler lavender. The variety *Syringa* x *chinensis* 'Saugeana' is a highly desirable selection, featuring lilac-red flowers. *Syringa* x *chinensis* was recognized with an Award of Garden Merit from the British Royal Horticultural Society in 1969.

Syringa x *chinensis*

80

Taxus baccata 'Repandens'
Spreading English Yew,
Weeping English Yew

STRUCTURAL INTEREST

Evergreen
Effective landscape height: 3-4 feet
Effective landscape spread: 6-8 feet
Zone 6
Taxaceae (Yew Family)
Native range: Europe, North Africa, western Asia

"Soft" and "graceful" are the adjectives that best describe this excellent garden plant. Although sometimes referred to as Weeping English Yew, I feel that "weeping" is a misnomer. The branches are not normally pendulous in the cascade-like manner of Sargent's Hemlock. Instead, they are generally ascendant to horizontal. However, the tip growth hangs down slightly, and all the side shoots on each branch are pendulous or at least not above the horizontal. When the plant grows at ground level, this produces a most graceful effect resembling a ground cover. When grown at the top of a wall or in a planter, the weight of the side branches eventually brings them down below soil level and an excellent cascade effect occurs. The needles are slightly longer and thinner than other varieties regularly available, and the color is a rich dark green.

One advantage of Spreading English Yew is that it will do just as well in light shade as in full sun. It is, of course, a perfect texture for contrasting with broadleaf evergreens. Its thick growth with both spiky and pendant qualities enables it to blend happily with other plants: horizontal, round, ascendant, or pyramidal in form. In fact, *Taxus baccata* 'Repandens' is of practically unlimited usefulness.

In a shady situation it makes an excellent ground cover to use with the broad, golden variegated leaves of *Aucuba japonica* 'Croton.' Such a planting might well include the pyramidal, small-leaved Perny Holly *(Ilex pernyi)* as a background. The branches of this Holly develop an arching character in the shade, which would pick up some of the charming rhythm of the Yew foliage.

In a sunny spot Spreading English Yew would make an excellent ground cover for association with three of the pyramidal bronze-leaved Hollies, *Ilex aquifolium* 'Ciliata Major.' In this case, a single plant of a Whitestem Raspberry (*Rubus cockburnianus, R. biflorus,* or *R. leucodermis*) among the Yew would add a strong note of winter interest. The milky blush of the Raspberry would echo the pink shades in the Holly leaves; its arching habit would relate well to the habit of the Yew.

In a larger area *Taxus baccata* 'Repandens' contrasts delightfully with the broad evergreen foliage of *Magnolia grandiflora.* One Magnolia, three plants of Corkbark Euonymous *(Euonymous alatus),* and a ground cover of Spreading English Yew would make a charming contrast of forms and textures. A single plant of the golden-banded grass *Miscanthus sinensis* 'Zebrinus' among the Yew would provide a chartreuse accent that would enliven the whole scene in summer. The form of the grass would echo the Yew's habit, and its seed heads in the fall would provide an interesting contrast both in texture and form with the red-foliaged, later corky-barked Euonymous.

Taxus baccata 'Repandens' requires a good, well-drained soil and resents root competition from other plants. Otherwise, it is an easy plant to grow. Because it is slower-growing than most Yews, it is seldom necessary to prune it.

Yews are the most universally planted evergreen shrub in the United States, and there are a number of varieties to choose from. Four species are commonly grown: *Taxus baccata,* which has 99 known varieties, hybrids, and cultivars; *Taxus canadensis,* which has 4; *Taxus cuspidata,* which has 20; and *Taxus* x *media,* which has 15.

Taxus baccata 'Repandens' was introduced into this country around 1887. It and *Taxus baccata* 'Fowles Variety' are the two hardiest English Yews commonly grown here and are certainly two of the most outstanding Yew varieties. *Taxus baccata* 'Repandens' received a well-deserved Award of Garden Merit from the Royal Horticultural Society in England in 1969.

81

Taxus × *media* 'Sentinalis'
Vermeulen Sentinel Yew

Vermeulen Sentinel Yew is the narrowest, dark green, vertical evergreen available for use in gardens in this area. An 8-foot plant may be no more than 16 inches across at the widest point. Rather rectilinear in young form, the plant becomes more cigar-shaped at maturity. The vertical branches are packed very tightly together and the bright green needles are thick on the branches. Each of the extensions is vertical but grows at differing rates. One branch may put on only 1½ inches of growth while an adjacent branch may grow 4 inches. This irregularity is definitely a part of this Yew's charm and explains the richness of its color impact; one's eye responds to black-green deep inside the plant, the dark yellow-green of the exterior growth, and the brighter, lighter yellow-green of new growth shoots. In addition, the plant bears red berries in the fall.

From a design standpoint, such a rich phallic symbol becomes strong accent material and must be used carefully for best effect. Matched pairs, fours, sixes, and eights are useful in formal situations, and clusters of varying heights may be useful in informal groupings. Its strongest use is, of course, as a single specimen. Companion plants of rounded or horizontal form work well with Vermeulen Sentinel Yew. Pendulous forms indicate a direction of motion in opposition to the Yew and set up an undesirable tension.

STRUCTURAL INTEREST

Evergreen
Effective landscape height: 8 feet
Effective landscape spread: 16 inches
Zone 5
Taxaceae (Yew Family)
Hybrid origin

Taxus x *media* 'Sentinalis'

A grouping of three *Taxus* x *media* 'Sentinalis' of varying heights would produce a striking effect against the gray-green of the moundy, broad-leaved Fragrant Elaeagnus (*Elaeagnus pungens* 'Fruitlandii'). A group of the flat, dark green Helleri Japanese Hollies (*Ilex crenata* 'Helleri') planted as a ground cover around the Yews would provide a handsome contrast.

A single Vermeulen Sentinel Yew planted in a group of five moundy, shiny-leaved Dwarf Chinese Hollies (*Ilex cornuta* 'Rotunda') would make a really strong statement planted against one of the horizontally branching Corkbark Euonymous *(Euonymous alatus)*. In a small-scale situation a single Vermeulen Sentinel Yew would make an especially fine solo impact in an all-gray planting: a ground cover of Woolly Lamb's Ear *(Stachys olympica)* might be accented with three clumps of *Salvia argentea* (with its larger rosettes of heavy, woolly leaves), and the planting backed with three plants of the gray-foliaged, Whitestem Barberry, *Berberis dictyophylla*.

The hybridization and introduction of Vermeulen Sentinel Yew is an interesting tale and a good example of the important role keen plantsmen play in modern horticulture. A Mr. Hicks of Hicks Nursery on Long Island collected seed at random from Yews in his nursery. Growing there were plants of *Taxus baccata, T. canadensis*, and *T. cuspidata*. Seedlings were sold to a Mr. Sexauer of Lake Grove, New York. There was considerable variation in the seedlings, indicating that chance hybridization among Hicks's plants had occurred. In 1933 the nurseryman John Vermeulen selected thirty plants that had "that tall slender look." *Taxus* x *media* 'Sentinalis' was one of seven that he decided were particularly worthwhile and introduced in 1946–1947. It is assumed that the parentage of this plant is *T. cuspidata* x *T. baccata*.

82

Tsuga canadensis 'Pendula'

Sargent's Weeping Hemlock,
Weeping Hemlock

STRUCTURAL INTEREST

Evergreen
Effective landscape height: 4½ feet
Effective landscape spread: 10 feet
Zone 5
Pinaceae (Pine Family)
Native range: New York State

This slow-growing, weeping form of one of our native Hemlocks *(Tsuga canadensis)* is a most useful garden subject. Sargent's Weeping Hemlock is a true weeper, having the peaceful but visually stimulating quality of a cascade. Unlike some "weeping" plants, there is nothing grotesque or freakish about it. The plant is generally twice as broad as it is tall, and the foliage is fine-needled and a dark yellow-green. As it matures, surface irregularities develop in its smooth form which enhance the whole picture, because of the attractive shadows created. With great age, the trunk and main stems become very muscled-looking and attractive as glimpsed through the pendulous fronds.

The first availability of *Tsuga canadensis* 'Pendula' occurred at a time when interest in unusual plants was running high in this country. Because of this fact and its hardiness, it was a frequent lawn feature of American estates of the late nineteenth and early twentieth centuries. Today it is equally popular as a specimen "softener" for the bold, simplified lines of contemporary architecture.

Sargent's Weeping Hemlock is especially attractive in conjunction with rocks and rock outcroppings. However, it does not grow well in impoverished, stony soil; fertile soil high in organic matter should be provided.

Aesthetically, Weeping Hemlock is most effective when seen just about at human eye level. This means that unless you are dealing with a really immense

old plant, it is best planted in a location above normal ground level. This might be as a specimen plant in a raised planter or grouped with other plants on a rising bank adjacent to the viewing area.

For gardeners enjoying contrasts in form and texture, it is a rich addition to the palette. Generally speaking, Weeping Hemlock is at its finest when backed with broadleaf foliage and provided with an interesting foreground planting.

A fine specimen of *Tsuga canadensis* 'Pendula' might be placed among some well-rounded rocks, with a background of three plants of 'Nellie R. Stevens' Holly (*Ilex* x 'Nellie R. Stevens'), with its very dark, broadleaf texture and orange-red berries. In the foreground, a ground-cover planting of the bright green Thyme *(Thymus serpyllum citridorus)* accented with one clump of the cabbage-like *Bergenia cordifolia* would provide strong interest.

Also, a Weeping Hemlock backed with a large planting of the spiky broadleaf foliage of *Yucca smalliana* could present a pleasing picture, with a foreground of red-foliaged Hen and Chicks *(Sempervivum)* ground cover accented with one *Sedum spectabile* 'Indian Chief.'

Another attractive combination would be a Weeping Hemlock backed with three dark-green-foliaged 'Otto Luykens' Cherry-laurels (*Prunus laurocerasus* 'Otto Luykens'), with a ground cover of Redleaf Ajuga (*Ajuga reptans* 'Metallica Crispa') accented with one clump of Variegated Liriope (*Liriope muscari* 'Variegata').

Sargent's Weeping Hemlock was discovered in the Fiskekill Mountains of New York by General Joseph Howland about 1857. It was first cultivated and introduced by Henry Winthrop Sargent (1810–1822), a student of the famous landscape architect Andrew Jackson Downing. The native Hemlock, *Tsuga canadensis*, is extremely variable; although this clone, 'Pendula,' is the best-known and most widely used variant, there are a host of others to choose from. In a monograph on Hemlocks, currently being prepared, there are 127 other major cultivars listed. Most of these are dwarf in nature and represent a host of potentially good garden plants for small properties. Needless to say, the slower a dwarf type grows, the more the nurseryman must charge for it.

83

Viburnum carlesii
Spice Viburnum

The Spice Viburnum is justifiably renowned for its highly attractive and fragrant blossoms. This is a fragilely branched, rounded shrub whose flowers appear before the foliage in late April or early May. The flower clusters open white, round-topped, and 3½ inches across. The peak of beauty is at the bud stage, when each floret composing the flower head is a tight, shiny, waxy pink bud. The fragrance is strong and delicious, being variously described as resembling cloves, daphne, and gardenias; it carries for at least forty feet. The fruit occurs irregularly and is dark blue. The leaves are dull green, grayish on the undersides; some turn reddish-purple in the fall.

Spice Viburnum is a welcome, early-spring-flowering dooryard plant because of its superior fragrance. Like so many spring plants valuable for the fleeting beauty of their blossoms, it has little to offer the balance of the year.

I once saw it used as the feature plant in each of four quadrants of a formal, four-square, box-edged parterre, underplanted with blue Periwinkle (*Vinca minor* 'Bowles') and a variety of diminutive spring bulbs. This was a charming one-season effect, and the pattern of the boxwood and four Japanese jardinieres on the corners carried the show the balance of the year.

Pink, blue, and chartreuse make a particularly exciting spring color combination. *Viburnum car-*

SEASONAL INTEREST

Deciduous
Effective landscape height: 5 feet
Effective landscape spread: 8 feet
Zone 5
Caprifoliaceae (Honeysuckle Family)
Native range: Korea

lesii can figure strikingly as the feature of such an arrangement using the pink hybrid Magnolia, *Magnolia* x *soulangeana* 'Verbanica,' as the background for the chartreuse puffs of Chinese Snowball *(Viburnum macrocephalum forma macrocephalum).* Spice Viburnum would repeat the rounded forms of these two in the foreground, planted in a sea of the blue creeping *Phlox stolonifera* 'Blue Ridge.'

Spice Viburnum was first discovered and described informally by William Richard Carles of the British consular service in Korea from 1883 to 1885. Its name and description appeared in a London journal in 1888. The form that we know (which does not come true from seed) was introduced from Korea into Japan in 1885; it was grown there and propagated by Alfred Unger of L. Boehmer and Company in Yokohama. Although dried specimens came to London from Carles in 1880, the first living plant was received at Kew in 1901. Five years later Boehmer's entire stock of it was sold to the firm of Lemoine (in France), which was responsible for its distribution.

When grown from seed, the offspring are often taller and rangier than selected garden plants and, although the fragrance is consistent, the flowers are of varying quality. As a result, the traditional practice has been to graft a desirable form onto *Viburnum lanata.* The latter suckers and there have been severe problems with disease at the graft union. Consequently some horticulturists have given higher ratings to some of the hybrids resulting from crosses using *Viburnum carlesii* as a parent—for example, *Viburnum* x *burkwoodii* (*V. carlesii* x *V. utile*), *Viburnum* x *carlcephalum* (*V. carlesii* x *V. macrocephalum*), and *Viburnum* x *juddii* (*V. carlesii* x *V. bitchuense*). The fact remains that although some of these have larger flowers and more attractive, glossier foliage, none of them has so fine a fragrance as *Viburnum carlesii.* Because it can be propagated from cuttings fairly well and techniques for doing so will probably improve, I continue to favor Spice Viburnum very highly above its children!

84

Viburnum ichangense

This large Asiatic shrub is valuable for its very showy, red berries, effective in September and October. The fruit is at the peak of its "performance" when the leathery, dark gray-green leaves are still in their prime. The very glossy red berries are small (3/16 inch) but clustered, eighty to ninety together, in heads which themselves often merge together on the plant. It is the combination of foliage and berries which makes this plant unusually beautiful. The better-known Linden Viburnum *(Viburnum dilitatum)* and *Viburnum wrightii* are similar, but their fruits are darker and with less sparkle and their foliage is not as good. *Viburnum ichangense* is slender-branched. The leaves are broad, pointed ovals. The flower clusters, which appear in May, are white and fragrant.

Companion plants with early fall interest present an opportunity for some really striking combinations. The rounded form of the Viburnum is brought into sharper focus when contrasted with open, ascendant forms of Dwarf Japanese Yew (*Taxus cuspidata* 'Nana') and Tea Crab Apple *(Malus hupehensis).* The Yew is, of course, dark green, and this color is echoed in the fruit of the Crab Apple, which is greenish-yellow to red. The fruits of the Crab Apple also create a teasing relationship with the red fruit of the Viburnum.

The round Viburnum form might also be associated with the spiky mounds of Yellowberry Firethorn (*Pyracantha coccinea* 'Aurea') and Fragrant Elaeagnus (*Elaeagnus pungens* 'Fruitlandii'). One clump of Plume Grass *(Erianthus ravennae)* added to this combination would provide a stimulating vertical accent. The yellow berries of the Firethorn would relate strongly with the gray of the Elaeagnus

SEASONAL INTEREST

Deciduous
Effective landscape height: 9 feet
Effective landscape spread: 12 feet
Zone 6
Caprifoliaceae (Honeysuckle Family)
Native range: central and western China

and *Erianthus* foliage and provide an appealing foil for the bright red and green of the Viburnum.

An exciting tricolor scheme might include purple as well as red and yellow. In addition to several plants of *Viburnum ichangense*, feature a single specimen Hardy-orange *(Poncirus trifoliata)*, with its green-yellow lemons. Plant the foreground with six or eight plants of the purple-fruited Japanese Beautyberry *(Callicarpa japonica)* and large drifts of the cheerful, yellow-flowered, fall bulb, *Sternbergia lutea*. Who said the garden must be dull in September?

Viburnum ichangense is undemanding in its requirements. Average garden soil plus occasional feeding is desirable. Fruiting is better in years with adequate summer moisture. Pruning should be limited to removal of dead wood and occasional thinning (in the case of very old plants).

This Viburnum comes from the Hupei province in China and was introduced first to England in 1901. It was collected by Dr. Augustine Henry, British collector in China from 1896 to 1900, and described by W. B. Hemsley in 1900 as a variety of *Viburnum erosum*. Eight years later Alfred Rehder at the Arnold Arboretum demonstrated it to be a species distinct from *V. erosum*.

85

SEASONAL INTEREST

Deciduous
Effective landscape height: 15 feet
Effective landscape spread: 15 feet
Zone 7
Caprifoliaceae (Honeysuckle Family)
Garden origin

Viburnum macrocephalum forma macrocephalum
Chinese Snowball Viburnum

For the entire month of May this handsome shrub puts on a spectacular show. Its snowball-like blossoms are greater in size than those of any other Viburnum, being 8–12 inches in diameter. The flowers have a marvelous chartreuse coloration in early May, gradually turning to pure white three weeks later. Unlike the wild form, the flowers are all the large, sterile kind and are so closely packed together in the head as to be unlike anything else in nature. The shrub is rounded and solid-looking, and clothed with 3½-inch-long handsome, pointed, oval, dark green leaves with a light green midvein. The current season's shoots bearing next year's growth buds and flower buds are coated with a greenish-white fuzz, giving the plant an appearance of special vigor and robustness.

During its chartreuse stage in early May, Chinese Snowball Viburnum combines well with the fine-textured, white-flowered *Spirea thunbergii*. This blend is a delightful combination with the Quince tribe and its many shades of red and pink. I recall with particular pleasure this combination with the soft pink *Chaenomeles speciosa* 'Apple Blossom' in the Winterthur Gardens in Delaware. In a larger-scale situation there, the chartreuse blossoms of *Viburnum macrocephalum forma macrocephalum* are a delightfully stimulating accent among the purply-pink blossoms of flowering Crab Apples— such as *Malus* x 'Red Silver,' *M. floribunda*, and *M. parkmanniana*. The blues of Grape-hyacinth *(Muscari armeniacum)*, *Tritilea*, and Virginia Blue-bells *(Mertensia virginica)* would make a wonderful carpet with any of the above, and the chartreuse blossoms of *Euphorbia Myrsinites* would provide a good repeat of the chartreuse Viburnum blossoms; the *Euphorbia* would be most effective as a restrained accent among the blue.

When the blossoms become full white in middle to late May, the plant combines beautifully with the blue-lavender of Chinese Lilac (*Syringa* x *chinensis*) and the soft, soft yellow of Warminster Broom (*Cytisus* x *praecox* 'Luteus'). This combination stands well on its own or can serve as a charming background for multicolored tulip plantings with yellow *Alyssum saxatile*.

The white blossoms usually continue to be effective as the blue and lavender, tall German iris and orange-and-tomato-colored Mollis Azaleas (*Rhodo-*

Viburnum macrocephalum forma macrocephalum

dendron x 'Kosterianum') reach their peak. Combined with a ground cover of fresh, fine fern foliage such as Hayscented Fern *(Dennstaedtia punctilobula)*, this can be as fine a picture as any of the earlier ones. There is probably no other spring-flowering shrub which has such a long season of interest and is effective in such a wide range of combinations. In addition, the solid mass of the plant, with its good foliage color and expression of vigor make it an asset all year.

I have found no cultural problems with the Chinese Snowball Viburnum. It has, in fact, surprised me in its ability to tolerate standing water in a poorly drained garden, performing just as well under these circumstances as Winterberry *(Ilex verticillata)*. *Viburnum macrocephalum forma macrocephalum* has made a fine espalier for me as well, seeming to be a natural for formal training.

This form of the plant is a "garden form" found in Chinese gardens and introduced to England by Robert Fortune in 1844 (for the Royal Horticultural Society). Fortune later discovered the less spectacular, flat-headed wild form with fertile flowers growing 20 feet high in Chusan, China, during his exploration there.

Viburnum macrocephalum forma macrocephalum received an Award of Merit from the Royal Horticultural Society in 1927.

86

SEASONAL INTEREST

Deciduous
Effective landscape height: 8-10 feet
Effective landscape spread: 10-12 feet
Zone 5
Caprifoliaceae (Honeysuckle Family)
Native range: China and Japan

Viburnum plicatum forma tomentosum
Doublefile Viburnum

Although Doublefile Viburnum is one of many white-flowered shrubs blooming in late May, it is uniquely distinctive in its floral effect. The bright green young foliage has already begun to unfold when the 4–5-inch flat white flower heads appear.

Each head is composed of a cluster of very tiny fertile flowers surrounded by a ring of larger (1-inch) sterile ones. These large outer florets are highly light-reflective. There is a wonderful jewel-like quality about the total blossom, which is accentuated by the way the heads are arranged in orderly double files on the upper sides of the nearly horizontal branches. Each head is perfectly horizontal as though checked by a carpenter's level and the flowers are closely spaced on the branches. The display is striking! The small fertile flowers in the center bear red fruits which later turn black. At least in my area this does not happen reliably and the fruits do not last long when it does. The leaves are apple-green, leathery, and deeply veined. It is a one-season plant but a backbone subject for that season.

Viburnum plicatum forma tomentosum can be used with the open, large-flowered white Azalea *Rhododendron* x *vuyk hybrid* 'Palestrina,' and the pendulous *Spirea vanhouttei* for a really delightful play on white in various forms. It can also be used with the butter-yellow "orange blossoms" of *Kerria japonica* and the lavender *Wisteria floribunda*, or with the purple-flowered Empress-Tree, *Paulownia tomentosa*, and the sharp yellow-flowered Tree Peony 'Golden Isles' (*Paeonia* x 'Golden Isles'), for a striking white, lavender, and yellow color scheme. In a large-scale situation, the wine-pink combination of 'Thundercloud' Plum (*Prunus cerasifera* 'Thundercloud') and 'Pink Pearl' Azalea (*Rhododendron* x *kurume* 'Pink Pearl') sparkles beautifully when combined with Doublefile Viburnum and a ground covering of blue *Scilla campanulata*.

Doublefile Viburnum has been cultivated as a garden plant in Japan and China for several centuries. It was first named and described in 1794 by Carl Peter Thunberg, a pupil of Carolus Linnaeus in Sweden, during his three-year stay in Japan. Robert Fortune first introduced it to England in 1865, and it was offered by nurserymen in the United States as early as 1872. It received an Award of Garden Merit from England's Royal Horticultural Society in 1969.

Viburnum plicatum forma tomentosum, close-up of flower

Viburnum plicatum forma tomentosum

87

SEASONAL INTEREST

Deciduous
Effective landscape height: 8-12 feet
Effective landscape spread: 12-15 feet
Zone 7
Verbenaceae (Vervain Family)
Native range: southern Europe, western Asia

Vitex agnus-castus 'Latifolia' *(Vitex macrophylla)*

Chaste-Tree, Monk's Pepper

This one-season flowering shrub is valuable both because the blossoms occur at a time when there is a dearth of bloom and because the blossom color is a good lavender-blue, a shade always in short supply in the garden. The 13-inch-long flower spikes literally cover the shrub during the third week in July. Superficially resembling the blossoms of the Butterfly-Bush, these flowers are stiffer and more spiky, giving *Vitex* strong structural qualities. This is, in fact, a reflection of its stiff, vertical, ascendant branching habit. The narrow, pointed leaves are clustered fan-like in groups of five. Seen close up the foliage color is a dark yellow-green. At a distance the total effect is more gray, a fact which tends to dissipate some of the floral effect.

There is a grouping of midsummer flowering shrubs at Winterthur Gardens (near Wilmington, Delaware) whose color impact is delightfully cooling and refreshing. This features the blue of *Vitex* with the architecturally handsome white blossoms of *Hydrangea paniculata grandiflora.* The combination is seen against a background of the bawdy pink powderpuff-like blossoms of the hardy Mimosa, *Albizia julibrissin* 'Rosea.' In the foreground is a planting of gracefully arching Butterfly-Bushes with blossoms in shades of pink and deep, deep purple (*Buddleia davidii* 'Black Knight'). This is sufficiently successful to bear copying. To add a ground cover of the 'Crimson Pygmy' Barberry (*Berberis thunbergii* 'Crimson Pygmy') would give a bit of tailoring to the whole scene, all of which would be most enjoyable as a close-up, potpourri kind of experience.

Vitex is equally effective when seen from a distance, especially when it is uphill of the viewer so that the lavender-blue blossoms can be seen against the lighter blue of summer skies. Whereas *Vitex* appears very spiky close up, it has much more of a soft, mounded character when seen from a distance. A few plants of *Vitex* clustered on a rise with a single twisty specimen of Japanese Black Pine *(Pinus thunbergii)* and a huge ground-cover sweep of the chartreusey-Golden Variegated Liriope (*Liriope muscari* 'Variegata') would make an unforgettable composition.

Because of the tendency for some wood to winter-kill in our area, *Vitex* is most effective as a cut-back shrub (that is, each winter the stems should be cut back to 4 feet or less). The following spring and summer the current season's growth reaches 6 feet by the time the blossoms occur, and the general appearance is neat and uniform, without need for cutting out dead wood. Plants allowed to grow naturally in the protection of cities do often, however, develop great character and can be quite charming, providing the owner is prepared to carefully hand prune dead wood after a severe winter. There is one in downtown Wilmington, Delaware, 12 feet high by 18 feet in spread. The main trunk is 12 inches in diameter and side branches are 6–8 inches in diameter. *Vitex*es are quite late in leafing out. Therefore, do not assume that the leafless stalks are dead until they have been thoroughly warmed by June sunshine. Ordinary to poor soil is adequate for *Vitex*. There are white and rose-colored forms.

Vitex is a Mediterranean plant, which was cultivated in England as early as 1570, and was mentioned by John Clayton and Thomas Jefferson as being in American colonial gardens. The Greeks still use the pliable shoots for basket-making. (The name *Vitex* comes from the Latin word *viere* to plait or weave.) According to Alice Coats (1965), Pliny attributed the origin of the plant's common name to the fact

Vitex agnus-castus 'Latifolia'

that "the dames of Athens during the feasts of the Goddess Ceres . . . make their pallets and beds thereof, to cool the heat of lust, and to keep themselves chaste for the time."

It apparently is an all-purpose shrub, however, because there is a strong belief in Mediterranean countries that it possesses aphrodisiac qualities, even going under the charming name of Monk's Pepper in some areas.

IV
GROUND COVERS

The total number of ground covers available to the landscape
architect is literally overwhelming. The thirteen chosen for
discussion here, therefore, must be regarded as a particularly arbitrary sample, a selection that I have found myself using frequently
to fill needs in my own garden and in designing gardens for
others. The list includes evergreen, deciduous, and herbaceous
plants. To any landscape planner, ground covers are tremendously
important design tools. They provide the low horizontal lines that
tie together all sorts of other plant shapes, textures, and colors,
creating unity where chaos might well reign. Together with lawn
grass, they are also tremendously valuable for defining the form
and shape of garden spaces. Those entries valued primarily for
their use in providing all-year structure to a garden are distinguished from those of strong seasonal interest. Most, of course,
serve both functions to some extent.

88

SEASONAL INTEREST

Deciduous
Effective landscape height: 30-36 inches
Effective landscape spread: indefinite
Zone 5
Gramineae (Grass Family)
Native range: Japan

Arundinaria viridistriata
Dwarf Golden Variegated Bamboo,
Variegated Ground-cover Bamboo

This vigorous, spreading ground cover is equally charming, but in distinctly different ways, if examined close up or seen at a distance. Seen closely, the vertical, 30-inch stems carry narrow (1-inch-wide), 7-inch-long leaves which are longitudinally striped with narrow bands of dark green, yellow-green, and butter-yellow. The width of the bands varies for different colors on the same leaf, and no two leaves have exactly the same pattern. The effect is charming and calls forth none of my past conditioning and prejudices against variegated plants. The effect from a distance is quite different, as the variegation blurs together netting out a very vibrant, cheerful chartreuse. This is a color not commonly available in ground covers, and since it is most effective during the summer months, it has a welcome cooling effect in its contrast with the duller greens of that season. As a ground cover, it gives a desirable vibrance and life to all the other plants in any grouping which it also pulls together.

In addition to contrasting effectively with other shades of green, I find its combination with oranges and wine-purples particularly stimulating. For orange try the annual *Tithonia rotundifolia* 'Torch,' the Trumpet-vine, *Campsis* x *tagliabuana* 'Madame Galen,' and the orange Day-lily, *Hemerocallis* x 'Shining Plumage.' For wine-purple try the annual foliage plant *Perilla fruticans* and the popular Redleaf Barberry, *Berberis thunbergii* 'Atropurpurea.'

There is one major drawback to this plant, which I must emphasize strongly. It is highly invasive! It spreads very rapidly by underground stems and cannot be controlled by any casual means. A friend who has done considerable work with Bamboos recommends surrounding the area in which you want *Arundinaria viridistriata* with an underground barrier. He prefers sheets of fiberglass (such as Filon) 24 inches wide, securely fastened together and placed with 21 inches below ground and 3 inches above. The sheets should be tilted with the top away from the planting area so that the pernicious roots will head upward once they contact the barrier. Should they start downward, they might still find their way out of confinement. More expensive but at least equally effective would be a masonry barrier. If you are fortunate enough to have a planter surrounded by masonry or a plant pocket in a terrace (paving on a concrete slab), you may well have a perfect location for Bamboo. Aside from needing an average well-drained soil, this plant has no demanding cultural requirements. The foliage is not terribly effective in the mid-Atlantic area until mid-June but is good from that time until frost.

Arundinaria viridistriata has been cultivated since the 1870's and was long known as *Bambusa fortunei aurea.*

89

Berberis thunbergii 'Crimson Pygmy'

'Crimson Pygmy' Barberry

When grown in full sun, this pincushion-shaped plant is exceedingly valuable for its good foliage color. Mature leaves are a bronzy, purple-red and serve as background for the orange-pink of the new growth. The overall effect is a rich wine color with highlights. The plants are dense, compact, and slow-growing.

SEASONAL INTEREST

Deciduous
Effective landscape height: 2 feet
Effective landscape spread: 4 feet
Zone 5
Berberidaceae (Barberry Family)
Garden origin

Berberis thunbergii 'Crimson Pygmy'

There are so few low-growing plants with good red color that I find *Berberis* 'Crimson Pygmy' most welcome as a "colored ground cover" and use it almost exclusively that way (see photograph). I set the plants on 4-foot centers and mulch the intervening areas heavily with crushed sugar cane until the plants have grown together. I have found such ground-cover masses most effective when grown on slopes where the planting is tilted toward the viewer. 'Crimson Pygmy' Barberry is also, of course, very useful as a low, compact hedging plant.

Although the foliage color combines well with many other plants, it is particularly striking when associated with blue-greens, as seen in Plume-poppy *(Macleaya cordata)*, Wilton's Creeping Juniper (*Juniperus horizontalis* 'Wiltonii'), Smoke-Tree *(Cotinus coggygria)*, and *Tamarix* 'Pink Cascade.' When planted with lighter pinks such as Beauty-Bush *(Kolkwitzia amabilis)* and the soft pink form of Crape-myrtle *(Lagerstroemia indica)*, it adds a depth and richness which is highly attractive.

The original plant was apparently raised by Messrs. Van Eyck of Boskoop, Holland, in 1942 and has been sold in Europe as 'Little Gem,' 'Little Beauty,' and *B. thunbergii* 'Atropurpurea Nana.' Under the latter name in England it received an Award of Garden Merit from the Royal Horticultural Society in 1969. As so often happens, a new American name, 'Crimson Pygmy,' was given the plant by J. J. Gruellemans when he began to market it from Wayside Gardens in Mentor, Ohio.

90

Bergenia cordifolia
Bigleaf Saxifrage

STRUCTURAL INTEREST

Evergreen
Effective landscape height: 12 inches
Effective landscape spread: 18 inches
Zone 2
Saxifragaceae (Saxifrage Family)
Native range: Siberia

This persistent-foliaged herb is extremely valuable to the gardener who is interested in attractive textural contrasts. The leaves are broad, shiny ovals, approximately 9 inches long by 7 inches wide. They come from a central crown, causing individual plants to have a slight resemblance to cabbage. The foliage color rather than being blue-green, however, is dark green with a yellow-green midrib and veining. The newer growth is lighter. Bright pink blossoms rise 20 inches high in April; the color can be a little shocking so early in the season. Some *Bergenia* fans simply cut off the blossoms, growing the plant only for its foliage effect. I find that the pink is perfectly happy if balanced with a yellow of equal intensity such as in *Narcissus* x 'Buttercup.'

Bergenia will grow in either sun or shade but performs differently in the two environments. In moist, partially shaded areas colonies form quickly. Leaves are lush, and winter coloration is limited. There is opportunity in such a situation to create a quiet textural subtlety. I recall a really charming path at the Munich Botanic Garden, which included large patches of *Bergenia* with sweeps of *Rogersia* in variety (broad but cut foliage), *Aruncus sylvester* (coarse foliage, foamy white bloom), Hydrangeas in variety, *Waldsteinias* (glossy, strawberry-like foliage), *Alchemilla mollis* (light green, frosty, geranium-like foliage and chartreuse blossoms), Christmas Fern *(Polystichum acrostichoides)*, and the variegated, strap-shaped leaves of *Liriope muscari* 'Variegata.' Thus, the eye was teased and pleased by contrasts in shades of green and shapes of leaves. (I have also seen *Bergenia*, less lush to be sure, making an excellent ground cover in the *dry* shade of large conifers in the gardens at Winterthur, Delaware.)

In sunny spots, by contrast, the growth is retarded, and the foliage takes on shades of wine, maroon, and bronze during the winter. With a backing structure of several native Cedars *(Juniperus virginiana)* and a specimen of the lush-foliaged Cutleaf Sumac (*Rhus typhina* 'Laciniata'), great ground-cover interest can be achieved by contrasting patches of *Bergenia* with Hayscented Fern *(Dennstaedtia punctilobula)*, the ferny-leaved *Aruncus atheisifolius*, the green-leaved Ornamental Fescue, *Festuca ovina*, and the lush, leafless, green-and-black-ringed stems of *Equisetum hyemale* (the primitive Scouring Rush).

Bergenia cordifolia is extremely hardy. Chewing insects are occasionally attracted to the foliage. The roots are very fleshy and stoloniferous. Therefore, if it is used as a ground cover rather than an individual clump, it will probably be necessary to dig it up and replant it every four to five years to keep the carpet as lush as you would like. The best time to do this is in the spring, just after flowering.

There are white- and purple-flowered forms as well for those interested in the blossoms. In addition, I admired the following alternatives in a British nursery, which should certainly be tried in this country: *Bergenia* 'Ballawley Hybrid' had exceptionally large foliage; *Bergenia delavayi*, from Yunnan, had dramatically red stems and foliage, even though growing in heavy shade.

The *Bergenia*s are native from India northward through western China to Siberia and Mongolia. *B. cordifolia* is the most hardy of the species. This species and the closely related *B. crassifolia* have been grown in western Europe since the mid-1700's. Prior to 1928 they were treated in garden literature under the genus *Saxifraga* (with which they are allied), or under the generic name *Megasea* (over which the earlier name *Bergenia* was found to have priority). Unfortunately, though long considered incorrect, these inaccurate names persist in some catalogs.

91

Ceratostigma plumbaginoides
Blue Plumbago

Cobalt to gentian blue flowers reminiscent of Phlox blossoms in shape make this herbaceous ground cover the star of summer and fall plantings. Commencing about the first of August, the flowers are borne in clusters at the top of the 15-inch growth. They contrast handsomely with the pinkish tubes, bronzy, pointed flower buds, and broad oval apple-green leaves. The foliage gradually takes on attractive red and bronze shades with the coming of cooler autumn weather.

Plumbago is late to leaf out, the first leaves often not appearing until mid-May, but makes a lush cover thereafter. It is an ideal overplanting for permanently planted spring bulbs and provides a whole second season of interest to such an area. Because blues are at a premium in the late summer garden and because its blooming season is so long (at least two months), it is a very valuable plant for the designer. It is effective as a ground-cover planting adjacent to the blue-green Juniper *Juniperus horizontalis* 'Wiltonii'; the two provide contrasting textures. As with most blues, it is at its best used with contrasting colors. In herbaceous planting try Plumbago with the purple form of Globe-Amaranth *(Gomphrena globosa)* and the White Spider-plant *(Cleome spinosa* 'Helen Campbell') or with the chartreuse-leaved Ivy *Hedera helix* 'Buttercup,' and the orange, Zinnia-like flowers of *Tithonia rotundifolia* 'Torch.'

Plumbago puts on its last burst of bloom just in time to make a striking picture with the pinkish-lavender of the Autumn Crocus *(Colchicum autumnale)* in its many forms. The latter combination requires very little maintenance and is rewarding

SEASONAL INTEREST

Deciduous
Effective landscape height: 15 inches
Effective landscape spread: indefinite
Zones 6–7
Plumbaginaceae (Plumbago, or Leadwort, Family)
Native range: China

because, once planted, the grouping will continue undisturbed for years.

Ceratostigma plumbaginoides tends to move about and can be considered invasive. However, it can be easily controlled either by occasional digging or using good-quality metal edging. Although it is tolerant of partial shade, it really blooms its best in full sun. Rich soil is desirable and good drainage is essential as it will freeze out in supersaturated soils. It can be divided easily in early spring.

In 1844 this plant was sent to England from Peking by Robert Fortune, who found it in a garden there (it had been collected in 1830 in Peking by the Russian botanist von Bunge, who described it a year later under the name *Plumbago plumbaginoides* and reclassified it in 1838 as *Ceratostigma plumbaginoides*). Fortune's introduction of 1844 failed to survive the first winter in England.

Two years later Lady Larpent at Roehampton received some plants from a Mr. Smith of Canton, who had found them growing out of the stonework on Shanghai's damaged ramparts. Sir George Larpent exhibited these at a London show in June 1847. The enterprising nursery firm of Knight and Perry acquired the stock with the stipulation from Sir George that it be named for her ladyship. This John Lindley did for them, in an 1847 issue of *Gardeners Chronicle*, calling it *Plumbago larpentae*. This was, of course, an invalid name botanically because of its earlier naming by von Bunge.

The plant does not now appear to exist as a wild growing population—nor has it since Western man has had access to China's flora. The absence of any native collections in herbaria of western Europe meant that botanists had small cause to study it. Hence, it was not until about 1909, when the German dendrologist Camillo Schneider investigated the genus, that it was realized that the same plant had existed under two botanical names for sixty-two years. English-speaking gardeners did not become aware of this fact until the publication of Liberty Hyde Bailey's *Cyclopedia of Horticulture* in 1914, sixty-seven years after Lindley's publication. Now, some sixty years later, the name *Plumbago larpentae* is still inaccurately used in some catalogs. No doubt this is a point of irritation to some botanists and a source of amusement to Sir George Larpent, in his grave.

92

Genista sylvestris 'Lydia'

Lydia Woadwaxen

This nearly leafless shrub makes a dense mat at a rather uniform 24 inches and presents a unique textural character all year. The twigs are gray-green and horizontal except at the tips, where they "curl" downward. There are no leaves at all on the heavier old growth. Those on the newer growth are small, minimal in number, and practically inconspicuous. In late May to early June the closely spaced branches are absolutely loaded with butter-yellow, pea-like blossoms, a really thrilling spectacle!

I prefer to use *Genista sylvestris* 'Lydia' in large ground-cover-like masses. The color of the flowers, as with *Forsythia* x *intermedia* 'Spectabilis,' is so intense that single plants simply poke distracting holes in any composition in which they are used. There can be no richer scene than a dry slope planted with masses of this deep yellow *Genista*, the orange daisy-like flower of *Coreopsis auriculata* 'Nana,' and the softer yellow daisy of *Anthemis tinctoria* 'Kelwayi.' Additional mass plantings of dark green foliage such as Helleri Holly (*Ilex crenata* 'Helleri'), *Calluna vulgaris* 'Rigida,' and the shrubby Ivy *Hedera helix* 'Conglomerata Erecta' would provide good color contrast for the gray-green *Genista* and a rich cornucopia of textural interest. Alone as a ground cover it would provide a perfect background for featuring such dark green, broadleaf evergreens

SEASONAL INTEREST

Deciduous
Effective landscape height: 2 feet
Effective landscape spread: 4 feet
Zone 7
Leguminosae (Pea Family)
Native range: eastern Europe

as *Ilex* x 'Nellie R. Stevens' or 'Otto Luykens' Cherry-laurel (*Prunus laurocerasus* 'Otto Luykens').

Genista sylvestris 'Lydia' is only barely hardy in this area (Zone 7); if given adequate wind protection and kept out of frost pockets, performance is completely satisfactory, however. This can be accomplished by careful choice of location, such as in front of a south-facing wall; if a windier spot must be used, a cover of pine needles held in place by erosion netting in the winter will bring the blossom buds through unscathed.

Genista sylvestris 'Lydia' was introduced to the United States in 1927. Dr. W. B. Turrill of London's Kew Gardens had found this plant growing on limestone rocks above Backova, Bulgaria, in 1926. In my area it appears to thrive best in sandy soil on the acid side.

This plant has been recognized with awards on three occasions by England's Royal Horticultural Society: Award of Merit in 1937, Award of Garden Merit in 1946, and First Class Certificate in 1957.

93

STRUCTURAL INTEREST

Evergreen
Effective landscape height: 6-12 inches
Effective landscape spread: indefinite
Zone 6+
Araliaceae (Ginseng Family)
Native range: Latvia

Hedera helix 'Baltica'

Baltic Ivy

Much is written these days about ground covers; and English Ivy and its form 'Baltica' are often dismissed lightly as being "ubiquitous." If your main tests of a ground cover are that it should cut down on maintenance, establish itself rapidly, and hold earth on slopes in either sun or shade, Baltic Ivy must go to the top of the list. This is the toughest, handsomest, most reliable evergreen ground cover I know. The individual leaves are three-to-five-lobed, shiny, and dark green—with light, gray-green venation particularly noticeable on old foliage. The new growth, by contrast, is yellow-green and provides highlights to any mass planting.

Soil should be prepared by incorporating peat moss and fertilizer with a power tiller. Potted plants are best, and should be planted from May to September 15, on 12-inch centers unless the area is steeply sloping, when the spacing should be reduced to 6 inches. Mulch with shredded or crushed bark and keep well-watered. Following this system an area will be completely covered in two growing seasons and is reasonably well-covered in one. It is a mistake to allow tree leaves to accumulate in Ivy plantings, as this smothers the stems and causes dead patches. For the same reason, established plantings which have become heavy with growth need to be cut back hard. I do this by running a rotary mower through the bed every two years just before the new growth starts in the spring and make sure to apply a 10-6-4 fertilizer at the same time and to keep the planting well-watered if the early season turns dry. By the end of June one cannot tell that the barber has been there!

Baltic Ivy may simply be used to hold a bank too steep to mow or to cover the ground under a large tree such as Norway Maple, where the lawn grass cannot be coaxed to grow. On the other hand, it may be used by the design-minded gardener to create smooth, flowing planting lines. Aesthetically, a ground cover such as *Hedera helix* 'Baltica' is the savior of the plant-collecting gardener. What would otherwise be a distracting collection of varying objects can to some extent be tied together by this evergreen carpet. For the sophisticate who enjoys tones and textures of green, a shaded setting might include Baltic Ivy contrasted with patches of moss, Japanese Silver Fern *(Athyrium goeringianum pictum)*, the dinner-platter foliage of *Petasites japonica*, and the light green, curling spikes of *Iris cristata*.

In England and central Europe, *Hedera helix* covers many acres of native woodland. Many clonal forms have been collected and named, for this plant has been used in gardens since ancient times. There is a certain amount of confusion as to names, and

Hedera helix 'Baltica'

to make matters worse many of these clones are unstable and lose their distinguishing characteristics after a few years. 'Baltica' seems to be completely stable. It was discovered by Dr. Alfred Rheder in pine woods near Riga, Latvia, and introduced to the Arnold Arboretum in Jamaica Plain, Massachusetts, in 1907. To the late Edgar Anderson, horticulturist at the Arboretum, goes the credit for recognizing the potential of this clone and promoting it to the trade.

It is only in recent years that Ivy has been considered useful as a ground cover, having been formerly used chiefly as a climber. This fashion was particularly prominent during the romantic and picturesque period of English landscape architecture, when it was even trained on fire screens, banisters, and around pictures. According to J. C. Loudon (1854), in some large drawing rooms during this period, Ivy, trained on wire parasols or espaliers, formed "a rustic canopy for small groups... who may sit themselves under its shade, in the same manner as parties sit under orange trees in the public rooms of Berlin, and of other cities of the Continent."

94

STRUCTURAL INTEREST

Evergreen
Effective landscape height: 2 feet
Effective landscape spread: 30 inches
Zone 7
Araliaceae (Ginseng Family)
Native range: Europe

Hedera helix 'Conglomerata Erecta'

This half-running, half-spiky shrub is a real eye catcher for textural interest. The acutely pointed, dark, lustrous green leaves are arranged in very orderly fashion by pairs, evenly spaced on the main stem. One of each pair is at the 12 o'clock position, the other at the 6 o'clock position. The viewer therefore sees (from the 3 and 9 o'clock positions) a distinct and charming pattern of leaf stems meeting the main branch.

This curiosity (only barely hardy in my area) is

best used in a wind-sheltered spot; it prefers either light shade or a western exposure. Early sun from the east is very likely to cause burning. Its main value is for its stimulating textural zap. In semishade it might be planted in patches which would contrast with the needly *Pachistima canbyi*, the coarse-foliaged Christmas-rose *(Helleborus niger)*, spiky *Iris cristata*, and the cabbage-leaved *Bergenia cordifolia*. In sun try it with the needly Veronica *(Conradina verticillata)*, the grassy *Festuca ovina* 'Viridis,' the succulent *Sedum telephium* 'Rosy Glow,' and the bright green, diminutive foliage of *Thymus serpyllum citridorus*—all low-growing plants.

Generally speaking, *Hedera helix* 'Conglomerata Erecta' is a great asset in the winter landscape, where its foliage and color work especially well with rusty and textured bark types such as Paperbark Maple *(Acer griseum)*, Japanese Cornel Dogwood *(Cornus officinalis)*, Korean Stewartia *(Stewartia koreana)*, *Parrottia persica*, American Cyrilla *(Cyrilla racemiflora)*, and Oakleaf Hydrangea *(Hydrangea quercifolia)*.

According to Dr. George H. M. Lawrence, this clone has been grown by English Ivy fanciers in America for the last thirty-five years or more. It is American in origin, a sport of the older 'Conglomerata,' a clone that differs from it in having leaves with rounded lobes and apex.

Hedera helix 'Conglomerata Erecta'

95

Hemerocallis x 'Hyperion'
Yellow Day-lily

The 5–6-inch canary-yellow blossoms of *Hemerocallis* x 'Hyperion' appear on 4-foot stems in late June and July. Although each flower lasts only one day, the bloom continues for nearly a month.

SEASONAL INTEREST

Herbaceous
Effective landscape height: 32 inches
Effective landscape spread: 4 feet
Zone 2
Liliaceae (Lily Family)
Hybrid origin

Hemerocallis x 'Hyperion'

I frequently use it as a ground cover, as the graceful, grass-like foliage appears in early spring and is relatively good all summer. I space the plants on 4-foot centers and mulch the area in between. In an amazingly short time the foliage is touching and the plants are able to choke out all weeds. Closer spacing would only require frequent division. Division, when necessary, can be done either in early spring or in August. Plantings will succeed in full sun or very light shade. Reasonably good, well-drained soil is all that is required. Very rich soil produces foliage that is too rank. Too much lime causes the foliage to turn pale green. The plant really is a low-maintenance dream come true. As Robert E. Lee wrote, "The average daylily is so hard to kill that it may one day become the symbol of abandoned or overgrown gardens" (Cumming and Lee, 1960).

A mass planting of Hyperion Day-lilies can be made more interesting by spotting in an accent plant of *Hemerocallis* x 'Shining Plumage,' with its rich orange-mahogany-red blossoms. Where low maintenance is not the primary consideration, a beautiful picture can be painted by associating masses of *Salvia superba* (with its rich blue-purple spikes) and masses of the tall, gray-foliaged *Artemisia albula* with sweeps of *H.* x 'Hyperion.' A larger-scale planting that would be very handsome might feature a grove of Goldenrain-Trees underplanted with blue *Hydrangea macrophylla* subsp. *macrophylla* and ground-cover masses of *Hemerocallis* x 'Hyperion' and Variegated Lilyturf (*Liriope muscari* 'Variegata').

Breeding and growing Day-lilies has been a craze during the past fifty years, and the United States has been the leader in boosting this plant. There are some 4,000 named clones in commerce. *Hemerocallis* x 'Hyperion' is certainly one of the best from a landscape viewpoint. It resulted from the cross 'Sir Michael Foster' x 'Florham' and was introduced in 1925 by Franklin B. Mead of Fort Wayne, Indiana. England's Royal Horticultural Society gave 'Hyperion' its Award of Merit (based on trials at Wisley) in 1931.

96

Liriope muscari 'Big Blue'
'Big Blue' Lilyturf

SEASONAL INTEREST

Evergreen
Effective landscape height: 16 inches
Effective landscape spread: 2 feet
Zone 7
Liliaceae (Lily Family)
Native range: Japan and China

Liriope muscari 'Big Blue' is an attractive evergreen ground cover that does not generally seem to be well known. This is unfortunate because it has some most desirable qualities. In the first place, *Liriope* has narrow (³⁄₁₆-inch), strap-shaped leaves, approximately 16 inches long, which rise upward from the ground for two-thirds of their length, then arch gently back downward near the tip. The effect is very much like that of a fine stand of lawn grass that has been left unmowed—each blade broader and darker green, however. (The texture is, of course, completely different from the traditional ground covers, Baltic Ivy and Pachysandra, and, as such, *Liriope* is extremely useful from a design standpoint.) Secondly, the plant has lavender-blue blossom spikes in late August and early September. Coming at a season when the choice of flowering material is thin, *Liriope* is a welcome addition. The blossom spikes slightly resemble Grape-hyacinths and are generally as tall as, or slightly taller than, the foliage. The florets are closely grouped on stems that are lavender to brownish in color; each floret is centered with a cluster of yellow stamens.

The fruit, particularly noticeable in October and November, consists of spikes of very shiny black berries. The gloss is so great that they are truly ornamental and much admired by flower arrangers.

Liriope muscari 'Big Blue' will thrive in most garden soils that are moderately to well drained. Thorough preparation of the soil with additions of organic matter and 10-6-4 fertilizer is desirable before planting. The plant's root system is composed of thick tubers with many fibers, and propagation is by divi-

sion. For a smooth ground-cover effect, plant one to two bib divisions (divisions having one or two sprouts) 6 to 8 inches apart in the spring. If a more clumpy effect is desired, larger divisions or container-grown plants spaced farther apart are recommended. *Liriope* will grow in either sun or shade. There is, however, one drawback to its use in sunny locations, at least at the northern end of its range. Under such conditions, the foliage is usually so badly burned from early spring sun that it is quite unsightly. This is, of course, only a temporary problem, as the foliage can be cut to the ground to be followed by fresh, new growth. New foliage on *Liriope* does not come particularly early in the spring, however, so the gardener must be prepared to wait until late May for a fresh effect. The significance of this fact is simply that if *Liriope* is to be used in a sunny situation, it is best to pick a spot that is not of prominent interest in early spring.

Liriope has a wide range of uses as a ground cover with various woody shrubs. For instance, in semi-shaded situations it is most attractive as an underplanting for Oakleaf Hydrangea *(Hydrangea quercifolia)*. In full sun it is a fine choice to combine with its blooming mate Franklinia *(Franklinia alatamaha)* and with the early fruiters Asiatic Sweetleaf *(Symplocos paniculata)*, which has bright blue berries, and Snowberry *(Symphoricarpos albus laevigatus)*, which has white berries.

In addition, a wide range of herbaceous and ground-cover plants combine well with *Liriope muscari* 'Big Blue.' In the shade an attractive pink, white, and blue combination would be the Hardy Begonia *(Begonia evansiana)*, the white August-lily *(Hosta plantaginea)*, and *Liriope muscari* 'Big Blue.' In a sunny situation the lavender-blue of *Liriope* might be contrasted with patches of the chartreuse-foliaged 'Buttercup' Ivy (*Hedera helix* 'Buttercup') and Plumbago *(Ceratostigma plumbaginoides)*, with its marvelous cobalt-blue blossoms.

It should be noted that there is also an excellent white-flowered form, *Liriope muscari* 'Monroi #1,' which makes an absolutely charming picture with its blooming companion *Caryopteris* x *clandonensis* 'Blue Mist.'

The real show stealer of the group is Variegated Lilyturf (*Liriope muscari* 'Variegata'). This plant is valued chiefly for its foliage effect, however, which hits its stride in late June when the new leaves have matured. Each strap-shaped leaf is longitudinally striped. In shade or semishade the center of the leaf is dark green, the edges yellow-green, the overall effect a cool and cheerful chartreuse. In sun the center band is yellow-green, the edges creamy white, the overall effect a creamy green. The blossoms are a light lavender. Although perfectly acceptable, because their intensity is weak by comparison with the intensity of the foliage color the flowers cannot be considered an outstanding feature of this plant. The foliage, on the other hand, is effective for two summer months and well into the winter.

Liriope muscari 'Variegata'

When dramatizing a dark green, needle evergreen, no plant provides a finer contrast than Variegated Lilyturf. I can think of nothing more charming than a fine old Yew topiary or a grove of Oriental Spruces *(Picea orientalis)* or Incense-cedar *(Calocedrus decurrens)* underplanted with this broadleaf ground cover. No words could describe such a scene better than "rich and lively." In its more chartreuse stage (when planted in partial shade or on the north side of a building) it is also very effective with blue-greens. I have used it most successfully in combination with the broad, blue-green foliage of Leatherleaf Mahonia *(Mahonia bealei)* adjacent to a plant of the light-green-foliaged Dawn-redwood *(Metasequoia glyptostroboides)*. This was accented with a few plants of the herbaceous *Ligularia clivorum* 'Desdemona.' The broad, oval, purplish foliage of *Ligularia* is an exciting contrast with both the *Liriope* and *Mahonia* foliages, and its stalks of orange-yellow daisies greatly enliven the summer scene.

In a shaded situation Variegated Lilyturf is the natural highlight plant for an exciting ground-cover symphony of color and texture. Visualize, if you will, the broad, fat, blue-green foliage of *Hosta sieboldiana*, the light green, fine-textured foliage of Hayscented

Fern *(Dennstaedtia punctilobula)*, the oval, dark green, cabbage-like leaves of *Bergenia cordifolia*, the strap-like chartreuse-tinted foliage of *Liriope muscari* 'Variegata,' the blushy, gray-green foliage and frothy, chartreuse flowers of Lady's Mantle *(Alchemilla mollis)*, the spiky, dark green, architectural leaves of Shrub Ivy *(Hedera helix* 'Conglomerata Erecta'*)*, the very shiny, kidney-shaped leaves of European Ginger *(Asarum europaeum)*, and the fingery, black-green foliage of Christmas-rose *(Helleborus niger)*. The need for flowering plants fades into insignificance in the face of such a rich visual experience!

97

STRUCTURAL INTEREST

Evergreen
Effective landscape height: 10 inches
Effective landscape spread: indefinite
Zone 6
Buxaceae (Box Family)
Native range: Japan

Pachysandra terminalis

Pachysandra, Japanese Spurge

In a day and age when "low maintenance" has become a key phrase in gardening circles, ground covers are a topic of considerable importance. Certainly Pachysandra is the very best evergreen ground cover we have for shady spots. It spreads by underground stems, making a very dense carpet. The broad, jagged-ended, wedge-shaped leaves are carried in whorls. This plus a very uniform growth height explains why a patch of *Pachysandra terminalis* has such a neat appearance and such a delightfully light-reflective quality. The white-green flower buds are followed by white flowers in May.

In addition to the maintenance advantages of ground covers like Pachysandra and Baltic Ivy, they are very strong design tools. In the first place, ground covers are, by nature, low horizontal lines and, as such, tie together all sorts of other plant shapes and textures, thus creating more of a unity. By virtue of the organization achieved, the picture is simplified and, thereby, has more impact. Secondly, ground covers are really the most important element with which we create planting shapes in a garden. This is a very important point because the creation of strong, carefully studied forms makes for a good design, whereas weak, sloppy shapes leave us with a weak and meaningless design. Forms made with Pachysandra's broadleaf texture contrast especially well with lawn grass, the other strongest texture usually present.

The unusual leaf shape of *Pachysandra terminalis* works well in a design sense with both fine and broadleaf textures—a rare virtue, indeed! It is an extremely good tie-together for such broadleaves as Azaleas, Rhododendrons, and Leucothoë. On the other hand, there is nothing more handsome than contrasting sweeps of Pachysandra and a fine-foliaged fern such as Hayscented Fern *(Dennstaedtia punctilobula)*. For me, however, Pachysandra is *most* effective in the wintertime. Its rich green carpet is an especially cheerful note at a time when lawn grass is, at its best, uninspiring. A wonderful play on greens results from using it with such small-needled, darker green conifers as Canadian Hemlock *(Tsuga canadensis)* or Oriental Spruce *(Picea orientalis)*. The biggest treat for a winter scene, however, is to feature tree trunks of strong winter interest in a sea of Pachysandra. A grove of trunks—all of one variety—can carry a wonderful impact when treated in this manner. Possible subjects would include the gray-barked Beeches, *Fagus sylvatica* and *Fagus grandifolia*, White Birch *(Betula verrucosa)*, River Birch *(Betula nigra)*, with its exfoliating pinkish-tan bark, Paperbark Maple *(Acer griseum)*, with its exfoliating bronzy bark, and the Japanese Redtwig Maple, *Acer palmatum* 'Senkaki.'

Where good drainage and adequate topsoil are provided, Pachysandra will thrive. There has been an occasional problem in the mid-Atlantic region with Euonymous scale, but this is controllable by spraying with dormant oil spray.

Pachysandra is a Japanese native and was introduced into Germany in 1882, and arrived in the

Pachysandra terminalis

United States about a decade later. It was another quarter-century, however, before its merits were fully appreciated; eventually it was accepted as superior to our native *Pachysandra procumbens*, and it became widely used.

98

Rudbeckia fulgida var. *sullivanti* 'Goldsturm'
Blackeyed Susan, Cone-flower

SEASONAL INTEREST

Herbaceous
Effective landscape height: 40 inches
Effective landscape spread: 4 feet
Zone 5
Compositae (Composite Family)
Native range: United States—Michigan to Missouri and West Virginia

This selected form of the American Blackeyed Susan is a real garden asset. The striking, black-centered, orange-yellow daisies appear in great profusion from mid-July to mid-August. There are usually additional scattered blooms until frost, and if moisture conditions are just right, there can be a real second bloom. This form is tough, spreads rapidly, and has real merit as a ground cover. The foliage (14 inches high) is composed of dark green, broad, pointed-oval leaves which do a good job of crowding out weeds. When in flower, the total plant measures 30–40 inches high. The flowers are a good 3–4 inches across, with faintly twisted, rich yellow (almost orange) rays.

Because 'Goldsturm' Blackeyed Susan is intense in color and bold in texture and is used most effectively as a ground-cover mass, care must be taken to balance sufficiently large masses of other colors and textures with it. The rich mahogany-orange of the Day-lily variety 'Shining Plumage' (*Hemerocallis* x 'Shining Plumage') and the lighter yellow of the Goldenrod variety 'Peter Pan' make one of several possible sunny color combinations with the *Rudbeckia*. The texture of the Goldenrod blossoms and the Day-lily foliage lighten the boldness of the

Blackeyed Susans; the long-stemmed blossoms of the Day-lilies give a quality of gracefulness to the whole scheme.

Experimenting with color combinations can be both entertaining and rewarding. In addition to the orange-yellow-mahogany direction described above, 'Goldsturm' Blackeyed Susans, it will be found, work especially well with grays and plum-reds and are a real "knockout" with chartreuse. In the plum-red direction try interlocking sweeps of 'Goldsturm' Blackeyed Susan, the feathery gray *Artemesia albula*, and the low, woolly, broadleaf Lamb's Ear *(Stachys olympica)* accented with a clump of three or four plants of the purplish-plum-colored *Perilla fruticans*. Or, on a larger scale, try the red-foliaged Barberry, *Berberis thunbergii* 'Atropurpurea' and the fine gray-foliaged *Salix elaeagnos*, with *Rudbeckia fulgida* var. *sullivanti* 'Goldsturm' as the ground cover. In the chartreuse direction, a single plant of 'Goldsturm' Blackeyed Susan might be featured in a sea of the chartreuse-leaved Ivy *Hedera helix* 'Buttercup.' This could be backed by a grouping of the feathery, light green *Kochia scoparia* accented by four spikes of soft yellow Mullein *(Verbascum* sp.). The light green and soft yellows of all of the other plants would by contrast dramatize the *Rudbeckia*'s intense color; the form of the Mullein (vertical spikes) and the texture (feathery) of the *Kochia*, by contrast, call attention to the compact habit of the *Rudbeckia* and broad-textured, ray design of its flowers.

Although *Rudbeckia* is not usually classed as a moisture-loving plant, it is usually far happier and produces more and larger blossoms when some attention is given to siting it where some moisture is available. There are no real growing problems. Spring division of plants is recommended every third year for best results.

Rudbeckia is another example of a native American herbaceous plant which makes an excellent garden subject. Forms of both *Rudbeckia* and Goldenrod *(Solidago)* have been selected for garden use. There are many others, however, particularly

Rudbeckia fulgida var. *sullivanti* 'Goldsturm'

among the meadow flowers, such as Joe Pye Weed *(Eupatorium purpureum)*, Iron Weed *(Vernonia novaboracensis)*, and Butterfly Weed *(Asclepias tuberosa)*, which have not been evaluated for garden use and which have great potential.

The British have recognized the merits of this plant with the following awards from the Royal Horticultural Society: Award of Merit (based on trials at Wisley) in 1952 and Award of Garden Merit in 1969.

99

SEASONAL INTEREST

Herbaceous
Effective landscape height: 6-9 inches
Effective landscape spread: indefinite
Zone 6
Crassulaceae (Orpine Family)
Native range: eastern Asia

Sedum kamtschaticum

For some reason we too seldom think of herbaceous plants as valuable landscape subjects. *Sedum kamtschaticum* is certainly one that should be valued more highly for its use as a ground cover. Not a *creeping* Sedum, this species has 6-inch-high *clumps* of broad, scalloped leaves, arranged in whorls, superficially resembling *Pachysandra terminalis*. This Sedum is, however, much more successful than *Pachysandra* in full sun and under dry conditions. The foliage color is a healthy, attractive, yellow-green, dark enough to show off the rich yellow blossoms, which occur for about two weeks in late June and sporadically thereafter during July and August. Blossoms are followed by attractive bronzy seed heads. These and the stems, which actually have a shrubby tendency and remain alive over winter, are not uninteresting at that time of the year.

In my own garden I have a grove of Umbrella-pines *(Sciadopitys verticillata)* planted on a soil mound. *Sedum kamtschaticum* thrives here and is most effective. The yellow-green, broadleaf Sedum is an excellent contrast and tie-together for the darker green, needly foliage of the *Sciadopitys*. Another striking combination for a sunny, dry situation would be to feature that "character" Pine, *Pinus densiflora* 'Oculis-draconis,' with its yellow-banded needles, and the dark green, round-leaved *Osmanthus rotundifolius* in a large ground-cover patch of *Sedum kamtschaticum*. The yellow-green of the Pine and the Sedum would relate to each other, while their texture would contrast. The dark green of the *Osmanthus* would anchor the whole planting, and its foliage would provide an interesting contrast with the other two plants. Adding one *Bergenia cordifolia*, with its cabbage-like rosette of leaves, would provide an interesting accent and complete an exciting play on textures and colors.

For ground-cover effect, small divisions of *Sedum kamtschaticum* should be planted 6 inches apart. This prevents too clumpy a look and minimizes weeding. I cut the stems back to the ground with hedge shears in very early spring. The fat buds for the new growth, formed the year before, are clearly visible and most attractive as they swell and break with the first warm weather.

The plant is widely distributed in coastal areas of northeastern Asia, and as its name suggests, was first known to botanists from collections made in the Kamtschatka Peninsula. It was introduced to gardens before 1850, first in St. Petersburg, and has been grown in the United States since the 1870's.

Sedum kamtschaticum

100

STRUCTURAL INTEREST

Evergreen
Effective landscape height: 3 feet
Effective landscape spread: 4+ feet
Zone 5
Agavaceae (Agave Family)
Native range: United States—South Carolina to Florida and Mississippi

Yucca smalliana
(*Yucca filamentosa*)
Adam's Needle, Silk Grass

This native American plant is among the most valuable tools of the garden designer. The long (1½–2 feet), narrow (1–2 inches), blue-green evergreen leaves are sharply pointed and nicely arranged in huge orbs or rosettes as much as 42 inches across. In late June huge flower spikes often reaching 8–10 feet, rise from the center of the plant. These conical flower clusters are composed of bell-like, waxy, yellowish-white flowers. The blossom effect is candelabra-like; the foliage has a very strong architectural quality all year.

Whether it is used as a structuring plant in an herbaceous border, for its evergreen quality in a grouping of deciduous shrubs, or for its broadleaf texture among needle evergreens, its architectural strength lends tremendous character to the setting involved. Because *Yucca* is extremely winter-hardy and tolerant of poor soil and drought, it is available for use under a wide variety of growing conditions and with a wide variety of other plant material. Occasionally in gardening we run into soil which is low in organic matter and poor in fertility and which when dry is usually dusty. This is described by knowledgeable gardeners as "dead soil." *Yucca smalliana* will grow well under such adverse conditions along with such other "toughies" as *Wisteria floribunda*, Warminster Broom (*Cytisus* x *praecox* 'Luteus'), Scotch Broom *(Cytisus scoparius)*, Japanese Pagoda-Tree *(Sophora japonica)*, Golden-Chain-Tree *(Laburnum vossii)*, Lorberg's Siberian Pea-Tree (*Car-*

agana arborescens 'Lorbergii'), *Lespedeza bicolor*, and Chaste-Tree (*Vitex agnus-castus* 'Latifolia').

If you have the urge to create a desert-type scene in a more northern clime, *Yucca smalliana* is a prime candidate. Mulched with water-worn pebbles, this picture could include varities of *Sedum, Sempervivum*, and *Cytisus* as well as the hardy Prickly-pear *(Opuntia compressa)*, and the annual Angel's Trumpet *(Datura meteloides)*.

There is an interesting affinity between this plant and moths and butterflies. *Yucca* flowers are extremely attractive to butterflies, and they frequently lay their eggs on its leaves. There is in addition a special family of night-flying moths on which *Yucca* depends for fertilization. This species of moth cannot exist without the *Yucca* and the *Yucca* cannot set seed without the help of the moth—or the hand pollination of man.

The natural range of all varieties of *Yucca* is confined to the hot, dry regions of the United States, Central America, and Mexico. It has also escaped from cultivation over much of the East coast of the United States in areas where it is not native. Unlike some other members of the genus, the two varieties most adaptable for northern climes, *Y. smalliana* and *Y. glauca*, keep their stems below ground. *Y. smalliana* increases and spreads by means of side growths from this basal stem.

There are curly, thread-like filaments, 6–10 inches long, on the margins of the leaves of some southwestern species, which were supposedly used by the American Indians in making clothes.

This plant received an Award of Garden Merit from the Royal Horticultural Society in England in 1969.

BIBLIOGRAPHIES

Books About Plant Exploration and Plant Introduction

Anderson, Alexander Walter. 1966. *How We Got Our Flowers*. New York: Dover Publications. An unabridged and unaltered republication of the work originally published by Williams and Norgate under the title *The Coming of the Flowers.*

Coats, Alice M. 1956. *Flowers and Their Histories*. London: Hulton Press.

——. 1965. *Garden Shrubs and Their Histories*. New York: E.P. Dutton and Co.

——. 1969. *The Plant Hunters*. New York: McGraw-Hill.

Cox, E. H. M. 1961. *Plant Hunting in China*. London: Oldbourne Book Co.

Herbst, Josephine. 1954. *New Green World*. New York: Hastings House.

Hiroa, Te Rangi [Peter H. Buck]. 1953. *Explorers of the Pacific*. Bernice P. Bishop Special Publication, no. 43. Honolulu, Hawaii: Bernice P. Bishop Museum.

Kingdon-Ward, Frank. 1960. *Pilgrimage for Plants*. London: George G. Harrap and Co.

Lemmon, Kenneth. 1968. *The Golden Age of Plant Hunters*. Edited by Peter Hunt. London: Phoenix House.

Whittle, Tyler. 1966. *Some Ancient Gentlemen*. New York: Taplinger Publishing Co.

——. 1970. *The Plant Hunters*. Philadelphia: Chilton Book Co.

Wilson, Ernest H. 1927. *Plant Hunting*. 2 vols. Boston: Stratford.

——. 1929. *China, Mother of Gardens*. Boston: Stratford.

Books About Garden Design

Bardi, P. M. 1964. *The Tropical Gardens of Burle-Marx*. New York: Reinhold.

Brattleboro Museum and Art Center. *Built Landscapes, Gardens in the Northeast* – Catalog of a Travelling Exhibition produced by the Brattleboro Museum and Art Center, Old Union Railroad Station, Maine and Union Sts., Brattleboro, VT, 1985.

Brookes, John. 1969. *Room Outside*. New York: Viking Press.

Grant, John A., and Grant, Carol L. 1954. *Garden Design Illustrated*. Seattle: University of Washington Press.

Hobhouse, Penelope. 1985. *Color in Your Garden.* Little Brown and Co., Boston and Toronto.

Jellicoe, Susan, and Jellicoe, Geoffrey. 1968. *Modern Private Gardens.* London: Abelard-Schuman.

Kassler, Elizabeth B. 1964. *Modern Gardens and the Landscape.* New York: Museum of Modern Art.

Lees, Carlton. 1960. *Budget Landscaping.* New York: Henry Holt.

Shepheard, Peter. 1954. *Modern Gardens.* New York: Praeger.

General Bibliography

A. H. Scott Horticultural Foundation. 1955–56. *Plant Notes.* 3d typewritten ed. Swarthmore, Pa.: Swarthmore College.

American Horticultural Society. 1962. *The Peonies.* John C. Wister, chairman, editorial committee. Washington, D.C.: the Society.

Bailey, Liberty Hyde. 1930. *The Standard Cyclopedia of Horticulture.* 3 vols. New York: Macmillan.

——. 1954. *Manual of Cultivated Plants.* Rev. ed. New York: Macmillan.

Bailey, Liberty Hyde, and Bailey, Ethel Zoe. 1941. *Hortus Second.* New York: Macmillan.

Bean, W. J. 1951. *Trees and Shrubs Hardy in the British Isles.* Vols. 2 and 3. London: John Murray.

——. 1970, 1973. *Trees and Shrubs Hardy in the British Isles.* 8th ed., rev. Vols. 1 and 2. London: John Murray.

Bloom, Alan. 1957. *Hardy Perennials.* London: Faber and Faber.

Bruce, Harold. 1968. *The Gardens of Winterthur.* New York: Viking Press.

Cumming, R. W., and Lee, R. E. 1960. *Contemporary Perennials.* New York: Macmillan.

Curtis, William. 1799. *Botanical Magazine* 13: plate 466 and adjoining note on *Chimonanthus praecox.*

den Ouden, P., with Boom, B. K. 1965. *Manual of Cultivated Conifers.* The Hague, Netherlands: Martinus Nijhoff.

Flemer, William, III. 1972. *Nature's Guide to Successful Gardening and Landscaping.* New York: Thomas Y. Crowell Co.

Flint, Harrison L. 1983. *Landscape Plants for Eastern North America (Exclusive of Florida and the Gulf Coast).* John Wiley & Sons, NYC.

Hamblin, Stephen F. 1929. *Lists of Plant Types for Landscape Planting.* Cambridge, Mass.: Harvard University Press.

Harper, Pamela and Frederick McGourty. 1985. *Perennials.* H.P. Books, Inc. P. O. Box 5367, Tucson, Arizona 85703.

Hansell, Dorothy E., ed. 1970. "Handbook of Hollies." *The American Horticultural Magazine* (Fall) 49: entire issue.

Hebb, Robert S. 1974. *Low Maintenance Perennials.* Arnold Arboretum of Harvard University.

Hillier, H. G. 1972. *Hillier's Manual of Trees and Shrubs*, Newton Abbot, England: David and Charles.

Hockenberry, Mary L. 1973. "Landscape Characteristics and a Key for Selected Ornamental Grasses." Master's thesis, Cornell University.

International Commission for the Nomenclature of Cultivated Plants of the International Union of Biological Science. 1969. *International Code of Nomenclature of Cultivated Plants.* J. S. Gilmour, chairman, editorial committee. Utrecht, Netherlands: International Bureau for Plant Taxonomy and Nomenclature.

Kingdon-Ward, Frank. 1954. *Berried Treasure.* London: Ward, Lock, and Co.

Lee, Frederick P. 1965. *The Azalea Book.* 2d ed. Princeton, N.J.: D. Van Nostrand Co.

Lindley, John, and Paxton, Joseph. 1850. *Paxton's Flower Garden*, Vol. 3. London: Bradbury and Evans.

Loudon, J. C. 1854. *Arboretum et Fruticetum Britannicum.* London: Henry G. Bohn. (See section on *Hedera helix*, p. 1004.)

Miller, Philip. 1768. *The Gardeners Dictionary.* 8th ed. London: Printed for the author.

Roper, Lanning. 1960. *Hardy Herbaceous Plants.* Harmondsworth, Middlesex, England: Penguin Books.

Royal Horticultural Society. 1965. *Dictionary of Gardening.* Edited by Patrick M. Synge. 2d ed. Oxford: Clarendon Press.

Still, Steven M. 1980. *Herbaceous Ornamental Plants.* Stipes Publishing Co., 10-12 Chester St., Champaign, Illinois 61820.

Taber, W. S. 1937. *Delaware Trees.* Publication no. 6. Dover, Del.: Delaware State Forestry Department.

Tatnall, Robert R. 1946. *Flora of Delaware and the Eastern Shore.* Wilmington, Del.: Society of Natural History of Delaware.

Thomas, Graham Stuart. 1976. *Perennial Garden Plants (or the Modern Florilegium)* J. M. Dent and Sons Ltd. London.

United States Department of Agriculture. 1973 *a. History, Progeny, and Locations of Crabapples of Documented Authentic Origin.* Agricultural Research Service, National Arboretum Contribution, no. 2. Washington, D.C.: the Department.

——. 1973 *b. International Checklist of Cultivated Ilex.* Agricultural Research Service, National Arboretum Contribution, no. 2. Washington, D.C.: the Department.

Van Hoey Smith, J. R. P. 1970. "Some Trees at Le Cosquer [Brittany]." In *International Dendrological Society Yearbook, 1970,* edited by Patrick M. Synge, pp. 58–9. London: International Dendrological Society.

Van Melle, P. J. 1955. *Shrubs and Trees for the Small Place.* Edited by Montague Free. Rev. ed. Garden City, N. Y.: American Garden Guild and Doubleday.

Welch, H. J. 1966. *Dwarf Conifers.* Newton, Mass.: Charles T. Branford Co.

Wister, John C., ed. 1947. *Woman's Home Companion Garden Book*. New York: P. F. Collier Son.

Wyman, Donald. 1965. *Trees for American Gardens*. Rev. and enl. ed. New York: Macmillan.

———. 1971 *a. Shrubs and Vines for American Gardens*. Rev. and enl. ed. New York: Macmillan.

———. 1971 *b. Wyman's Gardening Encyclopedia*. New York: Macmillan.

Zucker, Isabel. 1966. *Flowering Shrubs*. Princeton, N.J.: Van Nostrand.

INDEX

PHOTOGRAPHIC CREDITS

Arthur Hoyt Scott Horticultural Foundation
  Abies nordmanniana, 5
  Gymnocladus dioica, 16
Eaton, Jerome A.
  Poncirus trifoliata, close-up of fruit, 140
Flemer, William E., III
  Myrica pensylvanica, 132
  Quercus phellos, 31
  Sophora japonica 'Regent,' 37
  Viburnum plicatum forma tomentosum, 175 bottom
Hampfler, Gottlieb
  Hemerocallis x 'Hyperion,' 192
  Koelreuteria paniculata, 18
  Sedum kamtschaticum, 201
Henry Francis duPont Winterthur Museum, the Gardens Division
  Lonicera fragrantissima, 127
Henry Francis duPont Winterthur Museum, photos by
    Gottlieb Hampfler
  Corylopsis glabrescens, 104
  Diospyros kaki, 55
  Forsythia x *intermedia* 'Spectabilis,' 108
  Rhododendron schlippenbachii, 151
Kalmbacher, George, Taxonomist, Brooklyn Botanic Garden
  Malus x 'Red Jade,' in fruit, 66
Lees, Carlton B., Vice-President, New York Botanic Garden
  Bergenia cordifolia, 183
Lewis, Clarence E.
  Acer griseum, bark, 40
  Acer griseum, foliage, 41
  Amelanchier canadensis, 42

Aralia spinosa, general scene, 43
  Aralia spinosa, close-up of trunk and leaf blade, 44
  Cotinus coggygria 'Foliis Purpureis,' 50
  Caragana arborescens 'Lorbergii,' close-up of flower, 95 bottom
  Cladrastis lutea, 11
  Fagus sylvatica 'Laciniata,' 12
  Kolkwitzia amabilis, 124
  Leucothoë fontanesiana, 125
  Malus x 'Red Jade,' 65
  Myrica pensylvanica, close-up of fruit. 132
  Philadelphus coronarius, 139
  Tsuga canadensis 'Pendula,' 167
  Viburnum carlesii, 169
Lighty, Richard W.
  Cotinus coggygria 'Foliis Purpureis,' 49
  Ilex glabra 'Densa,' 117
Longwood Gardens, Inc., photo by Gottlieb Hampfler
  Oxydendrum arboreum, 73
Morris Arboretum
  Pinus flexilis, 29
  Stewartia koreana, bark and flower, 77, 78
Planting Fields Arboretum
  Syringa amurensis var. *japonica,* 79
  Acer palmatum var. *dissectum,* 86
Simon, Richard, Bluemount Nurseries
  Miscanthus sinensis 'Gracillimus,' 130
United States National Arboretum
  Sciadopitys verticillata, 35

All other photographs are by the author.

A Note About the Author

William H. Frederick, Jr., is principal in the landscape-architecture firm Private Gardens, Incorporated, of Hockessin, Delaware. A native of Wilmington, he began gardening at the age of eight, and after graduation from Swarthmore College and Dickinson School of Law realized that his interest in horticulture and landscape architecture outweighed any other. With his wife, he established Millcreek Nursery, a firm specializing in custom landscape work, rare plants, and specimen plants. Mr. Frederick has designed residential gardens in a number of eastern states, is the author of several articles on horticultural subjects, and has been active in direction of the Delaware Flower Show. He is a member of the Board of Trustees of the Ida Cason Callaway Foundation, which owns and operates Callaway Gardens in Pine Mountain, Georgia. Since 1970 he has been a member of the board of trustees of Longwood Gardens, Inc. and its president, 1970-1980. His spare moments are spent developing his own 20-year-old "garden in the making." Located in a 17-acre stream valley, the garden – like this book – reflects its owners' belief that there are a great many good garden plants, hardy and not necessarily rare, that are not now getting the use they deserve.

A Note on the Type

The text of this book was set in the film version of Garamond Bold, a modern rendering of the type first cut by Claude Garamond (1510-1561). A pupil of Geoffroy Tory, Garamond is believed to have based his letters on the Venetian models, although he introduced a number of important differences, and it is to him we owe the letter we know as old-style. He gave to his letters a certain elegance and a feeling of movement that won for their creator an immediate reputation and the patronage of Francis I of France.

The text was composed by Superior Printing, Champaign, Illinois. Color separations by Northwestern Colorgraphics, Inc., Menasha, Wisconsin.
Typography and binding design by Christine Aulicino